Diverse Pursuits

Essays on Drama and Theatre

Javed Malick

AAKAR

Diverse Pursuits: Essays on Drama and Theatre
Javed Malick

First Published 2020

ISBN 978-93-5002-648-9

Published by
AAKAR BOOKS
28 E Pocket IV, Mayur Vihar Phase I
Delhi 110 091 India
aakarbooks@gmail.com

Laser Typeset at
Sakshi Computers, Delhi

Printed at
Sapra Brothers, Noida

Contents

Introduction

Drama and theatre have interested me for most of my adult life. It started in early youth as a lay person's more or less casual interest in watching plays. I was fascinated by how a play was put together and was wonder struck at the way actors were able to bring characters alive on stage and thus carried the story forward. This, as I said, was still the casual and amateurish interest of an ordinary or lay playgoer. It was only, during my graduate studies for a Master's degree that it developed into a serious, sustained, and specialised engagement with the dramatic form and its rich and variegated history. Since then drama and theatre have been the main focus of my scholarly interest. My doctoral work lay in this field and dramatic literature was a major part of the courses that I taught during my career as a teacher.

In the course of my academic life, there were times when I was drawn to particular areas or topics and undertook an in-depth study of them. These studies usually led to written essays or papers which were presented in seminars or as lectures and were eventually published. This book comprises five such texts. Although they were published before in their earlier versions, they have been revised, in most cases substantially, and updated in the light of recent scholarship on the subject.

I have titled this book "Diverse Pursuits" because the essays here represent a diversity of areas that I have explored over many years. At first glance, they may seem somewhat far afield in relation to the topics they deal with as well as in terms of the historical and geographical areas they traverse. However, these discrete texts possess a generic affinity which connects them and gives this book a degree of cohesion. They are covered by a single rubric of "drama and theatre". This generic affinity is further reinforced by the fact that, in terms of the historical and formal categorisation of dramatic forms, the topics belong within the field of "modern", drama which is a distinctly contemporary, urban phenomenon. A commonality of standpoint also unites these texts and gives this volume an even greater degree of cohesion.

It will not be incorrect to say that this standpoint constitutes the theoretical underpinning of the texts that makes up this book. The guiding principle of this theoretical underpinning is best summed up by the two simple words with which Fredric Jameson opens his "Preface" to *The Political Unconscious.* The words, almost a slogan, are: "Always historicise!" Historicising, as he goes on to explain, *is an "absolute imperative of all dialectical thought"*[1]. In other words, my approach is informed by a dialectical understanding of culture and (or, more precisely, **in**) history. Although there is not much direct discussion of theory as such, my endeavour throughout is to view every example of artistic form and practice as socio-historically produced, shaped, and received.

The specific category of "modern" theatre is historically, institutionally as well as formally distinct from "pre-modern" (folk and classical) traditions. It arose with the rise of the bourgeoisie. Its origins are to be found in the 18th–19th century European drama. One of the essays in this book deals with this European example and examines the close connection between the evolution of this new form of drama and the rise of the bourgeois social order with its dominant ideology or world view. As described in the subsequent essay on Parsi theatre, this new idea of theatre came to India, with, and perhaps as an unintended consequence of, the arrival of the British colonial rulers and the introduction of English college education.

Nobody can deny that, even before the arrival of this European model, there was theatre in India in the form of numerous classical and folk forms and traditions. But, that theatre was significantly different from what I have identified here as 'modern'. Pre-modern traditional theatre was an occasional or sporadic cultural phenomenon. Dramatic performances took place during religious festivals or other special occasions. Moreover, traditional theatre was closely linked to courts, temples, or fair grounds. The dramatic texts themselves dealt, almost invariably, with mythical and folkloric or legendary materials which involved superhuman (often divine) figures and events.

My purpose here is not to underestimate the value and interest of traditional forms. However, these and all such classical and folk traditions of theatre in their pure form belong to earlier, pre-modern ages, to forms of society prior to our own. As such, they carry within themselves deeply (and not so deeply) embedded signs of those pre-modern social formations and therefore cannot truly be called contemporary in my sense of the term. In contrast to this, the theatre that writers and theatre artists like Dinabandhu Mitra, Girish Ghosh, Ardhendu Mustafi in Calcutta, and Dadabhai Patel, Idulji Khori, Ratan ji Thonthi in Bombay helped shape was distinct from the traditional theatre in the sense that it belonged to the public domain in terms of its venue and patronage. Also, it was a secular theatre in that, although the preoccupation with mythical and fantastic materials continued for a period–particularly on the stages of Parsi theatre–it eventually began, in serious examples of Indian drama, to give way to portrayals of human, social reality in expressly human and social terms. It was during this period that theatre gradually began to become contemporary. It is with this category of theatre that the essays in this book are concerned.

It is possible, nonetheless, to draw upon traditional forms and styles in order to fashion a theatre which is distinctly contemporary. There are several examples of this kind of theatre in India and abroad in which a specifically modern consciousness is creatively blended with the vitality and remarkable energy of traditional styles and performances. One of the finest examples of this kind of theatre from post-independence India is found in the work of Habib Tanvir which is the subject of one of my essays in this volume.

As for the essays themselves, one of the central concerns in the opening essay "**Bourgeois Worldview and Beyond: Alternative Traditions in Modern Drama**" is the problem of the historiography of modern drama and theatre. The reason it focuses on examples from the 18th to 20th century Europe is because that is where the origins of what is globally understood by the term "Modern Drama" are located. My essay sketches the rise of the bourgeois worldview and the origins of what Raymond Williams describes as the "general form of bourgeois drama", during the 18th century in Europe and goes on to examine its development through the subsequent period. It then looks at the ways in which this worldview and the dramatic form which embodied it were challenged during the latter half of the 19th century by a new variety which is generally recognised as the drama of liberal dissent. Further, it discusses how, in time, this liberal variety was itself challenged by what I call the radical alternative tradition. It offers a detailed study of these two major and, in certain ways rival, dramaturgic and performative paradigms–one associated with the Ibsenian and Stanislavskian tradition and the other with the works of Meyerhold, Piscator, Brecht, and Dario Fo. The essay argues that, while on a conscious level both paradigms reject the bourgeois social order, it is only in the latter that the order is philosophically and politically transcended.

The essay that follows, "**Decolonialising an Imperial Icon: Shakespeare on the Parsi Urdu Stage**", looks at the historical conditions in which a particular form of popular modern theatre emerged and, in effect, defied the cultural hegemony of the colonial masters. It examines how the socio-economic logic of a vernacular commercial stage affected Shakespeare's plays when they were adapted in Urdu for the Parsi theatre between 1870 and the 1900s. It was around 1870 that the major Bombay-based Parsi theatre groups became professional companies and turned to Urdu adaptations of Shakespeare's works. The essay looks at the history of this move and, through detailed textual analysis of several examples, demonstrates how the Elizabethan bard was desi-fied (or nativised) in order to satisfy the popular taste of its Indian audiences. The essay is the outcome of protracted and extensive research into an area where much of the primary sources are either lost or not available readily for detailed critical reading.

In the subsequent essay,"**Refashioning Modernity: Habib Tanvir and His Naya Theatre**" I discuss how a major example of contemporary Indian theatre drew upon the artistic resources of traditional forms of theatre and not only gave a different direction to Indian drama but also reconstructed the conventional concept of modernity in the post-independence cultural practice. This essay is the result of a sustained interest in Tanvir's work which began long before 1996 when my first written response to it appeared as the "Introduction" to Anjum Katyal's English translation of Tanvir's celebrated masterpiece *Charandas Chor*, and has continued till after the playwright-director's death in 2009. The essay traces the development of the work of one of India's foremost theatre persons with a view to understanding how he evolved that distinctive style which made his productions both traditional and modern simultaneously. It looks at the aesthetic and political factors that inspired him to follow a trajectory so different from the one that foreign trained theatre artists of his generation tended to follow. Tanvir's approach to the folk culture is examined through a detailed, chronological discussion of his major productions, from the early *Agra Bazar* to *Charandas Chor* and beyond. It argues that much of the richness and power of this theatre derives precisely from Tanvir's remarkable ability to establish a partnership between his own sophisticated and unmistakably modern consciousness on the one hand and the astonishing traditional skill and energy of his unschooled village actors, on the other.

The next essay, "**Trapped in Infinity: Beckett's *Waiting for Godot***" offers an overview of Beckett's life and writings. Most of Beckett's major work was done during a politically disturbed climate which eventually led to the Second World War. It shows how, from the beginning, Beckett followed a path of what I call increasing interiorisation in order to reach a point in his writing where no reference to any external factor–history, society, or even the self–would be required to make sense of what is written. The essay then goes on to offer a detailed textual analysis of *Waiting for Godot* in order to demonstrate how Beckett has cleverly created a play in which an enormous amount of physical action and theatrical energy is employed not only to compensate for the absence of a play but to actually reinforce a sense of stasis, vacuity, and inconsequentiality. The essay is an updated version of what originally appeared as the introduction to a student edition of Beckett's play published by Oxford University Press (New Delhi).

At the end of the book there is a relatively shorter piece, "**Drama And/As Theatre from Written Text to Performance Text**". It deals with the close connection between the written script and its stage production. It argues that a performance is much more than mere vocalisation or visualisation of the verbal or written script. It derives from my classroom work on the subject with students of English Honours.

These essays were written over a long period of time. At some point during that period, I was afflicted with a vision disability and required assistance in various ways–from locating and getting books from libraries to reading and, in certain instances, even typing. Dozens of persons, mainly young students and friends, offered to help. Unfortunately, it is not possible to name all of them. Sadly one of them is no longer with us. A playwright and dear friend, Shahid Anwar, who provided invaluable help with Urdu texts at various stages of my protracted work on Parsi theatre, died unexpectedly. Dr. Abid Raza Bedar, a rare breed of librarians, who headed the Khudabakhsh Library (Patna), was of enormous help in locating, photocopying and mailing the texts that I needed to look at. I am also grateful to Sahba Khan of the Raza Library (Rampur) who went beyond the call of duty to help me find some of the rare texts. I am indebted to my friend and colleague Svati Joshi who helped read and translate Gujarati texts. During the final stages, Anuradha Jain was of enormous help in preparing and collating the typescript as was my former student and now a young friend, Priyanka Kharbanda, who did the final tidying and copy editing of the manuscript. Another friend, Smruti Gargi Eswar kindly agreed to design the cover of this book. I owe a huge debt of gratitude to them all.

Finally, like my other works, this book could not be completed without Neeraj, a fellow academic and my partner in life. She was always there to provide the necessary emotional support and whatever practical help I needed. Her advice and critical comments were of crucial importance to me in my writings.

NOTES

1. Cornell University Press (1981), p. 9.

1

Bourgeois Worldview and Beyond: Alternative Traditions in Modern Drama[1]

In his book, *To Brecht and Beyond* (1984), Darko Suvin writes: "From the very large number of modelling possibilities, one or (at exceptional periods of strife) a few become dominant in a given socio-historical constellation or age" (4). Taking our cue from Suvin's observation, we can identify in 20th century Western drama two distinct and rival dramaturgic traditions or modelling possibilities. We can describe these traditions as: one, the dominant bourgeois liberal tradition and two, the radical alternative tradition. The axiomatic basis of the first is in the ideology of individualism, while the alternative tradition takes its inspiration from some form of historically and ideologically post-bourgeois thought, and embodies concerns which are categorically societal or supra-individual. The two traditions contended for supremacy throughout the 20th century, often major changes in the socio-political climate tilting the balance in favour of one or the other.

In what follows we shall discuss these rival currents at length. However, it must be pointed out right at the outset that neither of these two traditions is monolithic or homogeneous. Each covers a wide and diverse body of formal and stylistic experiments in playwriting and play-producing. In other words, in a finer distinction, it should be entirely possible to sub-divide each of these traditions into a number of specific trends that emerged in the course of history. But, since in this chapter our purpose is to identify and describe only the general trends of these two dramaturgic types for the strictly functional purpose of historical perspective, we will not concern ourselves with specific examples of internal variations, but shall remain focused on the two overarching paradigms and their underlying ideological assumptions. Besides, practical examples from the two traditions are not always and necessarily exclusive but at times they can, and do, overlap in terms of political orientation and even content.

Bourgeois Origins of Modern Drama

During my long career as a teacher, I taught courses in modern European drama for many consecutive years. One of the very first questions that I usually took up for discussion in my class was: What was specifically modern about this drama; or, more precisely, how does one distinguish it from the non-modern or pre-modern dramatic traditions. Drawing upon the existing body of scholarship, I improvised a way of studying the changes in the dramatic form in relation to the changes in society. I found it instructive to approach it through a system of two distinct yet inter-locking perspectives: a long perspective or view of the genesis and history of modern drama going back to the 18th, and in some ways even to the 17th century, and a short one dealing with its, and, for our purposes more significant, view of its major formal and ideological tendencies since the latter part of the 19th century. Thus, in the long view, I traced the origins of modern drama to the rise of the middle class to power and supremacy in Europe, while my short view encompassed the period of the rise of liberal dissent within the European middle classes.

What made this bi-focal approach pedagogically interesting was that it yielded a two-part, seemingly paradoxical proposition. One, that modern European drama and theatre, in all its dominant forms and traditions (except in what I have identified above as the radical alternative tradition), is socially and ideologically middle class. Obviously, this part of the proposition pertains to the long view mentioned above. The short view, on the other hand, pertains to the drama, since the rise in the late 19th century, of a dissenting minority within the ruling class and inspires a seemingly contradictory proposition: that all influential examples of that very drama have been consciously and categorically anti-bourgeois. In other words, while almost all serious examples of modern drama from Ibsen to, say, Beckett, have been characterised by an unmistakable anti-bourgeois moral stance, this dramatic tradition, in the ideological implications and orientations of dramaturgic and theatrical forms, as also in the composition of its audiences, continued to be circumscribed by bourgeois philosophical horizons. It distinguished itself, on the one hand, from the pre-bourgeois (particularly medieval and Elizabethan) traditions, and, on the other, from the 20th century attempts at a radical break and renewal as in the tradition from Mayakovsky, Piscator, and Brecht to Dario Fo, John Arden, and dozens of radical activist theatre groups that emerged during the euphoric 1960s.

The distinctive conventions of this middle class drama evolved through a long and complex process. English drama, which, during the Elizabethan period, was the glory of the European theatre, lost most of its artistic vibrancy and popular character in the course of the turbulent 17th century. Instead of reaching out to all sections of society, it shrank till it became the theatre of a small social elite. As Arnold Hauser, one of the most incisive historians of the period, points out, "Since the reign of Charles I dramatists had limited themselves more and more to producing for the theatre of the court and the higher ranks of society, so that the popular tradition of the Elizabethan age had soon been lost" (87). Thus, when the Puritans closed down the theatre after the revolution of 1642, English drama was already in decline. A few decades later, when the theatres reopened in 1660, what was produced was a severely devitalised kind of drama. This situation continued for more than half a century and not much in what was produced was remarkable or of lasting value or influence.

Following the Cromwellian revolution, which brought the English middle class to power, it was clear that the new historical reality required new forms of cultural expression. Writers forged new forms out of old traditions. For instance, although fictional narratives like Bunyan's *Pilgrim's Progress*, Defoe's *Robinson Crusoe*, and Swift's *Gulliver's Travels* built on the old traditions of the picaresque, by the middle of the 18th century, in the works of Samuel Richardson and Henry Fielding, increasingly more developed examples of an entirely new form of prose fiction called the novel emerged. Around the same time (mid-18th century), a new kind of drama also began to take shape in England and elsewhere in Europe. A new generation of playwrights emerged who, often, consciously, reworked old forms in order to make them reflect contemporary reality and the worldview of the emergent middle class. The most significant example of this was a new tragic drama, known as bourgeois tragedy which became widely popular during the middle decades of the 18th century. Although formally offered as tragedy, this drama was distinguished by the fact that it jettisoned the conventions and concerns of the traditional aristocratic tragic form with its predilection for protagonists of high social rank and for larger than life passions and grandiloquence. Instead, it employed, for the first time in the history of European drama, middle class protagonists whose tragic stories usually turned around sex, morality, money, and marriage.

The play which inaugurated this new form of tragedy in Europe was written in 1731 by an English dramatist, George Lillo. It was titled *The London Merchant, or the History of George Barnwell*. The play dramatised the tragic fate of a young man from a trading family who falls prey to an evil woman's charms and is led into murdering his loving uncle for money. Since he was using the traditional form of tragedy to convey a new kind of content, Lillo felt somewhat apologetic and found it necessary to offer an explanation to justify his "tragedy" about a young middle class man. In a dedicatory letter to his patron, Sir John Eyles, he wrote:

> What I would infer is this, I think, evident truth; that tragedy is so far from losing its dignity, by being accommodated to the circumstances of the generality of mankind that it is more truly august in proportion to the extent of its influence, and the

> numbers that are properly affected by it. As it is more truly great to be the instrument of good to many, who stand in need of our assistance, than to a very small part of that number.

Elaborating this further, he says:

> If princes, etc., were alone liable to misfortune, arising from vice or weakness in themselves or others, there would be good reason for consigning the characters in tragedy to those of superior rank; but, since the contrary is evident, nothing can be more reasonable than to proportion the remedy to the disease (250).

Lillo's play was followed in 1755 by Lessing's *Sara*, which broke new ground in the theatre and introduced bourgeois tragedy on to the German stage. Influenced by the novels of Richardson (in particular by *Clarissa Harlowe*), *Sara* was the first tragedy in German to be taken from contemporary life and, unlike Lillo's, to have been written in ordinary, everyday prose dialogue. Writing about this new variety of drama, Hauser notes:

> The tragic deed was an uncanny, inexplicable, irrational phenomenon in Greek drama, in Shakespeare and still, to some extent, in French classical drama; its shattering effect was due, above all, to its incommensurability. The new psychological motivation gave it a human measure and, as the representatives of the domestic drama intended, it was made easier for the audience to sympathise with the characters on the stage (92-93).

One of the notable features of the romantic German drama of the "storm and stress" movement was that it foregrounded the theme of the individual versus a hostile environment, a theme that was to become a pivotal motif in an entire current of significant modern drama from Ibsen and Strindberg to, say, Arthur Miller and John Osborne.

This Ibsenian tradition represented the full and finest expression of what Raymond Williams has described as the "general form" of bourgeois drama. In Williams' abstract model, this emergent form consisted of five factors: one, the subject matter became contemporary and, two, indigenous; three, the dramatic speech was no longer verse or formal prose but ordinary everyday prose (in Williams' own words "quasi-colloquial"); four, no longer confined exclusively to the life and actions of aristocracy, the drama became socially inclusive, so that all ranks and classes were now the acceptable subject of drama; and, five, all references to any supernatural or supra-human agency came to be gradually excluded and plays dealt with ordinary human reality and relationship in strictly human and secular terms (1981a, 166–67). These five constitutive factors can be reduced to three fundamental philosophical emphases: namely, realism, a secular worldview and a democratising orientation. These emphases define the new kind of drama and distinguish it from the theatre traditions of pre-modern periods. The emergent form thus can be said to herald the process of democratisation and secularisation of the dramatic form which reached its most significant culmination in the middle class drama in the late 19th century.

Two features that define middle class drama in its fully developed form are its axiological basis in the ideology of individualism and, to a lesser degree, its aesthetics of illusionism. Individualism, which forms the epistemological basis of the dominant European and American culture, particularly since the 18th century, is integrally allied to the materialist and atomist emphases of bourgeois theory and practice. It defines the horizon of the bourgeois worldview, revealing both its strengths (compared with earlier metaphysical modes and forms of thought) and its limitations (compared with what may be called post-individualist, particularly Marxist theory and practice). Illusionism, on the other hand, is the common artistic manifestation of this epistemology and endeavours to reproduce "mirror images" of observed life and setting, which not only blur the reader or spectator's awareness of the essential fictionality of an artistic text with a view to maximising and intensifying the emotional impact, but also restrict that text's artistic and cognitive range. Both these axioms are best illustrated in what is commonly described as the drama of naturalism.

Naturalism

Although naturalism developed as a conscious emphasis and stylistic term in drama only in the 19th century, it has a long and varied history, which has been usefully traced by Raymond Williams. He notes two main senses in which the term was used prior to its full scale development in drama. First, it was used in the late 16th century in "a form of conscious opposition, or at least distinction, between revealed (divine) and observed (human) knowledge" and as such signified "a philosophical position allied to science, natural history and materialism" (1977, 203). The early and general manifestations of naturalism in this sense can be seen in the tendency towards a consciously secular and social emphasis that goes back, in drama and fiction, to the 17th century (prose comedy, domestic drama) but becomes particularly pronounced in the 18th century "bourgeois tragedy" of which, as we saw above, Lillo's *The London Merchant* is a good example. It is reflected, in particular in the reliance upon observed (and, as Williams has pointed out, contemporary and indigenous) social life as the source of dramatic action.

The term naturalism was also used, in the mid-19th century, particularly in painting, to indicate a "method of 'accurate' or "lifelike reproduction" (1977, 203). This second meaning of naturalism, obviously related to what we have here identified as illusionism, continues to be the sense in which the term is popularly understood and used in relation to drama and fiction. However, according to Williams, naturalism in drama in its fully developed form combines both these senses; that is, it designates not only a method but also an ideological position. It indicates, in William's words, "a movement in which the method of accurate production and the specific philosophical position are organically and usually consciously fused" (203). This twofold emphasis of naturalism can be clearly seen in Zola's well-known defence of naturalist drama. He wrote:

> In effect, the great naturalistic evolution, which comes down directly from the 15th century to ours has everything to do with the gradual substitution of physiological man for metaphysical man. In tragedy, metaphysical man, man according to dogma and logic, reigned absolutely. The body did not count; the soul was regarded as the only interesting piece of human machinery;

> drama took place in the air, in pure mind. Consequently, what use was the tangible world? Why worry about the place where the action was located? Why be surprised at a baroque costume or false declaiming? Why notice that queen Dido was a boy whose budding beard forced him to wear a mask? None of that mattered; these trifles were not worth stooping to; the play was heard out as if it were a school essay or a low case; it was on a higher place than man, in the world of ideas, so far away from real man that any intrusion of reality would have spoiled the show (1968, 367).

Naturalism in this 19th century conception, thus, meant a secular and materialist emphasis in conscious opposition to the metaphysical and religious world view of earlier times. But it also meant a style of surface realism, a life like and non-emblematic reproduction of the "tangible world". However, it underwent a significant modification when it was combined with the idea of material determinism.

Determinism was a new emphasis which began with the enlightenment but developed to a fuller form in the theories of social and natural history in the course of the 19th century. For, although as early as the 18th century Montesquieu had, in *The Spirit of the Laws*, regarded environment not only as a background but also as a condition of human activity, and Denis Diderot had stressed the role of the milieu, it was only in the 19th century that social and natural environment came to be seen as a decisive, deterministic factor in human destiny. A leading proponent of determinism was Robert Owen, who wrote:

> The character of man is, without a single exception, always formed for him; ...it may be, and is chiefly, created by his predecessors; ...they give him, his ideas and habits, which are the powers that govern and direct his conduct. Man, therefore, never did, nor is it possible that he ever can, form his own character (1817, 91-92).

This new awareness of the importance of biological inheritance and material environment on one's life was a central feature of what came to be called Social Darwinism, which grew out of a general materialist orientation of bourgeois thought. This materialism, however, was mechanistic and naive compared with the more complex idea of dialectical materialism developed later by Karl Marx. For, the specific terms in which it developed in liberal thought during the 19th century carried with it a sense of inexorability that made it essentially a modern version of fate or destiny.

Naturalism with this determinist emphasis profoundly influenced the major dramaturgic forms and styles of the period. The consequence was that the physical environment, the setting, and the biographical past no longer functioned as mere realistic backdrops lending authenticity to the dramatised action but actually became crucial factors in that action. For example, the enclosed space of the room, within which the action was usually located, often assumed a formal and cognitive significance far beyond its simple illusionist function as an accurate reproduction of recognisable and seemingly authentic setting. It represented, in other words, the physical and social environment within which the inhabitants were forced to live out their destinies and which determined the range of their consciousness, choices, and the possibilities of life. In Williams' words, the major naturalist dramatists

> put on these rooms, prescribed in detail in a new form of writing which was much more than mere "stage directions", because such immediate physical environments were, in their view, necessary elements of the dramatic action. They were, in the fullest sense, living rooms: places made to live in certain ways: environments which both reflected and influenced their possibilities of life (1981, 169).

Thus, for example, in Strindberg's *Miss Julie*, the kitchen, the Count's boots, and, above all, the bell acquire a significance far beyond their functional value. They actually intervene in the action, directly or indirectly, as a representation of the external (or social) forces that control and define Jean's consciousness. Julie, too, is conceived, in the author's own words, as a

> victim of the discord which mother's "crime" has produced in a family, a victim, too, of the day's complaisance, of circumstances,

> of her own defective constitution, all of which are equivalent to the Fate or Universal Law of former days. (1965, 79)

The main problem with this kind of materialism was that it took a simplistic view of the relationship between human consciousness and the material and social environment. Positing an irreversible and unilateral process of natural and material cause and human effect, it failed to recognise, or sufficiently emphasise, that within certain limits men are also able to alter the circumstances of their existence and thus are capable of shaping their own collective destiny.

Individualism and Despair

The reason for this failure can be found in the ideology of individualism. While naturalism, as a philosophical position, unshackled the human gaze and enabled it to shift from a mysterious and distant god and supernatural forces to the human and secular world of knowable natural and social phenomenon, the ideology of individualism imposed a new restriction and confined that gaze, in social, economic, as well as cultural theory and practice, to the individual and its subjective standpoint. Beginning from the 19th century on, this practice of conceiving the world from the standpoint of the individual becomes the predominant feature of bourgeois thought and practice. It was during this period, as Williams points out, the concept of the individual as "the fundamental order of being" came to replace the earlier notion of an individual denoting a "single example of a group", and a new term, individualism, emerged to mean "a theory not only of abstract individuals but of the primacy of individual states and interests" (1976b, 135–36).

In the beginning, individualism was an emancipatory development. It offered a break from the static social hierarchy and absolutist feudal environment. As Arnold Hauser expresses it, "Western man had already become conscious of his individuality in the Renaissance," but it is only since the middle of the 18th century that "individualism as a challenge and a protest against the depersonalization inherent in the process of civilization has existed" (62). However, in the gradual development of liberal consciousness during the subsequent century, individualism degenerated into a restrictive epistemological phenomenon. The result was that, in Williams' words, "the point of reference became not a general order but the individual, who as such embodied all ultimate values" (1966, 68).

It is this individualism which lies at the basis of the dominant forms of drama since Ibsen and which determines the choice of subject matter as well as dramaturgic design. It is reflected, first and foremost, in the predominantly psychological and subjective definition of character, relationships, and conflicts. It is reflected also in the privatised and personalised mode–the restriction of dramatic action to personal and familial situations as well as the separation of this private and personal world from the larger, social world outside. But, above all, it is revealed (particularly in the more serious examples of mainstream drama) in a pervasive tragic awareness that the gap that divides these two worlds–the internal world of the individual and the external world of the society at large, with the latter wielding a hostile and overwhelming power over the former–is unbridgeable.

The privatisation of the scope of the dramatic action and the consequent lack of diversity in dramatisable relationships and events were accompanied in this kind of drama by the enlargement of the status of the dramatis personae (or agents) who are conceived and presented as fully developed individuals with seemingly complete psychological and biographical backgrounds. They become, for the first time in drama, characters in the strict sense of the term. As we saw in the example of Strindberg's *Miss Julie*, the individuality of these characters is consciously emphasised by setting them in a specific social and physical environment and giving them specific pre-histories. As the protagonists are usually conceived as unique individuals, the dramatic conflicts in such plays usually underscore the value of individual authenticity and freedom. The uniqueness of personality and its inner tensions and conflicts become the main focus of dramatic interest, making a play not the dramatisation of a fable but the exposition of a psychological state. Eventually, this subjective standpoint, which, in its final implication, internalises and de-socialises relations between people, leads directly to what Williams has called the drama of "subjective expressionism", which expresses "the action of a single mind at a level at which other persons have reality only in that mind's terms" (1981a, 270).

Concerned as this drama usually is with exploring the relation between the individual and its environment, the very privatisation of this dramatic action (the enclosed emotional space of the nuclear family, the walled-in physical space of the room) enhances the impression of the separation and expresses, to quote Williams again, "A precise contradiction in bourgeois social relationships: that the centre of the values was the individual and the family, but that the mode of production which sustained them–the world they went out into and returned from–was in quite different social range, much wider, more complex and more arbitrary" (1981, 171). Moreover, since the conventional limitations of the naturalist method forbade an emblematic mode of representation or rapid change of scenes, this complex social world could not be dramatised directly ("as in the older and simper actions of kings") and forever remained an outside, mysterious force that intervened in the dramatic action only through reports, messages, or visitors.

The history of modern drama, particularly since the latter half of the 19th century, is replete with protagonists who are in conflict with their social environment. They feel that it thwarts their individuality and denies them freedom. We see these unhappy characters protesting, with varying degrees of vehemence, against an uncaring society. But all their protests and anger is ultimately found to be futile, even impotent. One of the best visual expressions of this impotent anger is Osborne's Jimmy Porter who stands at his bed-sit window and angrily rants and shakes his fist at an indifferent world outside. Like Ibsen's Mrs. Alving, Strindberg's Jean, Miller's Willy Loman and Osborne's Jimmy, these rebellious protagonists are invariably broken in the end and what continues to prevail is the hostile environment.

When the bourgeois social and moral order is experienced (and emotionally rejected) from the standpoint of the consciously separate individual–that is, the individual thinking and/or acting alone against a common condition of compromise–it appears as a force that is external (because made and controlled by others), hostile (because threatening to individuality and its full and authentic development and expression), and overwhelming (because more complex and larger). It thus becomes an unacceptable, and at the same time, also an insurmountable fate. The tragic consciousness that pervades this drama, despite all its technical innovations and immense critical energy, is thus a direct result of this individualist approach to problems of collective social existence. That is why almost every significant example in this tradition, from Ibsen to Miller and beyond, invariably ends in a sense of defeat and despair.

Drama As Illusion

In one of his plays, John Arden describes the nature of theatre thus:

> All is painted, all is cardboard
> Set it up and fly it away
> The truest word is the greatest falsehood
> Yet all is true and all is play

Theatre, above all else, is a form of entertainment. If we look back in history, we find that the vitality of the medieval and Elizabethan theatres derived precisely from their ability to provide varied and wide-ranging kinds of experience in forms that invariably included and emphasised the principle of vigorous pleasure. These traditions, like popular dramatic traditions all over the world, regarded theatre as a form of game or sport. The very terms that were used to designate a dramatic performance indicated this ludic approach. For example, during the Middle Ages the terms commonly used for this purpose were game, play and sport in English, *Iudus* in Latin, *spiel* in German, and *jeu* in French. In India, too, popular terms for dramatic performance are often similar, e.g. *khel*, *tamasha*, etc.

This ludic emphasis is not merely a matter of terminology. It lies at the base of all popular or plebeian dramaturgic and theatrical practices everywhere in the world. It is evident in the robustly playful style of acting and staging, in the active and open interaction between the performers and their audiences. Dramaturgically, it is evident in the wide range of freedoms taken with respect to style, technique, and subject matter. Such freedoms allow playwrights to deal, with ease, dexterity, and inventiveness, with subjects of such vast magnitude as historical chronicles, the entire biblical story from *Genesis* to *Revelation*, and the epic narratives of the *Ramayana* and *Mahabharata.* It allows them also to mix within a single text kings and clowns, tragic and comic experiences, casual and formal styles, morally serious and merrily frolicsome tones, and critical and celebratory impulses. In speech as well as in activity, it can range freely between the everyday and the stylised, creating a delightful interplay of the empirically verisimilar and the artful. Using such devices as direct comment, and aside, it can involve spectators directly and actively in the performance. Such freedom, made possible mainly by an expressly ludic approach to the art of the theatre, makes for immense artistic and cognitive possibilities and richness.

Just as the communal and well defined, although often metaphysical, worldview of the medieval and Elizabethan dramaturgies is replaced in the individualist tradition of drama by a narrower, although expressly secular and rational, metaphysics of individualism, the earlier concept of the theatre as game and play is usually replaced in this drama by a correspondingly reduced notion of it as illusion. "In England in the Middle Ages", writes V.A. Kolve:

> one could say "We will play a game of the Passion" and mean what we mean when we say "We will stage the Passion." The transition from one to the other is more than a semantic change; it is a change in the history of theatre (1966, 14).

This changed conception of drama takes the form of artistic illusionism, which, in dramaturgic and theatrical practice, means a detailed reproduction of observed life in such a way that all traces of artistic construction (of a text's status as art) are carefully concealed. Such practice signifies a restriction of the artistic and cognitive potential of the theatre which directly corresponds to the process of individualisation and internalisation of experience noted above. Moreover, in its internalisation of experience and its suppression of the essentially ludic and collective aspects of the theatre and theatrical experience, this preoccupation with verisimilitude is also related, as Mikhail Bakhtin points out, to the modern prejudice against laughter, which in turn is related to the puritan heritage of looking down upon and suppressing plebeian or vulgar cultural forms. For,

> The Bourgeois nineteenth century respected only satirical laughter, which was actually not laughter but rhetoric. (No wonder it was compared to a whip or scourge.) Merely amusing, meaningless, or harmless laughter was also tolerated, but the serious had to remain serious, that is, dull and monotonous (Bakhtin 1968, 51).

Thus, the illusionist theatre's rejection of the earlier openly playful concept of drama is itself related to that process of individualisation and psychologisation of the carnivalesque that Bakhtin traces back to the emergence of the bourgeoisie's cultural forms.

Although illusionism reached its full formal development and became a dominant aesthetic principle only in the 19th century, the tendency towards it can be traced back to the Restoration. As early as 1672, Dryden, in his *Of Heroic Plays*, argued that various sound effects are essential in the theatre

> to raise the imagination of the audience, and to persuade them, for the time, that what they behold in theater is really performed. The poet is then to endeavor for an absolute dominion over the minds of the spectators (1912, 91).

The affinity of attitude between Dryden's desire to "persuade" the spectators by exercising "an absolute dominion" over their minds and Zola's ridicule in the passage quoted above of boy actors playing female roles is evident. It is this absolute control over the audience's thought and feeling that illusionist drama and theatre strives towards. It tries to affect this through a variety of means that involve not only the physical conditions of performance (kind of stage, lighting, seating, and so on) and style of acting (Stanislavski's method, for instance) but also the dramaturgic aspects of the text itself. Here also it is just as evident in a text's dependence upon the detailed reproduction of a specific physical environment–which transforms into a highly particularised and fixed location what in earlier traditions was always treated as a neutral, versatile, and communal playing area that could be made to designate any place with ease–as it is in that text's absolute reliance upon uniformly natural movements and everyday, colloquial speech. Above all, it manifests itself in a restrictive formulation of dramatic action, which requires that events be selected and arranged in a casual order so that the action would flow smoothly and, as much as is possible, without interruption from one event to the next, weaving a unilinear pattern of mounting intensity leading gradually but inevitably to the conclusion or impasse.

Obviously such a dramaturgic formulation is meant to intensify rather than diversify the experience and cannot permit much variation in the range of dramaturgic agents (who usually belong to a narrow range of socio-economic classes or milieus), the range of activities (which also remain uniformly "natural" and largely verbal), or the range of experiences and relationships (which remain largely emotional and familial, and either exclusively comic or exclusively tragic). The point is to so overwhelm the spectator with the emotional intensity of the dramatised experience that he will lose his ability to either view that experience critically or think of alternative possibilities within a given situation.

A crucial consequence of illusionism is that the process of production and communication of meaning becomes a mechanical, one-dimensional process, a one-way, univocal traffic from the stage to the auditorium. Banished from the world of the action and reduced to evesdropping through the proverbial "fourth wall", the spectators become passive recipients of the given experience and are so restricted in their optical and intellectual vision, and so involved in the emotional and subjective intensity of the presented action, as to have no perspective save the one the play chooses to dramatise. In both these effects, the illusionist theatre assigns to the spectator an intellectually passive role and renders him incapable of intervening, critically or imaginatively, in the dramatised experience. A play thus conceived loses the dialogic richness that the constant interjection of the spectator's own thinking can lend to the action that is played out on stage.

Dramaturgic and theatrical illusionism, then, consists in the practice of consciously trying to conceive, or de-emphasise, the essentially artful and playful nature of drama. Affecting both scripts and their staging, it results, for all the technical enrichment and intensity of feeling, in an impoverishment of the drama's intellectual and artistic resources. In seeking to be as unobtrusive and consistent as possible, it precludes all those forms, conventions, and devices–episodic structure, different forms of direct speech, poetry and songs, music and dance–which could allow drama and theatre, as in the Elizabethan age, to communicate the great variety and complexity of human experience. Its plots are so formulated that they seem to flow out of and into the empirical time and space of the performance, and this smooth, unilinear, and casual flow carries with it a sense of inevitability. Similarly, restricting the dramatisable activity to verbal and empirically verisimilar, rather than allowing it to range freely through a variety of colloquial and formal, verbal and physical, it not only reduces the theatre's ability to delight and entertain but curtails its semiotic possibilities as well.

The dominant tradition in drama, then, continued to combine, in varying forms and proportions, individualism and illusionism. In the serious and critical examples of modern drama–that is, the examples that reflected the greater degree of cognitive and moral seriousness, that often actively and critically explored the relations between people and their environment, and that, moreover, usually involved conscious attempts to break from the limitations of the official or orthodox forms of thought and art–these limitations may not be as obvious as they are in the lesser examples of commercial drama. The limitations are there, nonetheless, and they can be witnessed in the predominantly subjective and psychological preoccupation and the privatised and universalised (that is, absolutised, dehistoricised) modes that allowed the dramatic focus and the centre of values to be shifted from the collective and variegated world of social relationships to the interior, private world of the family and the individual and thence, as in the development from subjective expressionism to the Beckettian drama, a seemingly shared, but abstract, universalised, and subjectively perceived, category of"the human condition." The result, best exemplified by Ibsen's drama, is that, despite a rich proliferation of innovative forms and techniques, developed often in conscious opposition to the orthodox forms of social and artistic practice, no alternative mode of experience, no radically different response to the world, and therefore no explicit or implicit awareness of the possibility of a different and happier condition of human existence could be conceived.

Radical Alternative Tradition: Before and After Brecht

I have argued above that the ideological limitation of the bourgeois tradition can be transcended only when, as in Marxism, a person is seen not only in terms of his or her isolated and subjective self but also in terms of the web of relationships (personal and social) that define her/him, and, furthermore, when these relationships and situations are perceived in historical terms, that is, as subject to change and development. In such an approach, the particular and the general, the personal and the social experience and destinies, are seen in their dialectical relationships. Any particular situation comes to be perceived not only as an eternally and externally given universal condition but as a humanly and historically produced, and therefore similarly alterable, set of material and social circumstances. Such a complex world view requires an equally complex and dynamic form and style. One way in which a playwright may approach such a form is by consciously recognising the communal and playful nature and potential of his art and by conceiving the function of the theatre not as creating and maintaining illusions, nor as offering faithful reproductions or "slices of life" in all their emotional intensities, but as constructing, deliberately and emblematically, heuristic models of social life so that spectators are encouraged to undertake an intellectual and critical investigation of "the way people live together" (Brecht 1965, 12).

The epistemological shift that took place with the rise of Marxist theory and practice at the end of the 19th century replaced the bourgeois philosophy's mechanical and individualist form with the dialectical and collectivist one without losing the former's rational and materialistic emphasis. This shift also had a profound impact on the practice of playwriting and play-producing. An important consequence of this was that the socio-historical group or polity once again became the source and the centre of values, and the relationship between, human consciousness and physical environment came to be conceived in complex, rather than simply harmonious or simply antagonistic, terms capable of influencing and changing each other. This relocation of the epistemological focus is evident in the major examples of what I have here referred to as radical alternative tradition, which does not simply seek to dramatise issues and situations of communal and contemporary concern but also tries to do so within a historical and dynamic perspective. Above all, it focuses on social classes and their collective material interests rather than on individual heroes and their abstract ideals. The dramatic conflict in this kind of drama tends to arise out of the conflicts of interest between such socio-historical groups or collectivities.

The first major and sustained transnational appearance of the radical alternative tradition of the activist kind was in Russia and Germany during the first two decades of the 20th century in the wake of the world's first successful socialist revolution. Half a century later, in the 1960s and 70s, the radical activist climate that pervaded Western Europe and North America and which was largely triggered by the widespread opposition to America's brutal war in Vietnam, caused it to flower once again as a massive trans-Atlantic cultural phenomenon. In both instances, vigorous attempts were made to redefine the nature and function of the theatre, as an art form as well as a social institution, in the light of its essential artificiality as well as relation to contemporary socio-political concerns and aspirations, and to develop genuinely popular (or plebian) forms of dramaturgy and performance. These efforts–spanning several decades and many countries, and comprising the works of many writers, directors and theatre groups, caused symptoms of a radically alternative and globally influential current to emerge in European drama. Although each example of this richly variegated corpus of artistic theory and practice has its own distinctive features, its own mark, which sets it apart from the others, and although such differences could be of great significance in another context, each example also shares with the others certain basic features of ideological and artistic approach. It is precisely because of this identity of ideological and artistic orientation that it is possible to speak of them as constituting a coherent tradition.

The plays in this tradition are united by a twofold affinity: by their shared unease with the "legitimate" middle class forms and circuit; and, at the same time, by a common quest for alternative forms and circuits that are truly public and cognitively open-ended (i.e. more inclusive and diversified) as well as more entertaining. In practice, this has usually meant a dramaturgic and performance style that is able to integrate, in a vigorous and richly variegated presentation, the pleasures of storytelling and spectacle with those of critical contemplation and examination. In their attempt to achieve such a dramatic form, the radical playwrights demonstrate a common preference for the styles and conventions of the popular traditions of theatre. Notable among these features are episodic construction, social rather than psychological emphasis, and a playful, non-illusionist style–in other words, a kind of drama that can combine with ease a whole range of emotions and experiences (personal and political, tragic and comic, stylised and naturalistic) and often delights in playing with levels of (artistic) illusion and reality. All this has the effect of widening the scope of drama in terms of the magnitude of dramatisable situations and relationships as well as in the richness and variety of the theatre's artistic resources.

The radical alternative tradition is also characterised by its relentless search for new and truly popular audiences and by its desire to restore to the theatre its communal, public character and bring back to it those larger plebeian sections of society that the middle class theatre systematically excludes. This has usually resulted in either some radical re-construction of the naturalist stage or an outright abandonment of the fixed and enclosed locations of the conventional theatre (with its fixed and individually marked seats, polite atmosphere, financially and socially restricted admission, and so on). Performance may now be carried out in open air parks, noisy restaurants, factory gates, crowded marketplaces, and, busy shop floors, restoring to the theatre its public character and re-carnivalising the theatrical experience so that the relationship between the performers and spectators can be pointed, active and truly dialogic.

Theatre As Political Action: The Blue Blouse, Meyerhold and Piscator

Although it is possible to trace the trend towards politically meaningful, pro-people, kind of drama in Europe back to the last quarter of the 19th century, the more significant work towards developing what we have here identified as radical alternative tradition did not begin till the period immediately preceding the Bolshevik Revolution in Russia. By the beginning of the 20th century, particularly following the uprising of 1905, the opposition to the tyrannical Tsarist regime steadily spread to all sections of society regardless of class and ideological orientation. But it was the October Revolution which triggered an enormous upsurge of creative energy in the theatre circles in Russia as well as Germany. There was theatre not only in conventional playhouses but literally everywhere, in factories and trade union halls, in public buildings and squares, in workers' clubs and beer halls, and so on. A large number of theatre groups, big and small, professional and amateur, were actively involved in presenting revolutionary theatrical performances. A rich variety of theatrical forms flourished: poster plays, mass spectacles, political revues, knockabout farces and living newspapers. By the mid-1920s posters, cinema and theatre were reaching out to mass audiences. Theatre often took the form of a public trial with the audience as jury.

In this context, the work done during the early decades of the 20th century by directors like Meyerhold and Piscator and groups like the Blue Blouse was of particular significance. Their work had an enormous and far-reaching influence not only on the development of political theatre in Russia and Germany but also on the practice and theory of theatre in general the world over. In particular, Meyerhold and his modernist experiments, aided by significant creative inputs from Eisenstein, Tretyakov and the legendary circus artist, Lazarenko, helped shape the contours of the political theatre movement in the post-Revolution Soviet Russia.

The Blue Blouse was the largest and the most influential among the workers' theatre groups operating in the early years of the Soviet Union. It was a revolutionary theatre movement rather than a single group. It was started in 1923 by students of the Moscow Institute of Journalism who wanted to develop a dramatic newspaper offering stage versions of oral or printed reports. Soon this first amateur attempt grew into a professional movement and attracted a large number of playwrights, directors, composers, and designers. On the occasion of its fourth anniversary, it formed a nucleus of artists who endeavoured to work on the development of a new theatrical form based on questions of artistic and agitational work. They wanted a theatre which would serve as a "form of agitation, a topical theatre born of the revolution, a montage of political and general phenomena presented from the ideological standpoint... of the proletariat" and to function as "a variety platform, a special form of amateur art in the workers' club," characterised by its mobility and ability to perform under any conditions (3). The example of the Blue Blouse inspired several other groups to emerge all over Russia. The size of the Blue Blouse itself grew steadily and, at the peak of its popularity, it was said to cover nearly 7,000 workers' circles as well as several professional groups.

Stanislavski, the most influential theatre director of the time, was one of those who regarded a political message in stage plays as completely unacceptable. But his own favourite pupil, Meyerhold, whom several years later he was to describe as "my true heir in the theatre", had no such prejudice about using theatre as a political platform. Moving away from the master's preoccupation with psychological realism, Meyerhold started to experiment with a more blatantly theatrical and stylised form. His experiments eventually led him to a fully developed revolutionary theatre. Following the October Revolution his work acquired a greater sense of political immediacy and directness. All his innovations of the previous years were reworked in accordance with the requirements of the new situation. In the course of his experimentations, he not only developed forms of political drama, he also redefined many aspects of the art and craft of theatre in ways that seem like an early draft of what was to be developed more rigorously in later decades by Bertolt Brecht as "Epic theatre". He emphasised "three dimensional space, functional props, costumes and sets, rhythmic dialogue and movement. Moreover, he linked it to the traditions of popular spectacle: mysteries, commedia dell'arte, vaudeville, forms of storytelling, and fairground entertainments.

Meyerhold's work was part of the powerful outburst of creativity in post-Revolution Russia. His first post-Revolution production, *The Dawn*, was staged on the first anniversary of the October Revolution. It was, according to Edward Braun, "the first attempt to establish a comparable atmosphere of mass community within a conventional theatre...It exhibited a number of features that were soon to typify agitator theatre elsewhere: a text rewritten and staged to give it topical reference, the dismantling of the conventional performer-audience division, the merging of play into collective celebration, the conscious effort to dispel illusion, the use of a 'modernist' design in the effort to invoke the new spirit of revolution" (133). Meyerhold's other productions included, besides various innovative forms of agitational theatre, grand and massive predominantly celebratory shows or spectacles that were mounted in streets and public buildings during the euphoric years of the post-Revolution Russia. These spectacles involved casts of thousands and used clowning, acrobatics, dance, masks, huge symbolic props. The huge casts were usually divided into several units and each unit worked under a particular director. The productions dealt with equally grand subjects, such as, *The Play of the Third International*, *The Mystery of Freed Labour*, *The Blockade of Russia*, etc. It was also during this period that Meyerhold produced

Mayakovsky's political morality play, *Mystery-Bouffe,* on the occasion of the first anniversary of the October Revolution, and re-produced it in 1921 in a version substantially modified and updated with the author's help.[2]

During this period, Germany too witnessed widespread and vigorous attempts to link theatre with struggles and concerns of the plebeian sections of society. Erwin Piscator and Hermann Schuller co-founded a theatre called The Proletarisches Theatre (The Proletarian Theatre), which opened in Berlin on the occasion of the third anniversary of the October Revolution. In contrast to earlier attempts to bring art to the people, this was conceived by Piscator from the beginning as a theatre that combined agitation and political propaganda explicitly committed to promoting class consciousness and proletarian solidarity. In Piscator's own words, "It was not a question of a theatre that would provide the proletariat with art, but of conscious propaganda, nor of a theatre for the proletariat, but of a Proletarian theatre...We banned the word art radically from our programme, our 'plays' were appeals and were intended to have an effect on current events, to be a form of 'political activity'" (Piscator, 44–45).

In the wake of the massive euphoria unleashed by the October Revolution, theatre in these countries became more directly and unabashedly partisan. This even prompted some communist leaders to warn against mixing propaganda and art. But such was the extent of political enthusiasm at the time that artists tended to ignore the advice even of leaders as important as Lenin and Lunacharsky. Like so many others at that time, Erwin Piscator boldly declared: "We who had once regarded art as an end in itself, who had once supported art's claim to be omnipotent in comparison to the realities of the day, were now marching against that very idea under the slogan, 'No more art!'... The synthesis of art and politics implies final responsibility, implies placing every means, including art, at the service of the highest human aims" (66). Thus, theatre persons and playwrights—even the most significant ones like Mayakovsky, Meyerhold, and Piscator—openly used the stage for propagating revolutionary ideas and communicating political messages. It is possible that some of the work done in that surcharged atmosphere was formulaic and not of durable artistic value. But this huge outburst of energy certainly did bring forth some of the possible forms and features that the political theatre could build on during the subsequent periods.

Epic Theatre of Bertolt Brecht

The rise of the Stalinist regime in Russia and of Nazism in Germany caused the euphoric upsurge of revolutionary culture in Russia to decline and recede. The radical alternative tradition, too, suffered a serious setback but did not die completely. On the contrary, it continued to develop, in a quieter and more rigorous form, particularly in the works of Bertolt Brecht, whose dramatic and theoretical writings offer the best and most developed expression of the alternative dramaturgy. Brecht's most important contribution is that he refined and fine tuned the radical theatre practice and gave it a strong, systematic, and comprehensive theoretical foundation. Brecht was Piscator's younger contemporary but his work had a greater and farther reach and influence than Piscator's. It impacted every aspect of stage practice and performance. As Edward Braun points out, "whereas Piscator, the director, has made his more lasting impression in the field of dramatic writing, the lessons of Brecht, Germany's greatest modern playwright, have been most deeply absorbed by directors, designers, and actors" (162). This precisely is what makes him, to borrow Peter Brook's phrase, "the key figure of our time" (Brook, 80).

Brecht's reputation today rests mainly on his plays and theoretical writings of the period after his exile from Nazi Germany in 1933. Prior to it, beginning in 1918 in Munich, he wrote and produced a number of full length and one-act plays. They were mostly a lighter kind of social dramas or musicals, and lacked the political clarity and maturity of his later work. They did not carry any sign or sense of political immediacy that marked the activist theatre of Russia and Germany of that period. It is important to recall that, when Brecht began his career in the theatre, what is known as the post-war revolution was at its peak. Germany was in the grip of a massive and militant working class movement and there were clashes throughout the country. The conflict reached its most violent climax in 1918 and erupted in a full-fledged working class revolt, eventually leading to the arrest and execution of important communist leaders, including Rosa Luxemburg. And yet, Brecht's first major play, *Baal*, written in that very turbulent year, had nothing which would even remotely suggest an awareness of the raging political conflict. The play deals with a young debauched singer who seduces women wherever he goes and abandons them. Each of his victims eventually commits suicide. In the end, Baal himself dies alone. In Brecht's next play, *Drums in the Night*, the violent political environment did find a mention, but only marginally or peripherally. Although written some years later, Brecht set the play's action back in 1918 in Berlin which was the epicentre of the workers' revolt that year. He uses the widespread violence as the backdrop to the main plot in which a frustrated young soldier drunkenly follows the violent mobs through the streets. Brecht's other plays of that decade are also marked by a similar absence of ideological commitment and contain no direct reference to the contemporary political situation.

However, it can also be argued that Brecht had not really insulated himself totally from the political upheavals of the time. Those were his formative years. He was drawing upon various sources, such as fair-ground performances, skill and experience of the clown Karl Valentine. It is possible that in those seemingly apolitical plays of the early years he was trying to find a style and form of theatre distinct from the one that prevailed at the time. In other words, from the start, Brecht was trying to break free of the prevalent forms and conventions of middle class drama, a drama that belongs in what we have above identified as bourgeois individualist tradition. For example, shortly before his death he described what he was aiming at in his very first stage productions, *Baal* and *Drums in the Night*. He said: "We wanted to make possible a production which would break with the Shakespearean tradition common to German theatres: that lumpy monumental style beloved of middle class philistines" (1971, 439).

Nonetheless, Brecht acknowledged some years later that his understanding of politics during that period was "disgracefully slight" (Willet, 191). He seems to have become particularly aware of this around the mid-1920s during his work on a series about the rise of capitalism that he proposed to write. He was researching for the first play in the series which was to be set in Chicago when, according to his disciple and collaborator, Elizabeth Hauptmann, he began to read economics and discovered that the existing theatre was incapable of depicting the modern economics driven world. In Hauptmann's own words, "he was aware that the prevailing (big) form of drama was not suitable for depicting such modern processes as for instance the distribution of the world's wheat and the course of life of contemporary man". Hauptmann goes on to quote Brecht himself as saying, "when one sees that our world of today no longer fits into a drama, then drama does not fit the world". In 1926, after the staging of *Man is Man*, Brecht began to systematically and diligently read on socialism and Marxism, including *Das Kapital*. Hauptmann reports that it was in the course of these studies that Brecht formulated his theory of epic drama (Witt, 52). Thus, a fuller understanding of Marxism led Brecht to, in the words of Braun, "the realisation that the only dramatic means adequate for the elucidation of the complex working of the capitalist society was the Epic theatre" (169).

Elsewhere I have described two types of dramaturgic forms at some length: one, "character-based" and the other, "story-based" (Malick 1995, 41-52). The former type is best exemplified in the Individualist theatre since Ibsen and Stanislavski. In the character-based dramaturgy, every play revolves around a unique or exceptional individual. In this tradition, the focus of interest is predominantly on the individual character, on its emotional and psychological inner life. Plays in this tradition derive their power and richness from their ability to create and sustain an uninterrupted and mounting level of emotional intensity and to mesmerise the spectator into complete identification with the protagonist and with her/his experience or fate. Eschewing the traditional episodic or scenic division of action, this kind of drama also tends to divide the dramatic action into larger and fewer segments, usually 'Acts'. The finest and most influential example of this kind of dramaturgy is found in Ibsen. This preoccupation with the character is evident in Ibsen's famous description of the procedure that he followed while writing a play. "Before I write down one word," he said, "I have to have the character in my mind through and through. I must penetrate into the last wrinkle of his soul" (Cole, 170). Much the same effect is aimed at in Stanislavski's theory of psychological realism.

Needless to say, this disproportionate interest in the character as if he/she were an emotionally and psychologically complete real individual may enrich and enhance a play's emotional experience, but it also causes the drama's traditional storytelling interest to correspondingly diminish and devitalise. As we saw at the beginning of this essay, the tradition of individualist drama, to which character-based dramaturgy and theatre belong, is historically connected with the triumph of the bourgeois social order and its ideology of individualism. As against this, the pre-bourgeois dramatic forms, tended to be "story-based" and viewed characters, not as unique individuals, but as necessary functions of a narrative structure, as dramatic agents through whose agency a story is carried forward. It was largely the forms and conventions of these pre-bourgeois traditions that the radical alternative theatre drew upon in order to produce a new, collectivist kind of drama, a drama which employs an episodic or scene-based structure.

In his quest for a truly contemporary, post-bourgeois theatre, Brecht was from the beginning striving towards a story-based dramaturgy. As, Edward Braun writes, "[following *Edward II*] nothing in the theatre was more important for Brecht than the story (*Die Fabel*), and to ensure its clarity every action was made as concrete as possible" (164). This emphasis on telling a tale constitutes a central feature of what we today recognise as Brecht's epic theatre. His writings on theatre are replete with pronouncements which indicate that everything in the epic theatre must be subservient to telling, or in Brecht's own word, "showing", the story and foregrounding what may be described as parabolic interest. The entire idea of alienation effect or critical distance in Brecht's theory is ultimately related to the foregrounding of the story rather than the character. For example, his oft repeated instruction to actors is that they must 'show' or 'illustrate' a role, not live it. Braun points out that the idea behind Brecht's formulation of the epic theatre as 'acting from memory (quoting gestures and attitudes)', is that "the actors tell a story with foreknowledge of its outcome, and use the characters to 'illustrate' the narrative, rather than 'live' their roles" (168).

An entry in Brecht's diary indicates that, from the beginning, he took care not to depict his protagonists in such a way that the spectator becomes emotionally involved with them and begins to identify with their experiences and choices. He was already working towards what later came to be known as the estrangement effect. "There is one common artistic error," he wrote, "which I hope I have avoided in *Baal* and *Jungle*, that of trying to carry people away. Instinctively I've kept my distance and ensured that the stage realisation of my (poetical and philosophical) effects remains within bounds. The spectator's 'splendid isolation' is left intact, it is not *sua res quae agitur*, he is not fobbed off with an invitation to feel sympathetically, to fuse with the hero and cut a meaningful and indestructible figure while watching himself in two simultaneous versions. There is a higher type of interest to be got from making comparisons, from whatever is different, amazing, impossible to take in as a whole" (Brecht 1979, 159). About the same time, Brecht, with inputs from the famous Bavarian comic artist, Karl Valentine, had also started to experiment with his "demonstrative style of acting in which each gesture had significance and revealed something important about the character" (Braun, 165).

Thus, Brecht based his work, on the one hand, on an awareness of the severe artistic and ideological limitations of the dominant middle class tradition, and, on the other, like Meyerhold before him, on an equally conscious recognition of the immense potential of the "epic "styles and techniques of popular (pre- or non-bourgeois) forms of theatre and performance. He recognised that the established theater, in its commercial and socially complacent form, not only represented the world in an "inexact" way but also hypnotised spectators into accepting it as the only correct representation. "The one important point for the spectators in these houses", he observed, "is that they should be able to swap a contradictory world for a consistent one, one that they scarcely know for one of which they can dream". As for the serious form of middle class drama, he noted that in this drama "The field of human relationships came within our view, but not within our grasp" (1964, 188). This drama, Brecht argued, reduces social and historical conditions to a mere setting, or backdrop, to an action that itself remains predominantly subjective and private. "The feelings, insights and impulses of the chief characters are forced on us, and so we learn nothing more about society than we can get from the 'setting'" (Brecht 1979, 190).

Brecht was also aware of the tremendous potential of culture as a social institution. "It is precisely theatre, art and literature", he observed, which must provide the means "for a social, practical rearrangement of our age's way of life (123). Therefore, working increasingly from a consciously Marxist standpoint, he set out to formulate the idea of a truly post-individualist theatre–a genuinely political and collectivist theatre that would be more concerned with social relationships and contradictions and would base itself on the principle:

> that people's consciousness depends on their social existence, taking it for granted at the same time that this social existence is continually developing and that their consciousness is accordingly changing all the time (Brecht 1965, 35).

In other words, Brecht wanted a theatre that would not only reproduce the surface of reality but show it as a historical process in all its dialectical contradictions. It was to achieve this goal that he developed his theory of the epic theatre. In one of his many descriptions of this new kind of theatre, he defined it thus:

> The epic theatre is chiefly interested in the attitude which people adopt towards one another, wherever they are socio-historically significant (typical). It works out scenes where people adopt an attitude of such a sort that the social laws under which they are acting spring into sight.... The concern of the epic theatre is thus

> eminently practical. Human behaviour is shown as alterable; man himself as dependent on certain political and economic factors and at the same time as capable of altering them.... In short the spectator is given the chance to criticise human behaviour from a social point of view, and the scene is played as a piece of history. The idea is that the spectator should be put in a position where he can make comparisons about everything that influences the way in which human beings behave (1964, 86).

In developing the style and techniques of his dramaturgy, Brecht, like Meyerhold and others in the radical tradition but much more rigorously and systematically, built upon the conventions of popular theatre, both western and oriental. He studied and learnt from Elizabethan traditions and Far Eastern dramaturgy, from vaudeville shows and cabaret, from pantomimes and ballads. In all cases he drew upon their playful and deliberate style, their varied structure, and their immense gestural energy. He derived from them the principle of loose, episodic construction, communal and economic-political (rather than individual) focus, and humour, combining in a rich and uninhibited mixture direct and topical social comments, discussions, storytelling, jokes, songs and music. Brecht was firmly of the opinion that there was"a need for naive, but not primitive, poetic but not romantic, realistic but not ephemerally political theatre." He believed that the "contrast of art and nature can be made a fruitful one if the work of art brings it to a head, but without smoothing it out." Therefore, he saw in these features a great potential for revitalising the theatre. This could be done by making it simultaneously popular and realistic. By popular Brecht meant "intelligible to the broad masses, taking over their own forms of expression and enriching them/ adopting and consolidating their standpoint/representing the most progressive section of the people in such a way that it can take over the leadership" (1964, 154-55). And by realistic he meant:

> Laying bare society's causal network/showing up the dominant viewpoint as the viewpoint of the dominators/writing from the standpoint of the class which has prepared the broadest solutions for the most pressing problems afflicting human

society/emphasising the dynamics of development/concrete and so as to encourage abstraction (108-09).

Popular forms of drama and theatre also often produce what Brecht called the Verfremdung effect (variously translated into English as the effect, technique or stance of alienation, estrangement, or distancing), which in the epic composition of a play as well as in its performance, "allows us to recognise its subject, but at the same time makes it seem unfamiliar"; in other words, it "frees socially-conditioned phenomena from that stamp of familiarity which protects them against our grasp today" (192). Achieved through a variety of means–episodic or situational focusing which is fable-centred rather than character-centred, diversified style, and deliberate and repeated interruptions in the flow of action making representation and formulation alternate with and complement each other–it emphasises the artfulness and theatricality of the presented action while encouraging a complex and critical response on the part of the spectators.

This approach is clearly opposed to what we have above identified as the illusionist aesthetics which blurs the distinction between the fictional world of the play and the empirical world of the spectators and draws the latter, through encouragement of passive and emotional involvement, into the experience embodied in the stage action, thereby destroying their capacity to criticise it. On the contrary, the estrangement technique allows epic theatre to partly distance the spectator. The stage action is presented explicitly as an artificially and playfully arranged and mounted representation that must be viewed with a combination of sympathy and critical detachment. An excellent example of how Brecht prevents total identification with the emotional experience of a character and, instead, encourages a more complex response in which sympathy and critical distance are balanced is found in his *Mother Courage and Her Children*. At the end of the scene in which her deaf and dumb daughter, who has been assaulted by a soldier, returns badly bruised and traumatised Mother Courage curses the war. This is the only instance in the entire play where she denounces the war and we find ourselves sympathising with her. But this sympathy is short-lived because it is immediately undercut by the following scene which shows Courage wearing a necklace of silver coins and walking jauntily while singing a song in praise of the war.

Brecht's theory of a new kind of drama, which he had developed over long years of involvement in theatre both as a playwright and as a director, and which was to have a profound influence on the development of theatre both in the West and in other parts of the world, including India, is best illustrated by his own dramaturgic practice. It is evident in his non-moralistic and expressly socio-historical treatment of dramatic agents and situations, a treatment that emphasises not identity and consistency but contradiction and inconsistency. His plays usually embodied a complex interplay of perspectives, responses, and choices within determinate socio-historical situations. He is similar to other modern playwrights, even those in the individualist tradition, in so far as his agents are not heroes and villains, not absolutely good or absolutely bad paragons of virtue or vice. But they are also not conceived as psychologically or psycho-pathologically unique individuals, but clearly and openly presented as fictive constructs of complex social relationships. This is further reinforced by the "demonstrative", epic style of acting in which actors are required to "tell a story."

Furthermore, Brechtian drama, presents characters who are vacillating between the usually incompatible but necessarily internalised alternatives of a desired happy life versus cruel social alienation arising out of powerful and explicitly presented social forces (as a rule, other agents). Such agents are often forced to choose from several alternative courses, with some of them making a correct choice (as does Grusha in relation to the abandoned royal baby in *The Caucasian Chalk Circle*) and some making an incorrect one (like Mother Courage who loses everything she had hoped to save by treating war as business as usual). "The laws of motion for a society," Brecht believed,

> are not to be demonstrated by "perfect example," for "imperfection" (inconsistency) is an essential part of motion and of the thing moved. It is only necessary–but absolutely necessary –that there

> should be something approaching experimental conditions, i.e. that a counter-experiment should now and then be conceivable. Altogether this is a way of treating society as if all its actions were performed as experiments (1964, 195).

His own work in the theatre fully reflected this belief.

Return of Theatre as Political Action

I have been trying to trace the radical alternative tradition in drama and theatre since the early Soviet period. I hope I have made it clear that it is a long but not a continuous tradition. Closely tied up as it is with the rise and decline of radical (usually left wing) political movement or struggle, it fluctuates in both artistic vigour and popular appeal with the ebb and tide of that movement. So it was that in its "activist" form, this tradition underwent a massive resurgence in Europe and North America during the radically charged climate of the 1960s.

The euphoria amongst hundreds of thousands of young people all over the world during that heady seventh decade of the last century is best expressed by these famous lines of William Wordsworth:

> Bliss it was in that dawn to be alive
> But to be young was very heaven

Those young people are now well past their middle age, and often cynical, living as they are in the newly ordered, globalised and unipolar world of rampant conformism, consumerism, and careerism where there are few takers for radical ideas and socialist ideals. But, most of them cannot help remembering with nostalgia the revolutionary optimism and euphoria of those years which seriously challenged the established order everywhere. Although the promised "renewal of revolutionary politics as well as the arrival of a new revolutionary force" eventually failed to materialise, many things did come to a head during that period.

It was the revolt of workers and students in France which was the epicentre of a powerful radical ferment that triggered great excitement globally. Ten million French industrial workers had stopped work and occupied factories in what was perhaps the biggest ever trade union action in the post-industrial West. Thousands of students had left their classes and taken to the streets, occupying universities, erecting barricades and fighting fierce battles with the police. America's war in Vietnam had become increasingly unpopular and 1968 witnessed massive anti-war and anti-draft demonstrations, paralysing campuses in America and elsewhere in the West. The frenzy of police brutality at the Chicago Democratic Convention was an unprecedented event of state repression in the USA. But it only helped to increase the fury of the anti-war youth. Similarly, when the Soviet tanks rolled into Czechoslovakia to suppress "The Prague Spring" there was an international spate of protests. In England, the annual CND (Committee for Nuclear Disarmament) Easter March was turned into an anti-war demonstration and many universities (notably, The London School of Economics) were agog with students' radicalism. In Asia, too, China's (now controversial) "cultural revolution" was at its peak and had a wide reaching influence abroad. In India, the peasant revolt in Naxalbari inspired many academically brilliant and highly articulate students to champion the cause of an armed struggle against an oppressive Indian state.

In short, there was a worldwide explosion of youthful revolutionary energy. Many counter-hegemonic groups of ardently committed young men and women were all struggling for a radical and democratic reordering of the world and its social and moral institutions. Of course, in the end, no such reordering was achieved. The rebellious spirit of the period eventually waned giving way to the neo-conservative ethos of the subsequent decades. Nonetheless, during those tumultuous decades it succeeded in profoundly and lastingly influencing all aspects of social life and cultural endeavour.

One of the most prominent consequences of this revolutionary outburst was a veritable explosion of creativity and of counter-culture. There was a vehement rejection of orthodox or "straight" culture, along with other forms and institutions of the bourgeois social order. Established channels and circuits of cultural production and dissemination were rejected as bourgeois ideological tools of manipulation and control. An active, indeed an activist, conception of culture–that is, culture as a political weapon, or as an instrument of political action–flourished once more in almost every field of creative endeavour.

The impact of this anti-authoritarian spirit of the period could also be seen in theatre. It was not the time for safe, individualist-illusionist kind of drama. What the period produced was a powerful revival of the radical alternative forms and gave birth to many new groups, directors, and playwrights in America and Europe. These theatre artists participated in the protest activities. During the "hot spring " of 1968, along with students and workers, actors too went on strike and occupied major theatre buildings in Paris and Milan (such as the Odeon). Such was the enthusiasm that the Scottish playwright-director, John McGrath, drove to France with a message of solidarity from the British theatre workers. Some North American radical theatre groups notably, Lui Vadez's Spanish group El Teatro Campesino and Peter Schuman's Bread and Puppet Theatre, toured Europe. There were heated discussions in theatre circles about the social function of art in general and of drama in particular. The cultural theories of Mao, Marcuse and Gramsci were studied and debated. The authoritarian structure of some of the established companies was questioned by the younger artists associated with them, which sometimes resulted in their gradual democratisation. Several dictatorial theatre directors were actually ousted, and henceforth artistic decisions were made more collectively. The most prominent example of this was the removal of Ron Davis, the founder of the San Francisco Mime Troupe. According to Joan Holden, who took over as the company's artistic director, "there was a big fight over how much authority the director should have. People wanted more democracy. Davis made all the artistic decisions, and the people wanted to have a lot more to say" (Erven, 32).

After the example of widespread upsurge of radical theatrical activity in Russia and Germany during the 1920s, this was the second most powerful flowering of radical alternative theatre in the West.[3] The infusion of a powerful wave of fresh revolutionary ideas and ideals energised the theatre by effecting a radical change in both its concept and its practice. Among other things, theatre became bolder, more innovative, more flexible, more portable, more community based, and above all more involved with the immediate material and emotional life of its audience. Like in the early Soviet period, theatrical activity itself spilled out of the confines of the constructed, architecturally enclosed stage over to streets, neighbourhoods, shop floors, fair grounds, parks, marketplaces, and other such open public places. The idea was that these spaces belonged to the people and therefore, they were the most appropriate performance spaces for people's theatre. So, throughout the 1960s, theatre increasingly found its way to the streets and into politics.

There was an exciting intermingling of the twin concepts of political action as theatre and theatre as political action. For instance, Richard Nixon's inauguration as the 37th President of the US was opposed by a "counter inauguration", staged in the streets of Washington. Similarly, what ended in bloody mayhem during the democratic convention in Chicago, was originally planned, as Richard Schechner recalled a year later, "not as a confrontation with Richard Daley's gestapo but a carnival, a festival of life through which hundreds of thousands of young people would show how it was possible to take over streets and parks and celebrate an America to be born".

The May Revolution in France too was partly "staged" as a massive festival of graffiti and masks, songs and slogans, nudity and love making, speeches and spectacles, demonstrative actions and effigies, satires and lampoons. Besides actual theatrical performances–such as the short dramatic pieces interpreting daily news which were performed in the streets outside the Odeon theatre, or the impromptu agit-prop activity during sit-ins, teach-ins, rallies and demonstrations, what the rebels were staging was a gigantic celebration. As in the better kind of regular theatre, there was a great deal of fun and frolic which was at the same time a symbolic (although, at times naive) defiance of social, moral and political authority. what the rebels were staging was a gigantic celebration of love, humanity and solidarity. Jean-Jaques Lebel, a leading Parisian theatre activist of the time, described what he saw thus: "Everywhere people danced and trembled. Everywhere people wrote on the walls of the city or communicated freely with the total strangers. There were no strangers but brothers, very alive, very pleasant. I saw people fucking in the street and on the roof of the occupied Odeon Theatre and others run around naked on the Nanterre campus, overflowing with joy. The first things revolutions do away with are sadness and boredom and the alienation of the body" (Lebel, 113).

Just as agitational demonstrations and rallies became theatrical, theatrical performances became explicitly political, demonstrative and agitational. The new performance groups were looking for new kinds of audiences of the underprivileged and/ or disaffected people, women, proletariat, immigrants and youth. In this respect their concept of popular theatre was different from that of, say, Jean Vilar, the father of the Avignon Theatre Festival and director of the Theatre Nationale Populaire in Paris. Vilar's was a homogenising, populist concept of people (it was criticised as such by Jean-Paul Sartre). Such an approach conceives of theatre as "a place of communion where all social groups meet to receive their regular dose of national cultural heritage through the designated classics" (Erven, 13-14). The new radical movement in drama, on the contrary, regarded the theatre as "a place where the oppressed classes in society are made conscious of the injustice of their predicament" and, as Brecht had once suggested, the spectators are prompted to "intervene actively in life".

The radical theatre of the 1960s was not only searching for new kinds of audience but also new kinds of contact with the audience. Like their predecessors in the Soviet Union and Germany, they did not want the performance to be one-way traffic from the actor to the spectator as it is in middle class conventional theatre. They did not desire an audience of passive spectators who would merely "consume" the experience and go back home to their "normal" lives, undisturbed by what they saw and felt. Radically altering the traditional performance-audience relationship, they worked towards making the spectators active participants, collaborators, even co-authors who would help "write" the performance text. For example, Judith Malina and Julian Beck, founders of the Living Theatre group, who were living in exile in Europe since their brush with the US forces of law and order in 1963, wanted their audiences to "suddenly discover that they are no longer the 'privileged class' to whom the play is 'presented' but are needed by the actors for the very accomplishment of the play". This kind of approach to the theatre audience is an important characteristic of political theatre which wants people to challenge the established social order and its moral and philosophical assumptions. The tradition of this kind of approach goes back to Meyerhold, who envisaged a theatre that pre-supposes "the existence of a fourth creator in addition to the author, the director and the actor–namely the spectator". And it comes down to Augusto Boal's concept of "spect-actor" as formulated in his later work (Boal, xxx).

Along with the abolition of the conventional performer-spectator relationship, the new radical groups also tended to abolish the tyranny of the individually authored, scripted and fixed texts. Instead, scripts and performances were evolved or developed collectively through discussions and exercises. The concept of theatre workshop, a method which is now universally used by theatre groups not only for preparing a production, but also for training actors, was developed (partly under the influence of the theory and practice of Polish director, Jerzy Grotowski). These radical groups usually functioned as a collective and tried to forge a strong and direct bond with the audience. There was an insistence on the immediacy and directness of concerns. Specific problems and issues impinging on the material and emotional life of the community were chosen as the main themes and were dramatised from an openly partisan standpoint without any recourse to liberal ambiguity in the name of art.

Performances often dealt with current political events which were dramatised and interpreted critically in a form reminiscent of the "Living Newspaper" of the early Soviet period. The capitalist political order, and the value systems on which it is based and which it promotes in myriad ways, direct and indirect, frequently came in for scathing criticism. That political criticism in theatre can sometimes really hurt the power structure, and performances can actually make a difference is amply demonstrated by the censorship, persecution, and even brutal assault that political theatre workers were often subjected to.

An excellent example of how some of the European and American radical theatre groups of the period were subjected to repressive measures is found in the famous case of the Living Theatre. The group was invited by the Avignon Festival to perform its celebrated creation, *Paradise Now* ("a didactic practising of joy", ending in a procession through the streets). After a few performances, the group was told to stop the show and substitute some other play because the Festival authorities and the local administration feared that it would disturb the peace and order of the town. Rather than agree to perform *Antigone* (as suggested by the Mayor and the Festival administration) or desist from giving free performances, the group decided to withdraw itself from the Festival. In a hard hitting public statement, they gave eleven reasons for refusing to comply. Two of the reasons for this refusal were:

> 1. Because you cannot serve God and Mammon at the same time, you cannot serve the people and the state at the same time, you cannot serve liberty and authority at the same time ... you cannot play *Antigone* (which is about a girl who refuses to obey the arbitrary dictates of the state and performs a holy act instead) and at the same time substitute *Antigone* in a place of a forbidden play.
> 2. Because the time has come for us at last to begin to refuse to serve those who do not want the knowledge and power of art to belong to any but those who can pay for it, who wish to keep the people in the dark, who work for the Power Elite, who wish to control the life of the artists and the lives of the people" (Beck, Section 83).

That particular phase of radical ferment is over. Leftwing resistance is no longer trendy. As often happens in any such large scale and more or less spontaneous social upheaval, most of the agitprop groups which had suddenly sprung up during the late 1960s had little understanding of what constituted a truly popular political theatre. They could not last long after the ebbing of the revolutionary euphoria. But then there were several significant exceptions and they continued to survive. Their very survival—despite enormous financial and organisational difficulties and dwindling public support, despite serious devitalisation of left-wing political culture in many parts of the world since the 1980s—testifies to their tenacity and resilience. At any rate, that period had a profound and lasting influence on the political theatre and has significantly enriched its concept and practice. Its influence can still be discerned in the better known groups and artists the world over. The works of Dario Fo, John McGrath, John Arden, Augusto Boal, Richard Schechner, Eugenio Barba, Bread and Puppet Theatre, San Francisco Mime Troupe, Ariane Mnouchkine's Theatre Du Soleil, and several others, owe much of their artistic vigour to the electrifying climate of that period.

The most significant of them all was Dario Fo who was also one of the finest examples of radical alternative theatre artists.

Theatre of Subversive Laughter: Dario Fo

> The job of theatre is not to document filth, but to transform it into fertiliser, and generate messages of hope for young people.
>
> Dario Fo

An outstanding political performer and playwright, Dario Fo was the most popular and one of the most frequently produced artists of his time. In collaboration with Franca Rame, he developed a particular style of theatre which is undoubtedly one of the finest examples of radical alternative drama. Like his predecessors in this tradition, Fo's theatre, too, was defined by two interlinked features: one, a strong predilection for the culture and traditions of the ordinary people; and, two, a commitment to left-wing politics, to a revolutionary endeavour for an egalitarian rearrangement of society. From the former, it derived its astonishing vitality and subversive humour, and from the latter, it's incisive foregrounding of a radical, revolutionary consciousness. The consequence was a theatre at once hilariously funny and provocative, full of theatricality and sharp political comment: in short, a theatre which was not only relentlessly subversive of the existing system and its underlying ideological assumptions, but also distinguished by its remarkable artistic vitality and galvanising political immediacy.

Fo's connection with the pre-bourgeois cultural traditions was stronger, deeper, and more comprehensive than that of any of his predecessors in the alternative drama. He systematically built his work upon the old and nearly extinct popular traditions of performance. He was exposed to some of it since his childhood. The area where he grew up was rich in the traditions of *fabulatori*, traditional storytellers. As a child he was fascinated by the fantastic stories told by the local fishermen which talked of a strange, topsy-turvy underwater world where priests confessed their own sins, women got drunk and peasants beat up the landlords. Fo also had his first exposure to politics during that period. It was during his boyhood that the fascists rose to power in Italy and the Second World War broke out. He witnessed the growing anti-fascist activities among the local people. These two early influences–an interest in the traditional cultural forms and a commitment to anti-fascist politics–were to help shape his work as an artist. However, it was not till several years later that Fo began to be seriously interested in left-wing politics. His interest in the popular, plebeian cultural forms, too reached a fuller development after he came into contact with Franca Rame, who was herself a distinguished actress and militant feminist playwright coming from a family of traditional travelling performers going back three hundred years.

By the end of the 1950s, Fo had committed himself entirely to a career in the theatre and began to write and perform for the established theatres and television channels. For seven successive years, between 1959 and 1967, which is usually described as his "bourgeois period," he wrote a full-length play each season for the conventional commercial stage. Besides these, Fo also wrote and performed a TV series called *Canzonissimo*, which became one of the most popular shows on Italian television. Many of these productions, including *Canzonissimo* broke box-office records in Italy and made Fo and Rame among the most highly paid theatre artists. By the mid-1960s, his plays were translated and performed throughout the continent and he was established as one of the most frequently produced and commercially successful living playwrights in the whole of Europe.

This was the time when, like other parts of Europe and North America, Italy too was going through a politically turbulent period. The state was becoming more repressive in the wake of an increasingly militant anti-authoritarian movement of students, intellectuals and workers. In Italy, the late 1950s and the early1960s witnessed not only an attempted revival of fascist dominance but also militant protests against such manoeuvres. For instance, in 1959, a new Christian Democrat ministry led by Fernando Tambroni was installed with the support of a neo-fascist party which openly traced its antecedents back to Mussolini's regime. Emboldened by this, the latter indulged in openly provocative activities which, in turn, inspired widespread protesters in some places, killing several persons. A general strike was called which was enormously successful and forced Tambroni to resign. Italy's three main trade union federations, which had hitherto been divided due to ideological differences, joined together into one massive working-class movement. The Christian Democratic state was thus constantly challenged by an ever growing working-class struggle involving widespread strikes and protests against, among other things, censorship of arts and culture.

Fo's plays and revues of this period, written and performed with his characteristic profusion of humour and irony, reflected the political conditions of the time. True, he was writing for the conventional circuit and for conventional middle-class audiences. But, as Angela Montgomery points out, "Throughout this period, [he] was developing his own peculiar brand of explosive satire, which found its voice more and more in the grotesque expression of the domination and exploitation of the proletariat by the ruling classes, and in its references to popular culture. His theatre became increasingly 'political'" (206). In short, his plays of this so-called bourgeois period were equally poignant and unsparing in its satirisation of contemporary politics and society as his later work.

Despite commercial success and enormous popularity that he enjoyed, Fo and Rame began to feel uncomfortable working in the relatively safe circuit of commercial entertainment at a time when a massive wave of radical cultural turmoil was raging throughout the Western world. They decided that they would no longer be a 'jester of the bourgeoisie' and stopped entertaining those "whose values they did not share" and, instead, began to perform for workers, students, and other sections of the common people (Schecter, 145).

Poignancy, directness and immediacy in theatrical communication were of paramount importance for Fo. He saw political significance in the predominantly physical form of theatre that he practised. "I try to create images rather than words, which cause people to feel a sense of crisis in the relationships between the self and society," he once said. As a performer, he consciously built upon the traditions of the medieval strolling players, and the actors of commedia dell'arte. Like those traditional artists of the past he possessed an incredible skill for improvising and adapting a text according to the demands of the specific context of a performance.

In Fo, the functions of playwriting and play-performing were not divorced but combined. He liked to describe himself primarily as a performer who also "made" (rather than wrote) his own scripts. He did not see his theatre as the playwright's (or literary) theatre, but viewed it primarily as the actor's theatre. In other words, his was not what he referred to as "the theatre of words" but one of performed action, that is, of mime, movement, and gestures. Himself an outstanding performer, Fo created productions which almost invariably revolved around a protagonist whose role demanded immense range in performance skill. As a performer, he was often described–and, indeed, described himself–as a clown. This linked him and his work in the theatre, not only to the medieval tradition of the jongleur, but also to the modern tradition of political clowning from Durov to Charlie Chaplin.

Fo did not consider the written script as sacrosanct, nor as a rigidly fixed or finished text, but merely as a rough verbal outline of the action or scenario, which was always open to future additions, adaptations and improvisations. He wanted his plays to be improvised and adapted in keeping with the environment and the conditions of performance. That is why Fo always encouraged "adaptation" rather than "translation" of his scripts into other languages. He had no objections to his scripts being altered, even substantially, if it suited the context of performance and as long as it's political thrust was not undermined or distorted. He viewed scripts, in his own words, as "living and adaptable material," which, in the words of the Swedish Academy's Nobel Prize citation, "are open for creative additions, dislocations, continually encouraging the actors to improvise."

All this gives us a measure of how intensely and uncompromisingly political an artist Fo was. He used his art to serve specific political causes. From the beginning, he sought to develop a kind of theatre which did not merely reflect, but interrogated and even actively participated in the collective life and struggles of his audiences and becomes a form of collaborative political action. He not only wrote and performed in response to important and immediate political issues of his times but also participated in organised popular struggles around those causes and concerns. For a large part of his career, he worked closely with revolutionary groups and movements and devised productions to further those movements and what they stood for. In other words, like the radical artists of the early Soviet Union and of the 1960s, he practised an activist kind of theatre which communicated directly with its audiences about their own lived collective experience.

Working not from some liberal, populist viewpoint but from what Brecht called a "fighting conception of people and popularity," Fo recognised that to be able to reach out to large masses and to speak to them directly, it is not enough to merely put their problems and concerns on stage but that one must also endeavour to do so in the idiom of the people's own traditional forms. It is with this objective in mind that he retrieved from centuries of feudal and bourgeois suppression, neglect, and scorn, traditional forms of plebeian culture, in particular, the socially subversive traditions of the strolling players. He refashioned or adapted these forms for contemporary usage and modelled his theatre on them. He closely identified with the strolling players of the Middle Ages, the jongleur, "who," he said, "went from place to place, clowning in the square in pieces which were grotesque attacks on the powerful." He described the strolling performer as "a figure who came from the people, and who from the people drew anger and transmitted it through the medium of the grotesque." Fo believed that for the common people, traditionally, the theatre was the "spoken news paper in dramatic form," and functioned not only as "the chief medium of expression, of communication, but also of provocation and agitation through ideas" (Hood, xv–vi).

As someone who mainly wrote grotesque farces and satirical comedies on serious political and topical themes, Fo made it a point to keep his audiences laughing while also making them see, ideally with a sense of indignation, the injustices and hypocrisies of the system. He was not an ordinary clown but a subversive one, who like the jongleurs, irreverently mocked and burlesqued the sanctimonious seriousness of the existing institutions and values. In one of his statements about the nature of his own theatre, Fo said: "I do the same thing as a clown. I just put some drops of absurdity in this calm and tranquil liquid which is society, and the reactions reveal things that were hidden before the absurdity brought them into the open" (Bazzoni, 283). That is why most of his plays centrally involve clown-like characters whom he has obviously created for himself. These clown-figures–of whom the madman of *The Accidental Death of an Anarchist* is perhaps the best-known example–make us laugh at figures of authority and, by representing the exercise of power as a grotesque farce, demolish their supposed sacredness.

This produces that critical distance which Brecht advocated. It allows Fo to encourage the spectators to an objective and active contemplation of serious issues. He declared that his theatre, like the popular theatre traditions, used grotesque farces because satirical laughter helped prevent the generation of catharsis in the audience. He wanted the anger and outrage at an unjust society to remain intact in the spectator's mind and not be purged. As he said, "We want them to keep their anger inside them...so that they can take action and get involved in the struggle" (Mitchell, 64). His brilliance in combining urgent political concerns with elements of story-telling, pantomime, satirical songs and ballads, and grotesque farce not only made his plays simultaneously provocative and highly entertaining, but also allowed them to embody and communicate what Terry Eagleton has described in another context as "the vulgar cheerfulness of social hope."

It is for this reason that Fo, for example, constructed *Anarchist*–a play which arose out of the real tragedy of the custodial death of an innocent person–as an open-ended "tragic farce." True to this paradoxical categorisation, the play offered a hilarious but, nonetheless, deeply disturbing experience. In his "Author's Note" to Gavin Richards's English adaptation of the play, Fo himself wrote: "It is obvious that the theatrical theme and, above all, the enormous success which it enjoyed, produced a violent reaction in the centres of power. So we were subjected to provocation and persecution of all kinds, sometimes more grotesque and comical in their repressive stupidity than the very farce which we were performing" (Hood, xvii). It was through the grotesque antics of a madman, who is a quick-change artist, a "histrio-maniac" (indeed a clown), that the hypocrisy and the brutality of a police state are so scathingly exposed. The play thus demonstrates both the power of performance and the performance of power. The non-illusionism of the form prevents any easy, self-righteous and moralistic response just as the absence of a neatly defined or rounded conclusion to the dramatised action makes it necessary that the performance be completed by what Fo termed a "third act" of a discussion among the audience and the performers. The comical quality of the play also helps to keep the audience alert and in a pleasurably relaxed state of mind and body. This, in turn, helps to free them from "deadly" earnest individualist preoccupations and fosters an awareness of the generic and historical bonds that make them into a community.

By the end of 1973, Italy found itself in the grip of a severe economic crisis. There was acute recession, widespread unemployment and galloping inflation. The prices of electricity, transport and essential provisions (such as pasta, milk, sugar, and meat) had increased almost by fifty per cent. In the wake of this inflation, lower-income consumers, supported by trade unions, resorted to what was called *autoridizzioni* (self-reduction) and refused to pay more than what they felt was the right price for things. Beginning in Turin, the *autoridizzioni* movement grew in strength and popularity and spread to other parts of Italy. This was popularly described as "proletarian shopping". Fo responded to it with his wildly hilarious play *Can't Pay, Won't Pay*! which was produced and performed to huge audiences all over Italy. Based on a farcical plot, the play concerns a group of working-class women who, faced with a hike in prices of food items, help themselves to whatever they want from the supermarket. To hide the fact from their "moralistic" (Catholic) husbands, they conceal the stolen things inside their skirts. On being questioned, they pretend to be 'suddenly' pregnant. The result is a farcical comedy which has the audience laughing throughout the performance.

Fo's most important work was done in (and sustained by) a climate of euphoric revolutionism and ideological struggle. With the waning of that period and the advent of an unmistakably right-wing tilt in the political balance in Europe, his drama too lost much of its political edge, its immediacy and militancy. His subsequent plays, although still politically significant, lack the urgency and the sense of militant activism of his earlier, almost agitprop plays. In Italy, despite an acute economic crisis, the strength of trade unions had severely depleted. By the end of the 1970s, the alternative theatre circuit that Fo and Rame had helped develop had virtually disappeared, and they were obliged to return to the conventional theatre.

However, Fo and Rame were not seasonal artists, nor was their political radicalism a temporary and opportunistic phenomenon. They could not possibly stop writing or performing politically meaningful plays just because history had taken a turn to the Right. It is remarkable how they continued to fight against the general condition of despair and to seek out urgent political subjects for their work. Fo's *The Tiger* (1978), an allegorical monologue based on a Chinese fable, reflected his unflinching optimism at a time when all seemed lost. In Fo's own words, the play is "a hopeful play just at a time when negativity and a general collapse of ideas seemed to be dominant forces in our everyday lives." The play took a fresh and critical look at the revolutionary left, even Maoism, with its moral that unthinking loyalty to anything, even to a political party, is the enemy of reason and of revolution.

By the mid-1970s the massive explosion of radical activism which had overtaken Western Europe and North America had waned. In the subsequent decades, particularly, with the disintegration of the Soviet challenge, international capitalism seemed triumphant. This was the resurgence of multinational capitalism and consumerism. It was also the beginning of a period of despair for the Left globally. The prospects of a revolution that had seemed to loom so prominently on the political horizons during the late 1960s, had receded significantly and the left-wing ideas seemed to have become less popular or fashionable. Consequently, the massive resurgence of radical alternative theatre activity that had mushroomed then, and continued to flourish in Europe and North America for nearly two decades, also declined.

Although many of those artists and groups who had ardently dedicated themselves to a politics of social change and to a quest for a politically significant and genuinely contemporary form of people's theatre, are still around and more or less active in the theatre, they no longer possess the same artistic vibrancy and political immediacy or optimism. What is more, no new persons or groups of major significance seem to have emerged in recent decades. If one were to believe those post-modern Cassandras who prophesy the "end of history," "end of ideology," and the consequent death of the "transgressive" kind of political art, Fo's could well be the last great example of its kind in the West.

However, we should be careful not to rush to any final verdict. It is instructive to remember that the political theatre of the radical kind has often been pronounced dead in the past too. But, as often, it has risen phoenix-like from the ashes during periods of intense political struggle and protest. The growing awareness of the inequities and contradictions inherent in the new, uni-polar world order could well be a hopeful sign in this respect.

NOTES

1. Sections of this essay draw on my book, *Toward a Theatre of the Oppressed: The Dramaturgy of John Arden* (University of Michigan Press, 1995) and from the Introduction in my ed. *A Critical Companion to Dario Fo: Accidental Death of an Anarchist* (Worldview, 2014).
2. Following the death of Lenin, Meyerhold's preoccupation with the tendentious, activist kind of theatre began to weaken. In 1925, he staged a satirical play, *The Warrant*, which, according to Edward Braun, had "a mournful tone.... It was a significant change in mood from the derisive lampoon that had gone before [and] "marked Meyerhold's effective rejection of placard-drama and his return to the theatre of disturbing complexity." Stanislavski was deeply impressed with the play and commenting on the last act, said, "In this act Meyerhold has accomplished what I myself am dreaming of." (Braun, 143)]
3. Interestingly in 1969, Delhi too witnessed what was perhaps its first street theatre–although performed on the conventional stage of the Delhi University Tagore Hall. Improvised wholly by a group of student activists, the play called *India 1969*, satirised the degeneration and corruption of parliamentary politics.

WORKS CITED

Bakhtin, Mikhail. 1968. *Rabelais and His World*. Trans. Helene Iswolsky. Cambridge: Mass.: MIT Press.

Bazzoni, Jana O'Keefe. 1991. "Alter Egos: Clown Power and Enactment in Pirandello and Fo." *Companion to Pirandello Studies*. Ed. John Louis Digaetani. New York: Greenwood.

Beck, Julian. 1972. *The Life of the Theatre*. San Francisco: City Lights.

Boal, Augusto. 1992. *Games for Actors and Non-Actors*. Translated by Adrian Jackson. London: Routledge.

Braun, Edward. 1982. *The Director and the Stage: From Naturalism to Grotowski*. London: Methuen.

Brecht, Bertolt. 1979. *Bertolt Brecht Diaries 1920-1922*. London: Methuen.

___ . 1971. *Collected Plays*. Volume I. Eds. Manheim, Ralph, and John Willett. New York: Vintage.

Brook, Peter. 1977. *The Empty Space*. Harmondsworth: Penguin.

Cole, Toby, ed. 1998. *Playwrights on Playwriting: From Ibsen to Ionesco.* New York: Cooper Square Press.

Dryden, John. 1912. "Of Heroic Plays." Essays, pp. 87–94. London: Dent, and New York: Dutton.

Erven, Eugene Van. 1988. *Radical People's Theatre*. Bloomington: Indiana University Press.

Hauser, Arnold. 1951. *The Social History of Art*. Trans. Stanley Goodmann. 4 vols. New York: Vintage.

Hood, Stuart. 1988. "Introduction". *Mistero Buffo*. London: Methuen.

Kolve, V. A. 1966. *The Play Called Corpus Christie*. London: Arnold.

Lebel, Jean-Jaques. 1969. "Notes on Political Street Theatre, Paris: 1968-1969." *The Drama Review* (Summer). 110–118.

Lillo, George. 1975. *The Beggar's Opera and Other Eighteenth Century Plays*. London: Dent.

Malick, Javed. 1995. *Toward a Theater of the Oppressed: The Dramaturgy of John Arden*. Ann Arbor: University of Michigan Press.

Mitchell, Tony. 1984. *Dario Fo: People's Court Jester*. London & New York, Methuen.

Montgomery, Angela. 1994. "The Theatre of Dario Fo and Franca Rame: Laughing All the Way to the Revolution." In Brian Docherty, ed. *Twentieth Century European Drama*. New York: St. Martin's.

Owen, Robert. 1817. *A New View of Society*. 3rd ed. London: Longman.

Piscator, Erwin. 1968. *The Political Theatre*. Trans. Hugh Rorrison. London: Eyre Methuen.

Schechter, Joel. 1985. *Durov's Pig: Clowns, Politics and Theatre*. New York: Theatre Communications Group.

Strindberg, August. 1965. "Preface" to *Miss Julie*. Trans. Elizabeth Sprigge. New York: Avon.

Stourac, Richard and McCreery, Kathleen. 1986. *Theatre as a Weapon: Workers' Theatre in the Soviet Union, Germany and Britain, 1917-1934*. London: Routledge.

Suvin, Darko. 1984. *To Brecht and Beyond: Soundings in Modern Dramaturgy*. Brighton: Harvester.

Willet, John. 1959. *Theatre of Bertolt Brecht*. London: Eyre Methuen.

Williams, Raymond. 1961. *The Long Revolution*. London: Chatto and Windus.

___. 1966. *Modern Tragedy*. London: Chatto and Windus.

___. 1976. *Keywords: A Vocabulary of Culture and Society*. Glasgow: Fontana.

___. 1977. "Social Environment and Theatrical Environment." In *English Drama*. Ed. Marie Axton and Raymond Williams, pp. 203-23. Cambridge: Cambridge University Press.

___. 1981. *Culture*. Glasgow: Fontana.

Witt, Hubert. 1975. *Brecht As They Knew Him*. London: Lawrence & Wishart.

Zola, Emile. 1968. "Naturalism in the Theatre." In *The Theory of the Modern Stage*. Ed. Eric Bentley, pp. 351-72. Harmondsworth: Penguin.

2

Decolonialising an Imperial Icon: Shakespeare on the Parsi Urdu Stage[1]

Urdu does not possess anything like a sustained tradition of translating, adapting, or staging Shakespeare. I do not say this accusingly or, for that matter, apologetically. I do not think that the situation in most other Indian languages is significantly different. But in Urdu, barring a few occasional translations here and there, I do not know of any systematic attempt, by any individual, group, or institution to render all, or even a significant part of Shakespeare's work into the language. However, a century ago there did exist something like a popular tradition of adapting or translating, and staging Shakespeare in Urdu. It is mainly to that period that a large part of the existing corpus of Urdu language Shakespeare belongs. In fact that period can be regarded as the veritable golden age not only of Indian Shakespeare but also of Urdu drama in general. For, it was during this period that, at least in terms of quantum and popular reach, playwriting in Urdu and stage adaptations of some of Shakespeare's major plays reached a scale that was not witnessed ever before–or, for that matter, ever since.

The theatre that made this possible was what came to be called Parsi theatre. The last decades of the 19th century were marked in India by the rise of this entirely new and immensely popular cultural phenomenon. Many professional theatre companies, some big and nationally acclaimed and some small but locally popular, operated and did lucrative business throughout the undivided subcontinent. This entire phenomenon was subsumed under the term "Parsi theatre" which today denotes an institutionally and historically specific category as well as an artistic concept. It is used to describe the many different commercial theatre companies which operated throughout Indian during a particular period. The term is also used to describe a style, a set practice, based on a specific body of dramaturgic and performance conventions which were developed and perfected by these companies. This theatre came to be called Parsi simply because the first efforts in that direction were made by some former students of Bombay's Elphinstone College who happened to be Parsi and who also owned the biggest and most successful of these companies.

In the chapter that follows, I have attempted a general overview of the Urdu adaptations of Shakespeare's plays that were staged during the late 19th and early 20th century by Parsi theatre companies. I begin by describing how and why these English-knowing, Gujarati-speaking young Parsi directors turned to Urdu language drama and how Urdu adaptations of Shakespeare were obtained and staged by them. The radical significance of this practice is examined in the light of the dominant cultural politics of the period. This is followed by a more detailed discussion of specific examples such as Khori's *Khurshid* (1872), widely recognised as the first ever Urdu play to be offered from a professional public stage and which turns out to be an unacknowledged and partial adaptation of Shakespeare's *Cymbeline*. Karimuddin Murad Barelvi's *Khudadad* (1890) which is an adaptation of *Pericles, the Prince of Tyre*, and several other subsequent plays till about the early years of the 20th century. These texts will be discussed in terms of their genesis and their proximity to Shakespeare's original. Detailed textual comparison will be undertaken with a view to elucidating the artistic strategies that were employed in these and other adaptations in order to make the Elizabethan bard more acceptable to the Indian audiences.

As recent historical and literary scholarship shows, the iconicity of Shakespeare, which was a central component of English studies in India since the 19th century, was a colonial construct. It was used to inculcate a sense of British cultural supremacy among the colonised peoples. This colonial project was undoubtedly successful, but only up to a point. Its success can be witnessed, for example, in the highly worshipful attitude towards Shakespeare's work and worth on the part of some of the early (and, of course, 'scholarly') translators/adapters. To cite one such example, is Mohammed Athar Ali Azad Kakorwi's *Jaam-e-Ulfat*, a 1902 translation of *A Midsummer Night's Dream* in rhymed verse of very uneven quality. The author, who was the Nayab Tehsildar of Pandaru in Gorakhpur district, saw Shakespeare as a mediator who would bring the British and Indian nations together in friendship and harmony. In his Preface the author writes: "I will consider my effort worthwhile, if this translation proves instrumental in making the public familiar with Shakespeare and produces in our country an interest in the works of this rare and unique genius. This is because in my view it is things like this which will in the end help establish those harmonious relations which are essential between the English and the Indians and which are unfortunately rare today. I firmly believe that two hearts which consider the love and reverence of Shakespeare a matter of pride will never be unfamiliar and out of tune with each other" (5).[2]

Azad's views on the Elizabethan bard could not have been any different from those of the students of Elphinstone College, who, too, were taught the same kind of reverence and awe. As we shall see shortly, they too had learnt to view Shakespeare as virtually a transcendental figure beyond history, geography or culture. However, Athar Ali Azad was a government functionary who merely translated Shakespeare's text. In all probability he had no knowledge or experience of staging or watching plays. It was different with those young Parsi students who, after graduation, went on to involve themselves in practical theatre and, as we shall see, in the process learn to play with, rather than worship, the great colonial icon.

Origins of Parsi Theatre

The genesis of Parsi theatre, like that of the modern Indian stage in general, is closely bound with the British presence and cultural influence in India. It can be traced through two lines of descent, which, however, are not mutually exclusive: one relates to the influence and example of the visiting European companies as well as the amateur productions by and for the British residents; and the other to the enthusiasm for theatre generated among Indian college students by their British educators. This is how it was in Calcutta which was the East India Company's first port of call. But it was particularly true of the rise of theatre, especially of the Parsi theatre, in Bombay.

Well before the rise of the first Parsi theatre companies, there had existed in Bombay an exclusively British theatre, called The Bombay Amateur Theatre. Built around 1770 on the model of Drury Lane, it was situated on the Bombay Greens. Besides hosting the itinerant European performers, this theatre offered amateur productions of English plays (mostly farces, occasionally Shakespeare, sometimes double-bills of Shakespeare, abridged to fit the time limit). These productions were by and for the entertainment of the white population from the local trading, military and civil establishments. It flourished for a few decades but then beset with frequent financial crises, was forced to close down in 1835. The building was auctioned off to pay the debts and was eventually demolished.

Ten years later, a wealthy businessman, Jagannath Shankarsheth, who had received his higher education in England, initiated a campaign for a new theatre. Thus, with some support from the East India Company, a new Bombay Theatre came into existence in 1846. It began with productions in English. However, since Shankarsheth and his Indian associates had generously donated land and money for the new theatre, the British authorities agreed to allow it to be used for staging vernacular plays as well. A drama group called The Hindu Dramatic Corps of the Marathi playwright Vishnudas Bhave of Sangli was invited to offer plays in Marathi. Inspired by this example, a group of local Parsis–including Dadabhai Nauroji–formed the Parsi Dramatic Corps in 1853 and began to stage plays in Gujarati. Its first production was the famous legend of *Rustam-Sohrab*, derived from Firdausi's *Shahnama*, which was first performed in October 1853 (Mehta, 130).

This love of theatre among the young was significantly enhanced during the subsequent years when, another tradition began to take shape furthering the growing interest in drama among the city's native elite. This was the tradition of student drama which originated in Bombay's Elphinstone College. Established in 1856, its administration and faculty consisted largely of persons of British origin. However, most of its students came from the affluent local families. These included several Gujarati-speaking Parsis. English Literature in general, and Shakespeare in particular, occupied a central place in the curriculum. Among the faculty were some theatre lovers. From time to time, they encouraged and helped their students to prepare and stage productions of Shakespeare and other playwrights. In his memoirs, titled *Maro Natakiya Anubhav* (*My Experiences of Theatre*), Jahangir Khambata mentions some of the plays that were produced during those early years by the students of Elphinstone College:

> When Sir Alexander Grant was director of Public Instruction and Mr. K.M. Chettfield was the principal of Elphinstone College, "The Merchant of Venice" was staged very successfully. The respectable judge of the Small Cause Court, Mr. Rustamba Mehervanji Patel played the role of Antonio, which was greatly appreciated. Dadabhai Patel played Bassanio. Adelji Khori played Shylock and Mr. Hormasji Ardeshar played Portia. Once the Elphinstonians staged "Two Gentlemen of Verona." Nasarvanji Patel was Valentine, Barjorji Modi of Surat, retired judge of Small Cause Court played Proteus; Jehangir Adelji Dawar, the famous professor of French played Thurio; Mr. Khardeshji Siravai, chief of our Income Tax office played Launce; Mr. Hormasji Bhabha of Mysore, Director of Public Instruction was Silvia; Principal Dosabhai Wadia played Julia; Sergeant Lt. Col. Kirtikar played Glamour (157–58).[3]

These young men were so enthused by their experience that upon graduation, many of them got together and formed clubs and amateur drama groups and continued to produce plays in English and, later, in Gujarati. One such group was Gentlemen's Amateur Club which, according to Abdul Aleem Nami, was founded in

1860 by Faramji Dalal and Kavasji Nasarvanji Koherdaru (26). In Kumudini Mehta, there is a mention of a Parsi Elphinstone Dramatic Society, composed mainly of students and ex-students of the college, which began with small plays in English and went on to stage their first Shakespeare production, *The Taming of the Shrew*, in 1861. From Khambata's memoirs we further learn that the Club was founded by C.S. Nazir and in the course of its existence it staged a number of Shakespearean plays, among which were *The Taming of the Shrew*, *Merchant of Venice*, *Othello* and *The Two Gentlemen of Verona*. Recalling his own impression of these productions, Khambata adds: "Nazir's brother-in-law Nasarwanji Navroz Parekh played Amelia in Othello which I saw. His brother Col. Dhanjibhai Navroz Parekh played Desdemona. Another gentleman, Mr. Jamshedji Oonwala played Portia in *Merchant of Venice*, the performance that I will never forget. Nazir himself was a great scholar of English and an excellent actor and I have seen him play Katherine in *The Taming of the Shrew*" (15).

Interestingly, Mehta, too, highlights the significance of Nazir's contribution not just during those early years of amateur activities but also during the subsequent decades of the professional Parsi theatre. Referring to him as "the moving spirit behind every activity", she adds that Nazir "combined the duties of playwright, actor and manager. During the "sixties he concentrated mainly on amateur productions in English. He was also later actively connected with the Victoria Nataka Mandali which specialised in Gujarati and Hindustani plays." He wrote a Gujarati play *Kadak Kanya ne Khisela Parnya,* based on *The Taming of the Shrew*. "In the 60s he wrote most of the Epilogues and Prologues to the productions of the Society. ...For a full 38 years, he kept a sustained and intimate association with the theatre. He was either, proprietor, agent or actor in most of the big theatre ventures of the later decades of the [19th] century" (178-80). We also learn from Mehta that during the early years of drama activities, the young actors were trained by the British professionals residing in Bombay. "For example, in the beginning [an Englishman named] Hamilton Jacob was director and manager of the Parsi Elphinstone Dramatic Club" (181).

Beginning from 1860, new amateur drama groups continued to mushroom, and often also disappear after a short existence. By the end of the decade, there were several such groups operating in Bombay. Ever since their inception, these amateur drama enthusiasts had worked exclusively with English language plays, performing Shakespeare and English comedies and farces. Although they were trained and helped by their British mentors and supported by eminent members of the local Indian community, the reports in the media were usually not quite encouraging. In one such response, the commentator said, "although the performance was in English... the gesticulations were decidedly oriental" (Mehta, 183). Comments like this must have made these young men increasingly conscious of the limitations of trying to do Western plays in an alien language. They must have realised that, no matter how well they costumed themselves in Western clothes and how hard they tried to reproduce Western intonation, accent, and mannerisms, the Indianness of their voices and bodies could not be erased or concealed. This is probably why, gradually, there was a shift from productions in English to plays in Gujarati. Although in due course of time the Parsi theatre acquired its own playwrights who wrote original plays in Gujarati, initially they made do with translations of Shakespeare. Khambata mentions three Shakespearean productions in Gujarati during the 1860s: *Othello, Cymbeline,* and *Romeo and Juliet.* The last named play was translated by Dosabhai Framji Randhelia who, as we shall see below, some years later wrote the Gujarati adaptation of Shakespeare's *Pericles* as well (Khambata, 14-15; 22; 26).

Explaining this transition, Mehta writes, "The passion for a new kind of drama could not be satisfied by merely presenting a Shakespearean production annually. For the theatre conscious, the next logical step was to attempt translations of English plays and their adaptation onto the vernacular languages. Later, with more experience they could try their hand at original plays in the mother tongue. It is therefore not surprising that Adelji Khori who had played Iago in 1865 and Petruchio in 1867 associated himself closely with K.N. Kabraji and wrote some of the earliest Gujarati plays such as *Hajambad ane Thagannaj*" (191-2). About this play by Khori,

Khambata informs us, "it was nothing but a selection of scenes from Shakespeare's various plays. [Khori] put them together with such brilliance that even a good writer would be surprised" (88).

Emergence of Professional Companies

Closely following this shift from English to Gujarati language productions was the transition from amateur to professional status. The move to set up professional theatre companies, as we see below, was a shift of profound and far-reaching consequence. According to Nami, the origins of the first professional group called the Victoria Nataka Mandali was in the Parsi Victoria Club founded in 1867 with Kaikhusro Navrozji Kabraji, Framji Gustavji Dalal, and Shahpurji Bangali among its members. In 1869, the group decided to become professional and rechristened itself Victoria Nataka Mandali (26–27). However, Khambata describes the beginning of the Victoria group somewhat differently. He locates it in the efforts to raise funds for reviving a Parsi gymnasium. According to him, "The late Mr. Kekushru Navroji Kabraji took the lead and decided to stage a play to raise funds for the Parsi gymnasium which was in a bad shape. He collected the choicest actors like Dadabhai Thunti, Faramji Dalal, Pestanji Wadia and Hervanji Baliwala. A committee of 12 members was formed which selected "Much Ado About Nothing" and translated it into Gujarati. I had gone to see the play to see all the well-known actors together. It was staged a few times to raise funds and revive the gymnasium. ...People appreciated the play very much which encouraged Kabraji to start a theatre group. In fact, this was the beginning of the Parsi professional [*dhandhadari*] theatre. There were four partners–Dadabhai Thunthi, Faramji Gustadji, Kavasji Nasarvanji Koohiyardaru, and Horamji Modi... The first play was "Bejaan Manijeh" written by Kabraji based on the Shahnama" (30–31).

As mentioned, the Parsi theatre had its origin in the student drama of Elphinstone College in Bombay in the early 1860s. The share-holders, directors, managers, and actors of the major theatre companies till well into the 1900s were mostly old Elphinstonian Parsis. It was during their student days, that these theatre enthusiasts had their first exposure to the life of the stage and the works of William Shakespeare, several of whose plays they had performed under the direct supervision and tutelage of their British teachers. Their attitude to the bard in this initial contact, carefully mediated as it was by Englishmen, was that of immense awe and reverence. The following extract from an epilogue specially written for a performance of *The Taming of the Shrew*, in 1867, staged by the Parsi students of Elphinstone College shows how they were taught to approach the greatness of the Elizabethan bard with utmost humility:

> Bethink ye, that your sweet Avonian swan,
> Still flutters strangely over Hindustan,
> We know not yet the fulness of its tone,
> Its modulations are not yet our own,
> We fain would hope that, as it flies along,
> 'Twill scatter, sybil-like, its leaves of song
> And o'er our parent East new triumphs win,
> With but that touch which makes the whole world kin.
>
> (Mehta, 190)

The implied addressee of the Epilogue–as suggested by '*your* sweet Avonian swan'–are obviously the British. The lines, perhaps written for them by one of their teachers, strongly resemble the sentiment expressed by Athar Ali Azad Kakorvi in the passage quoted above. They emphasise the complete acceptance on the part of the young native actors of the authority and universality of the received version of Shakespeare. Taught to be aware of the huge chasm between the high culture of the colonial literary genius and the as yet 'undeveloped' culture of the colonised, they apologise for not being able to master the fullness of its tone and modulations.

However, when, after graduation, some of these men went on to build an all-India theatre movement and to produce plays first in Gujarati and then in Urdu, what happened was something entirely different. For, as they moved from the early attempts at amateur drama to forming professional theatre companies and were freed from the anxiety of mastering Shakespeare's "tone and modulation", their approach to the sacred swan of the Elizabethan period became significantly less worshipful and more playful. It ultimately, came to be driven predominantly by profit motive. It could not be any different because the theatre, which is the most public of all art forms, has a logic of its own whereby the cultural and social context of the production determines the nature of the play-text and its performance conventions. The founding fathers of the Parsi theatre were well aware of this. As company owners and artists in the 'business' of entertainment, they had a great regard for, and often quoted Samuel Johnson's famous dictum about the relationship between the stage and its patrons:

> The drama's laws, the drama's patrons give
> For we that live to please, must please to live

In the course of their theatre practice, they soon discovered that the awe and reverence with which they had learnt to approach Shakespeare's works was not compatible with the demands and the logic of a commercial vernacular stage. As a result, the Parsi theatre Shakespeare, mediated as it was by the box-office interests of the company owners and the 'low brow' cultural predilections of its 'native' audiences, did not conform to this ideal of a culturally monolithic icon and its sacredness. Instead, it represented a hybridised, even a deviant and fractured, text in which the European influences and native popular traditions of dramaturgy and performance were interwoven.[4]

Adapting Shakespeare, Freely

The heyday of the professional Parsi theatre was broadly from the 1870s to 1920s. It was during this period (particularly during the *fin-de-siecle* years) that a number of plays from Shakespeare's opus were adapted in Urdu (or, if you like, Hindustani) and staged by professional theatre companies. These adaptations were unique both in their popularity and in the fact that they took great liberties with the original. They departed so radically from the Shakespearean text that it would be more accurate to call them appropriations rather than translations or adaptations. This appropriation had the effect of nativising the revered Elizabethan icon and virtually turning him into our own "desi bhai" (fellow Indian).

The geographical reach and popular appeal of Parsi theatre continued to expand through the last quarter of the 19th century. By the end of the century, it grew into an entertainment industry of such enormous proportions that, in retrospect, it can only be compared to the commercial Bollywood cinema of the later period. It will not be wrong to say that this process of a radical increase in its reach and appeal was triggered when the professional companies decided to produce plays in Urdu.

The first move in this direction was made by a young and dynamic theatre enthusiast, Dadabhai Sohrabji Patel (popularly known as Dadi Patel). A former student of Elphinstone College, he had been active in theatre since his undergraduate days. He came from a reputed business family, and was able to combine, in almost equal measure, a shrewd business sense and a passionate love of the theatre. The theatre, he seems to have recognised, was not only an entertaining cultural activity but also potentially a profitable commercial undertaking. At the beginning of the 1870s, when this young man took over the directorship of the Victoria Natak Mandali, his first move was to commission and produce a Gujarati adaptation of Shakespeare's *Pericles*, of which we will speak later. The point of interest here is that soon Dadabhai's business instinct prompted him to recognise the greater commercial value of Urdu, which was at that time virtually the country's cultural lingua franca, and, as such and in contrast to the restricted box-office appeal of a regional language like Gujarati, had a nation-wide appeal. So he decided to stage a play in Urdu and started to look for an appropriate script in the language.

Dadabhai's decision to turn to drama in Urdu could have been partly inspired by the widespread impact and success of certain earlier stage productions in the language. The most celebrated and talked about of these was Amanat Lakhnawi's operatic composition *Indersabha* which was first staged in Lucknow in 1852. The production was so successful that its fame and influence reached the far corners of the undivided subcontinent and even beyond.

For, it was not only performed in almost every town and city of India but travelled also to Ceylon, Burma, and Malaysia. A measure of the play's influence and popularity can be gauged by the fact that Amanat's text was translated and published in numerous languages. It even inspired many other writers to write plays modelled on it (Hansen, 3–34). The Urdu critic Ishrat Rahmani describes at some length how, during the 1850s following the example of *Indersabha*, several Urdu theatre groups were established and flourished in Dacca and Murshidabad in Bengal (125–31). Nor was Bombay untouched by the popularity and fame of *Indersabha*. The play was first staged in Bombay during the 1860s. The form and style of this musical composition, with its profusion of poetry, songs and dances strung together by a thin story line, can also be evidenced in the operatic style that characterised Parsi theatre plays during its more commercial Urdu phase.

Apart from the example of *Indersabha*, there was a relatively minor and local instance of playwriting in Urdu. This is mentioned by Imtiaz Ali Taj in the introduction to his annotated Urdu edition of *Khurshid*. Taj quotes Abdul Aleem Nami who claims that the first play in Urdu was *Raja Gopichand aur Jalandhar* which was originally staged as a comic afterpiece to follow Marathi plays. It was written by Dr. Bhauji Lad for the Hindu Dramatic Corps and was performed by Marathi-speaking actors who had no difficulty in performing it as it was written in a popular idiom. The play was staged in November 1853 at the Bombay Theatre and was well received. On popular demand, a second part was staged a month later. Again, on January 5, 1854, both parts were staged together. They were staged again in February 1855. Following the popularity of this play, Dr. Lad wrote another play, *Sita ki Shadi* which was staged at the Bombay Theatre in November 1855 (21, 25).

Thus, there were attempts at playwriting and play producing in Urdu before Dadabhai's arrival on the scene. However, historically interesting though these attempts were, they were sporadic and did not add up to a serious and sustained tradition. It was another few decades before such a tradition of Urdu theatre became possible. The credit for staging the first full length play in the language thus belongs to Dadabhai Patel who broke out of the practice of offering plays in Gujarati alone and turned to those in Urdu.

Since no Urdu writers were locally available, Dadabhai invited his friend and fellow Elphinstonian, Adelji Khori to write a play for him in Urdu. As a student, Khori was an active member of the Elphinstone Dramatic Club and had participated in its productions. He had played Iago in 1865 and Petruchio in 1867. Later, he was closely associated with K.N. Kabraji and wrote some of the earliest Gujarati plays, including some adaptations of Shakespeare, which were successfully staged (Mehta, 192). According to Jehangir Khambatta, Patel wanted the company to produce plays in Urdu. "But the owners did not approve of this proposal because all the actors in the company were Parsi and could not speak Urdu. In their view, a long period would be needed to train the actors in Urdu speech...however despite these difficulties, Seth Dadabhai did not lose heart and suggested to his close friend Adelji Jamshedji Khori, who was a Gujarati playwright, that he write a play in Urdu" (89).

Khori was not proficient in Urdu and therefore declined his friend's request. But there was no one else that Dadabhai could turn to. So he persisted till he succeeded in persuading Khori to prepare a script in Gujarati with a view to getting it translated into Urdu later by someone else. The Gujarati script that Khori eventually offered to Dadabhai was titled *Sona na Mol ni Khurshid* (literally, Gold-Priced Khurshid). It was translated by Behramji Firdunji Merzban as *Khurshid* and successfully staged by the Victoria in 1871. Thus, *Khurshid* became the first ever fully fledged Urdu play to be produced from a professional stage. There is no evidence to show that Khori's original Gujarati version was ever performed or published, though Merzban's Urdu translation in Gujarati script did manage to survive.[5] It was this text that was transcribed into Persian script and published in 1969 from Lahore with notes and introduction by Imtiaz Ali Taj.

The language of Merzban's translation is what conservative Urdu purists would scoff at and regard as hybrid. It is a language in which Hindustani, Gujarati and Persian vocabulary and phraseology intermingle. While the songs, which occur frequently in the play, are in refined Persianised Urdu and are usually in the form of *ghazals* (a conventional form of poetry with strict rules of rhyme and meter), the dialogue between characters is full of non-literate expressions and inflections drawn from everyday colloquial registers of western India. Despite the mixed nature of its style, the play has dialogic immediacy which gives it its dramatic quality and power. Syed Imtiaz Ali Taj, himself a reputed Urdu scholar,was impressed by Merzban's effort and praised it. According to him, Urdu was alien to Merzban and he was unfamiliar with its idiom. His ears were unattuned to standard Urdu either at home or outside. Whatever Urdu he learnt was from his reading of Urdu writings. On this limited grounding, to try one's skills on a difficult form, to find appropriate dialogues for different characters, to warm up the text with effective articulation of emotions was not easy for a beginner. Taj goes on to observe that in Merzban's translation the dialogues of kings, queens, slaves and commoners are varied in style, and that the style of the soliloquy too is not as artificial as it could have been in this first Urdu play and as it was in many inferior plays of the later period. He is especially effective in writing emotional lines. The text has a high declamatory tone and short but quite effective sentences. There is an abundance of similes and metaphors which point to a poetic style of prose. Without knowing colloquial Urdu, Merzban based this first Urdu play on a language which despite the interference of Gujarati idiom and syntax, was not without dramatic flow and force. This language may be uncharacteristic of high Urdu literature but it does testify to Fardunji Merzbanji's artistic taste and creativity (Taj, 73-75).

Khurshid (1871, *Cymbeline*)

My discovery of *Khurshid*'s Shakespearean connection was sheer serendipity. It was the early days yet of my research into the subject. I picked up Khori's play for reading mainly because of its reputation as the first ever Urdu play to be staged by a professional company of Bombay and also the first example of serious playwriting in the language. Neither Khori's preface nor Taj's introduction, nor any of the existing critical material on *Khurshid* had prepared me for what I found there. Karimuddin Murad Barelvi's *Badshah Khudadad* which was written and produced in 1890, almost two decades after *Khurshid*, was generally believed to be the first Urdu adaptation of Shakespeare.

So, when I picked up Khori's play for reading I did not expect to find any Shakespeare there. I was nonetheless struck by its style and episodic construction which vaguely reminded me of the Elizabethan playwright's work. The play is in five acts as against the more usual three-act division that I had found in later Parsi theatre plays. I also noticed that the basic structural unit, as in Shakespeare, is the scene. Each act is divided into a number of short scenes.[6] Other elements which to my mind seemed reminiscent of Elizabethan dramaturgy were the epic sweep of time and place, and the use of the verbal conventions of what I have elsewhere identified as the non-illusionist stage, such as asides, soliloquies, and the characters' self-presentation. Above all, the figure of the clown or the wise fool in the *maskhara* who, at least on a few occasions, debunks the official versions of the social/political reality, had some resemblance to the Shakespearean Fool. Besides, on occasions, there is an attempt to take the dialogue to a larger, more philosophical level–something that the Parsi theatre plays of the later, fully commercialised era seldom did. This, too, could have been a Shakespearean influence.

As I have said above, there is no acknowledgement of any debt to Shakespeare anywhere either in Khori's preface to the play or in the works of subsequent scholars. In his preface, Khori claimed that he had derived the plot from what he called a "Hindu katha" (tale) *Kamawanti*." In the course of my research, I tried in every possible way to locate this tale, but Khori's acknowledged source remained elusive. However, it seemed probable that Khori was referring to one of those traditional, folkloric narratives that were widely popular throughout the 18th–19th centuries in India and were known as *dastaans*. That Khori, like all other contemporary writers, was familiar with the popular narrative literature of the period is borne out by the fact that at least three of his plays that were translated and staged in Urdu–e.g. *Gul Bakaoli*, *Hatimtai*, and *Noor*

Jehan–clearly derive from such traditional sources. So it is entirely possible that Khori took a traditional story and grafted on to it borrowings from some Shakespearean text, probably a romance. For, *dastaans* have remarkable similarities with the Western stories of heroic adventure and love which Shakespeare drew on for his romances.

Suggesting that the genre of romance is best defined not by "formal characteristics" but rather by "certain recurrent motifs, and also...a recognisable attitude towards the subject matter," Stanley Wells observes that "Shakespearean romance frequently includes the separation and destruction of families followed by their eventual reunion and reconciliation; scenes of apparent resurrection; the love of a virtuous hero and heroine; and the recovery of lost royal children" (49-50). Another critic, James McManaway, observes: "In [Shakespeare's] romances, there is little attempt at narrative logic or probability: incident appears for its own sake. Characters are two-dimensional and static: the good are very good and the evil have no redeeming feature. In a setting that is remote in time or place, or both, there are shipwrecks, rescues from the sea, miraculous restorations from apparent death, infants exposed to the elements, and above all, recognitions and reconciliations and the healing of breaches or the righting of ancient injuries usually through the agency of splendid young people, but with the direct intervention of the gods. The themes are patience, constancy, and forgiveness, and the dramatic interest is focused upon recognition scenes" (1259).

Not only did this description of the defining features of the romance aptly fit Khori's play but also bore a striking similarity to the definitions of the *dastaan* that Urdu scholars offer. For example, Quamarulhuda Faridi describes it as "a style of narration [in which] military and social adventures of the exemplary hero and his friends, imaginary matters of [female] beauty and erotic love as well as extraordinary happenings are related...the central character of the *dastaan* is, as a rule, an exemplary and static character who does not evolve but is endowed with all his/her qualities from the very outset. The hero is usually a person of considerable social prestige and power: a prince, a nobleman or a trader" (52).

The generic affinity between these two culturally and geographically distinct narrative traditions, as well as the fact that both Khori and Patel were actively involved in reading and producing the Elizabethan bard since their college days, prompted me to revisit Shakespeare's romances. Like *The Tempest, Pericles*, or *Cymbeline*, Khori's play too is a tale of love and adventure. As a punishment for defying her cruel princely husband, a woman of matchless beauty is sold for an enormous amount of gold to a young trader who is himself a virtuous prince in disguise. The two instantly fall in love. Separated through the villainous design of an evil and lecherous Kotwal (police chief), they stumble through a series of misfortunes, and are finally reunited and live happily ever after. Major formal characteristics and motifs of romance and *dastaan* literatures are all here. We have an exemplary heroine who is a paragon of beauty, virtue, constancy, and intelligence. We also have separation of lovers and siblings and their eventual reunion as well as motifs of erotic love, adventure, of heroism, apparent death and resurrection, and of "righting of ancient injuries".

On closer scrutiny of Shakespeare's romances, I discovered that in writing *Khurshid*, Khori had liberally and unmistakably borrowed from *Cymbeline*. It is probable that he did, in fact, derive the plot-idea of a beautiful woman being auctioned off for her weight in gold from some traditional Indian source, as he claims in his preface. For, scenes of beautiful young women being auctioned in public was not an uncommon feature of traditional oriental narratives. However, in adapting it for the Parsi stage, Khori clearly drew upon Shakespeare and drastically modified the original by interpolating large sequences of Cymbeline into it. Several characters, events, and even whole scenes in *Khurshid* are clearly modelled on Shakespeare's text. Furthermore, at times, Khori's dialogue reads like a direct translation from Shakespeare.

Let us look at some of these unacknowledged borrowings.

Khori's Kotwal closely parallels Shakespeare's Cloten. At certain points in the story he comes very close to the latter both in words and actions. He woos the heroine with a love song (a ghazal) just as Cloten in *Cymbeline* hires musicians to serenade Imogen.

Later, like Cloten (3.5.21–59), Kotwal also dons the clothes of the heroine's lover and sets out in search of her. He is killed and decapitated by one of the two princely brothers as is Shakespeare's Cloten. His headless body is likewise found by Khurshid (as by Imogen) who mistakes it for the body of her lover. Khurshid herself is a version of Imogen. With certain significant differences of character, her experience largely parallels Imogen's. She is also obliged to disguise herself as a man while searching for her lost lover. As in Shakespeare, Khurshid's disguise plays an important role in the resolution of the play.

The parallel is evident also at the level of the dialogue. On several occasions, Kotwal almost reproduces Cloten's lines. For example, Shakespeare's 3.5.81–83 where Cloten interrogates Pisanio (servant to Posthumus) about the whereabouts of his master, is reproduced in *Khurshid* in Act 2, scene 1, where Kotwal seeks the whereabouts of Firoz Shah from the latter's friend, Bahadur Khan. The following examples from the two plays will, I hope, make this even clearer. The excerpts from *Khurshid* have been given in a rough English translation in the right-hand column while matching lines from Shakespeare's original are given in the left column.[7]

Cloten: Where is thy lady? In a word, or else Thou art straightaway with the fiends. (3.5.81–83)	Kotwal: Why, you infidel...tell me, where have your master and that woman Khurshid gone? Tell me which way they went? Or else, your head will be wrenched off your body.
Cloten: For since patiently and constantly thou hast stuck to the bare fortune of that beggar Posthumous, thou canst not, in the course of gratitude, but be a diligent follower of mine. Wilt thou serve me? (116–19)	Kotwal: Do not think about your master any more. He has been rendered poor and wretched after the purchase of Khurshid. You will not profit from it any more. There is more profit for you in my service. Do you understand?

Cloten: With that suit upon my back will I ravish her; first kill him, and in her eyes. There shall she see my valor, which will then be a torment to her contempt. He on the ground, my speech of insultment ended on his dead body, and when my lust hath dined—which as I say, to vex her I will execute in the clothes that she so praised—to the court I'll knock her back, foot her home again. She hath despised me rejoicingly, and I'll be merry in my revenge. (130–45)	Kotwal: Wearing these clothes and disguising myself as a trader, I will first kill that trader fellow Firoz Shah. Then I will go to Khurshid and, through false pretences and tricks bring her under my control. Kill that trader fellow and in his own dress meet that obstinate wench. Afterwards, disclosing my real identity, torment her and bring her under control. And finally marry her. Only then will my anger rest.
Cloten: Be but duteous, and true preferment shall tender itself to thee. (150–51)	Kotwal: If it be so, bring me the clothes of your master. If I succeed in achieving my goal, I'll reward you with wealth.
Pisanio: Thou biddest me to my loss, for true to thee Were to prove false, which I will never be To him that is most true. To Milford go, And find not her whom thou pursuest. Flow, flow You heavenly blessings, on her. This fool's speed Be crossed with slowness; labor be his meed. (3.5.154–59)	Bahadur Khan: The town's name that I have given to this vile Kotwal is incorrect. He won't find it even if he spends his whole life searching for it. God! How can I betray one at whose table I have dined? And, have my friend murdered by giving his whereabouts to this tyrant? How can I, an ordinary creature, do what would embarrass even Satan. No, never.

Yet another scene that is closely paralleled in Khori is Shakespeare's Act 2 , Scene 2, wherein Iachimo is smuggled into Imogen's bedchamber in a trunk. In Act 3, Scene 1 of *Khurshid*, Babak, a professional burglar, similarly steals into the bedchamber of Gulchehra, a beautiful princess, and robs her of a valuable piece of jewellery. The speech that he makes has distinct echoes of Iachimo's lines in Imogen's bedchamber:

Iachimo:	Babak:
The crickets sing, and man's o'erlabored sense Repairs itself by rest. Our Tarquin thus Did softly press the rushes ere he wakened The chastity he wounded. Cytherea, How bravely thou becom'st thy bread, fresh lily, And whiter than the sheets! That I might touch! But kiss, one kiss! (11-17)	How sleeps and dreams this heavenly beauty on the white garden bed. In the garden of Eden, mother Eve too lay like this lost in the paradise of dreams as Satan prepared the snare of evil for her. Yes, I might kiss this rosy cheek. Just one kiss.
Iachimo: 'Tis her breathing that Perfumes the chamber thus. The flame o' th' taper Bows towards her and would underpeep her lids To see th' enclosed lights, now canopied Under these windows, white and azure-laced With blue of heaven's own tinct. (11-23)	Babak: Aha! What flagrant flame arises from her lovely body. Her breath fills this room with its sweetness. Look, how this flaming lamp sharpens this light to brighten the lamps of her eyes.

I may also mention that the precious ring that Babak steals from Gulchehra turns up again in the play's last scene and, much in the manner of the discovery of Imogen's bracelet on Iachimo, helps resolve certain misunderstandings in the story. The festive ending of the play–where the long separated kin (brothers and sisters, fathers and sons) and lovers are reunited and multiple marriages are announced–too, is strongly reminiscent of the recognition scenes of Shakespeare's romances.

Thus *Khurshid*'s debt to Shakespeare is unmistakable. As I said above, it is probable that Khori derived the basic plot idea from some traditional Indian tale. However, familiar with both the *dastaan* form and Shakespeare's romances, he must have recognised the fundamental generic affinity between the two and, therefore, was able to combine materials drawn from two diverse sources. For, a distinctive quality of Khori as a playwright seems to have been his ability to inter-weave, with remarkable dexterity and skill, whatever he took from Shakespeare into tales which are distinctively Indian– or oriental–in flavour, texture, and sensibility.

Khori's talent can also be witnessed in the fact that traces of Shakespeare are found in his two subsequent plays as well, namely, *Noor Jehan* and *Hatimtai,* although *t*he plot of neither of these two plays has anything to do with the bard. Like *Khurshid*, these plays, too, were originally written in Gujarati. Naurozji Meherbanji Khan Saheb 'Aram' translated them into Urdu for Alfred Company and Victoria Company in 1872. There is a scene in *Hatimtai*, where the physical features of the heroine's suitors are mocked and ridiculed in a conversation between her and her nurse. This scene has a distinct echo of the sequence in The *Merchant of Venice* (1. ii. 34–110) where Portia and Nerissa are engaged in a similar exercise. Similarly, *Noorjahan*, a typical *dastaan* of adventure and extraordinary happenings, has traces of *Pericles*, *The Tempest* and *A Midsummer Night's Dream*. There is something of Portia about Dil Aram, a major female character in the play. The main villain of the play, Zalim Singh appears to be a negative version of Shakespeare's Prospero. He is a magician who rules over the island of Surkhab. With the help of extraordinary creatures under his command (demons and genies), he gets people, particularly young women, transported from distant lands to his magical island. The play also contains a sequence which is strongly reminiscent of *A Midsummer Night's Dream*. In this scene, the hero is being chased by two women who claim to be equally in love with him. The complication is eventually sorted out, as it is in *Dream* through the supernatural agency of a group of frolicsome fairies who pour a magical potion into the mouths of the sleeping lovers.

Badshah Khudadad (1890, *Pericles*)

Victoria's example of *Khurshid* was promptly followed by the other major theatre company of the time, the Alfred, and soon plays in Urdu became the dominant trend in Parsi theatre. In the beginning, the theatre companies, which were mostly based in Bombay, were obliged to make do with Gujarati-speaking Parsi writers (such as Merzban and Aram) who had some degree of proficiency in Urdu and Persian. However, by the 1890s, as scores of big and small professional companies dotted the country's cultural map and the stage offered one of the most lucrative career options, the situation changed significantly. Playwriting became a flourishing industry and to obtain the services of established writers companies offered high, competitive salaries and rewards. As a result, writers from the Hindustani-speaking parts of northern India began to flock to theatre companies in Bombay and elsewhere in search of employment. Anybody and everybody who could write and versify tried his skill on the dramatic form–albeit with varying degrees of success.

These playwrights borrowed their plots from a variety of sources–from Indian and Central Asian folklore and popular narratives to mythology, history, and classics. William Shakespeare was one such source. In the course of my research, I was able to identify scores of texts which are direct (and occasionally indirect) translations and adaptations of Shakespeare. Written between 1870 and 1910, they cover 23 different plays from the Elizabethan playwright's opus and include his comedies, tragedies, histories, and romances. Almost each of these 23 Shakespearean texts was translated/adapted more than once and by different authors, although not all of them were staged or even stageworthy. Also, some of them are quite clearly no more than a rehash of already existing texts by more successful and established authors like Karimuddin Murad, Mehndi Hassan Ahsan, or Agha Hashra Kashmiri.[8]

However, for nearly two decades after *Khurshid*, Parsi theatre restricted itself almost exclusively to staging traditional narratives of heroic adventure, magical happenings, and erotic love. The next direct Shakespeare adaptation was made only in the late 1880s when Karimuddin Murad was commissioned to write *Badshah Khudadad*. This adaptation of *Pericles* is of special interest because of its peculiar genesis as well as its greater fidelity to the original text.

We have said above that the Parsi theatre plays demonstrated a penchant for freely combining indigenous material with plots, scenes, and motifs taken from Shakespeare. In comparison, Murad Barelvi's play, which, incidentally, is also the earliest formally acknowledged (and possibly staged) Shakespearean adaptation in Urdu to have survived, is relatively less liberal in its approach and free from such direct interpolations of indigenous material. One possible reason for this can be found in the origins of this text. Despite the fact that the Urdu text was written in 1890, it is rooted in a source which predates even Khori. But more of this later. What is important to mention here is that, its relative freedom from direct interpolations notwithstanding, the play does conform to some of the strategies that were later developed and typically employed in the Parsi theatre to assimilate Shakespeare to popular Indian taste and sensibility.

In 1882, when Dadabhai Ratanji Thoonthi broke off from the Victoria and decided to launch a company of his own called the Mumbai Natak Mandali, he felt it would be a good and profitable idea to produce plays in idiomatically and grammatically correct Urdu. He therefore dispatched his friend Pistonji to a tour of UP and Delhi to scout for talented authors. It was during these tours that Pistonji came across an interesting man called Karimuddin, who was employed as a maulvi in a madarsa in Bareili. Born in 1842, Karimuddin was not only a trained scholar of Urdu, Persian, Arabic, and Islamic theology, but also possessed a degree of proficiency in Hindustani music, both vocal and instrumental. Besides, he wrote poetry under the pen name of Murad. Greatly impressed by Murad's versatility, Pistonji wrote about him to Thoonthi who asked him to immediately hire Murad as the resident author of the company and bring him along to Bombay. Karimuddin Murad thus became one of the earliest Urdu writers from northern India to be employed by a Parsi theatre company.

His career in the theatre was successful but rather short. He seems to have written only four plays between 1883 and 1890. Each of the first three plays was based on a traditional *dastaan* and had a long run. Thus, *Gul Bakaoli* (1883) ran for one year; the second play *Gulistan-e-Khandan-e-Haman* (1885) for two years; and the third, *Chitra Bakaoli* (1887), for eight months. However, his luck ran out with his last play, *Khudadad* (1890). He had just completed the play when the company broke up as a result of internal differences. The play, therefore, was probably never produced (Nami, 159-60).

Remarkably, the prototype for Murad's *Khudadad* was not the Shakespearean original but a Gujarati adaptation of it. The person who commissioned and produced the Gujarati version was none other than Dadabhai Patel himself who a year later commissioned and produced Khori's *Khurshid.* When, in 1869-70, Dadabhai was invited to lead the Victoria Company, which at the time was locked in a tough competition with the Alfred Company, his first move was to stage a Gujarati adaptation of Shakespeare's *Pericles, the Prince of Tyre*. The adaptation titled *Khusro na Khavind Khuda urf Dad-e-Dariya*, written by Dosabhai Framji Randhelia, a sub-editor in the influential Parsi journal *Rast Goftar*, who had, on an earlier occasion, also translated *Romeo and Juliet* for an amateur group.Randhelia was paid Rs. 100 for his adaptation of *Pericles* which was further revised and polished by Kaikhusro Kabraji. The adaptation was staged in 1870. According to Khambata, the production was highly successful. The scenes depicting the sea were 'beautifully staged. The spectacle of the stormy sea violently rocking Pericle's boat was particularly breathtaking. It was staged by using a complicated device of wooden rectangles with painted screens with stage hands hidden behind them to gently or violently shake them. Khambata also mentions 'excellent performances' by the cast including, most interestingly for our purposes here, Dadabhai Ratanji Thoonthi, who was to be Murad's employer a decade and a half later, in the title role of Khusro (41; also Nami, 18-19).

It is this Gujarati text which was given by Thoonthi to Karimuddin Murad to translate into Urdu. *Khudadad* thus was the first example of a Shakespearean adaptation in Urdu arrived at through a complex and collaborative process involving a college educated, Shakespeare-loving Parsi director and a non-Anglicised and non-English-knowing writer from northern India. However, since Murad was steeped in the cultural and poetic traditions of Urdu and was himself an accomplished poet, it is highly probable that what he produced was more than a mere literal translation of the Gujarati original. It would have been interesting to compare Randhelia's Gujarati text with Murad's Urdu rendering of it. But, unfortunately, the Gujarati text does not seem to have survived. Interestingly, there is no authorised version of Murad's Urdu translation either. The text that has survived is, in all probability, a pirated version of Murad's work. It was published under the name of Mahmood Mian Zarif and has no date. Zarif, by several accounts, specialised in plagiarising other people's work and published them under his own name. He does not seem to have had any knowledge of English and, as far as is known, did not work for any theatre company. It is reasonable, therefore, to assume that the Zarif text is a plagiarised version of Murad's text which is itself derived from Randhelia's Gujrati original. Although Zarif has inserted his own *takhallus* (pen-name) 'Zarif' or 'Zarifoo' into the verses wherever it is possible (and even where the metre does not permit it), the text seems largely free from the more serious kind of textual impurities that pervade such pirated versions (Nami, 118-119). Nonetheless, it is fair to attribute the play's authorship to its two authentic progenitors. I will therefore refer to them henceforth as a single hyphenated identity, as Randhelia-Murad

In this context, it is interesting that Murad's *Khudadad*, in some ways, is a good deal more faithfully Shakespearean than the works not only of the preceding writers like Khori and Aram but also of the subsequent writers like Ahsan and Hashr whose works, while broadly adhering to Shakespeare's plot outline, refashion it with liberal interpolations of material either invented or drawn from indigenous sources. In contrast, Randhelia-Murad's text desists from adding new materials and, instead, prunes Shakespeare's original of whatever was presumably considered superfluous or not acceptable in the Indian cultural context. To begin with, it does away with Shakespeare's Chorus, of which there are seven instances in *Pericles*. It also deletes some scenes and rearranges some others so as to allow the main sequence of events–Pericles's flight, marriage, shipwreck, separation from wife and daughter, and their final reunion–to unravel in a monolinear movement. Needless to say that this also has the effect of simplifying and streamlining the Elizabethan playwright's typically diversified, multilinear pattern.

Shakespeare's play begins with Pericles who, during his visit to Antioch as a suitor for the princess, discovers the incestuous relationship between her and her father, King Antiochus. The discovery of this relationship and the consequent threat to his life causes the young protagonist to flee not only from Antioch but even from his own kingdom of Tyre. In Shakespeare, this action is played out in the first two scenes. Both of which are jettisoned in Randhelia-Murad's *Khudadad* and, along with it, the father-daughter incest motif which was presumably considered too strong for Indian sensibility is also removed. It is not irrelevant to point out here that that this discomfort with the incest motif and its deletion from an adaptation of *Pericles* is not really peculiar to the Parsi theatre. There has been a tradition of such omission during the 18th and 19th centuries in England too. Observing how the 18th century editors of Shakespeare felt uncomfortable with certain scenes, James McManaway points out: "The attitude of the age is illustrated by George Lillo's *Marina* (produced in 1738), which is built chiefly on Acts IV and V on the assumption that only the last part of the play is by Shakespeare. Edmond Malone restored the play in his edition of 1780 but with some reluctance. And critics and producers have continued to find the incest and brothel scenes highly objectionable until recent years."

What is particularly remarkable about *Khudadad* is the way in which the gap created by this omission is filled in by borrowing from another Shakespearean text. Antiochus's incest and tyranny in Shakespeare provide the dramatic motive for Pericles' flight which takes him through a series of adventures and misadventures. Having jettisoned this reference altogether, the Indian adapters were obliged to supply a new motive for the hero's voyages. In an ingenious move, they did it by borrowing a motif from *King Lear* and reworking it to serve his purpose. Just as Edmund's villainy in Lear (I,ii and II,i) sets his father, Gloucester, against his loyal and dutiful (incidentally, also legitimate) son, Edgar, and causes the latter to flee, in *Khudadad*, a villainous minister, Azlam, deliberately misguides the king about his son, Khudadad, and turns him against the latter. Like his Shakespearean counterpart, Azlam also cunningly misinforms Khudadad that his life is in danger and thus forces him to flee the kingdom.In a shrewd move, what *Khudadad* borrows from Shakespeare is not the details of the Gloucester-Edgar subplot. It merely takes the basic idea underlying it and refashions it in the style, which seems to be typical of the early phase of the Parsi theatre productions. The opening episode in Murad is given in two short and crisp scenes which are entirely in rhymed verses to be sung to specified traditional tunes.

The play opens with a ghazal of five couplets in which Khudadad laments that somebody has instigated his father against him and as a result his father is seeking the son's head. Therefore, he must flee the kingdom and set sail for wherever his destiny takes him. As soon as Khudadad finishes seeing Aslam, the chief minister of king Firozshah (Khudadad's father) enters and informs him in six-rhymed couplets that the king is after Khudadad's blood, he has already sent soldiers to arrest him, and that Khudadad must flee the kingdom without delay to save himself. This is followed by another ghazal by Khudadad which is sung as an aside. It informs us that Khudadad is aware of Aslam's villainy in instigating his father against him for his vested interest. Then he breaks out of his aside and in one rhymed couplet tells Aslam that he would go and hide somewhere away from the palace. Aslam departs and Khudadad sings yet another ghazal of six couplets in which, besides repeating what he has said in earlier ghazal, he declares his intention to go and wander around the world. This is followed by a very short scene, also entirely in rhymed couplets in which a group of soldiers accompanied by the clown (*maskhara*), enter complaining that they had come to apprehend the prince but couldn't find him. Although the debt to Lear is not mentioned anywhere, it is not difficult to see where this motif came from.The parallel with Gloucester-Edmund-Edgar story is obvious. The only difference here with Shakespeare's original is that while Gloucester and Edgar are both duped by Edmund, Khudadad is fully aware of the minister's villainous scheme and yet, quite implausibly, agrees to flee from the kingdom.

Thereafter the action in *Khudadad* moves straight to the shipwreck. The fugitive protagonist arrives in an unfamiliar country–Shauquistan, ruled by Almas Shah. On hearing of a competition for the hand of the local princess (Arzoo), he decides to participate in it and, winning the contest, marries her. Here again a new twist is given to the episode. First, instead of the triumph in which the knights participate and show themselves off (as in *Pericles*), the suitors merely present themselves before the princess. Second, instead of the shield with their mottoes, the suitors offer letters to the princess, which describe their minds and interests. Third, a comical touch is sought to be given to the scene through the agency of a court jester who, through his asides, ridicules the outward appearance and ethnic characteristics of each suitor. The scene is, perhaps, a variation on the Portia-Nerissa conversation about the suitors in *The Merchant of Venice* (I, ii; 34ff), a scene that Khori too had incorporated into his *Hatimtai*.

For a few subsequent scenes, the adaptation follows the same sequence of events as does Shakespeare's original. Khudadad, happily married, stays on in Shauquistan; the news of his father's death is received as is the information that his last wish was that Khudadad should take charge of the kingdom after him; and finally, Khudadad and the family set off for the hero's own kingdom. The subsequent scene begins with a dumb show and a theatrical spectacle (described by Khambata) of a ship in a turbulent sea depicting what corresponds to the action in Shakespeare's III, i: Khudadad's ship is caught in a violent storm; his wife Arzoo dies in childbirth; her body is encased in a chest and cast into the sea. The scene ends with Khudadad's lamentation (in three couplets) which further establishes Arzoo's death.

Continuing to adhere to Shakespeare's arrangement of events, the subsequent scene depicts the discovery of Arzoo in a trunk and her revival by a clever hakeem (doctor). Arzoo declares her resolve to become a 'jogin' (often found in Parsi theatre plays as an Indian equivalent of a nun) in a sequence of Urdu ghazals, Persian couplets and Hindi dohas. Khudadad leaves his motherless infant, Aoon, in the care of the king and queen of Iran. The daughter, Aoon, is kidnapped by thieves. However, here the adaptation skips the brothel scenes and the action moves directly on to Aoon's rescue from a brothel. It may be mentioned here that in *Pericles* three scenes are set in the brothel which dramatise, in the main, Marina's purchase by a bawd, attempts to force her into the profession, and her nobility and resolve to remain chaste–which moves some men to help her escape. In *Khudadad*, however, these details are omitted. Aoon is simply rescued from 'kutni's' clutches and placed in a respectable doctor's (hakeem's) house. In a further abridgement of the Shakespearean text, the hakeem is already present on Khudadad's ship which allows the action to move straight to the requisitioning of Aoon's services to cure Khudadad of his deep depression.

In Act V of *Pericles*, Pericles notes Marina's resemblance to his wife and says that his own daughter 'might have been' like the girl before him. This is an example of the care Shakespeare took to make the events in his plays plausible, for Pericles has not seen Marina since she was an infant and cannot possibly recognise her in youth. However, the adapter of *Khudadad* does not seem to have any such concern with plausibility and makes Khudadad say straight away that the young woman before him looks like his own daughter (III, i). Also in Shakespeare, the process of recognition unravels slowly. In Murad, the recognition of Aoon by Khudadad and their reunion is accomplished quite briskly. The scene ends with Khudadad's ghazal in which he thanks god for reuniting him with his daughter and declares his resolve to go to 'Ibadatgah' (literally, place of worship) and to serve the pious women of the convent.

The play's ending, too, is rather brisk and business-like. The scene opens with Arzoo's ghazal in which she laments her plight. This is followed by the song of women (Shakespeare's vestal virgins) who are on their way to the church. Arzoo joins them in their singing and goes out with them. Khudadad, Aoon, and their entourage enter and sing a song offering thanks to God for reuniting father and daughter. The subsequent scene, which is also the last scene of the play, takes place inside the church. 'Men and women' enter (Khudadad and Aoon among them) and each group sings alternate couplets and a song expressing their devotion to God. Rather suddenly, without any preamble, Arzoo turns to Khudadad and in five rhymed verses asks him who he is, where he is from and why he has come there dressed as a devotee. Khudadad, in three rhymed couplets, tells her his story. Arzoo faints (as does Thaisa in *Pericles*). Khudadad is bewildered and sends for the hakeem,who reveals to him Arzoo's identity and revives her. Thus, there is no protracted question-answer sequence as in Shakespeare to confirm the truth of this. Hakeem's verdict is accepted without any further ado. Arzoo comes around and sings two-rhymed couplets to thank God for reuniting her with her family. The scene ends with a group song in which the entire cast thanks the audience for coming to see their play and prays for their happiness and for fulfilment of their wishes. The song replaces Shakespeare's epilogue in which the moral of the story and the exemplary qualities of the main characters are extolled.

Thus, despite various deletions, abridgements, and rearrangements, *Khudadad* remains largely free from interpolations of any indigenous material and, therefore, basically faithful to Shakespeare. This suggests the hand of someone who had direct access to the original text. In other words, the contribution of Randhelia and Kabraji is unmistakable. Nonetheless, the Urdu version of the adaptation does carry a strong suggestion of Murad's contribution as well. It can be best evidenced in the profusion and the quality of the verses. These verses and the diction employed in them are of a quality that only a writer who had Urdu as his first language could have achieved. Moreover, it is not just that the play abounds in ghazals, songs, and other poetic forms, but, as my resume of the play's text above indicates, and quite unlike *Khurshid*, is predominantly conceived and written in terms of songs and verses, containing very little prose dialogue. Characters sing not only to communicate their strong emotions to the audience but also in ordinary conversation with each other. These songs are written and sung to specific, mainly folk, tunes. This gives *Khudadad* a strongly operatic flavour reminiscent of the *Indersabha*.

Ahsan Lakhnawi

By the time Murad joined a Parsi theatre company, the practice of bringing authentic Urdu language writers from the Urdu Hindi heartland of Uttar Pradesh and Delhi had become the norm. Before the end of the century, a number of truly talented poets and writers, such as Vinayak Prasad Talib, Narain Prasad Betab, Mehndi Hasan Ahsan Lakhnawi, and Agha Hashra Kashmiri, were employed by various companies as their resident authors. Of these, Ahsan and Hashr, who arrived in Bombay about a decade after Murad, were particularly accomplished writers. They were both skilful poets and were steeped in the poetic and musical traditions of northern India. They continued the style of writing that employed a profusion of poetry and songs. With their arrival on the scene, the literary level of playwriting was significantly enhanced and the operatic tradition of the mid-19th century Avadh, too, found a stronger expression. It will not be incorrect to say that, together, these two writers contributed the most towards the development of that characteristic style which made the Parsi theatre such a popular and commercially successful phenomenon.

The *fin-de-siecle* years when these two playwrights made their debut, were marked by a surge in Urdu adaptations of Shakespeare. Between 1898 and 1907, major Parsi theatre companies of Bombay staged at least eight major adaptations. Of these, four were by Ahsan and four by Hashr. These plays constitute a significant part not only of the work of the two playwrights but also of the entire body of Shakespearean adaptations on the Parsi stage. The earliest extant adaptation of a Shakespearean tragedy as well as the first ever adaptation of a Shakespearean comedy were done by Ahsan, who was also responsible for making a more frequent use of *ramishgaraan* (dancers and singers) to embellish his plays. Along with Hashr, he pioneered the practice of interpolating a comic subplot parallel to Shakespeare's main plot. No such interpolation is found in Khori or Murad. Besides, Ahsan's adaptation of Hamlet is the only tragedy in the entire history of Shakespearean adaptations on the Parsi stage which conforms to Shakespeare's ending. All other adaptations of tragedies–including Ahsan's own adaptation of *Romeo and Juliet* and Hashr's *Lear*–are given happy endings.

Ahsan was born in Lucknow, the birthplace of Wajid Ali Shah's *Radha Kanhaiya* and Amanat's *Indersabha.* From early years, he seems to have been drawn to poetry and theatre. His interest in theatre was probably kindled and reinforced by the fact that he lived close to a building called Afzal Mahal, which was the usual venue for performances by local and visiting theatre companies. We also learn from Ishrat Rahmani that Ahsan was fond of Hubab Rampuri's plays–particularly the ones based on traditional tales of love and adventure–and even tried, albeit without success, to take Hubab's guidance in writing plays (185).

The beginning of Ahsan's career as a professional playwright remains unclear. He was still based in Lucknow when he wrote his first play titled *Zahar-e-Ishq* based on Shauq's masnavi, which, according to one view, was probably staged as *Dastavez-e-Mohabbat* by Dorab Shah's company in 1897. However, Ishrat Rahmani thinks it more likely that Ahsan's first play was not staged and that it was his *Chandravali,* which was written on the request of Dadabhai Thoonthi and was inspired by the success of Karimuddin Murad Barelvi's *Gul Bakavali*, which made Ahsan famous among the Parsi companies (187). According to Nami, when Cowasji Khatau visited Lukhnow with his company and heard of the fame of *Zahar-e-ishq* and *Chandravali*, he offered employment to the young writer and brought him to Bombay (2:194–5). The first plays that Ahsan wrote in Bombay were adaptations of two major tragedies of Shakespeare: *Hamlet* as *Khoon-e-Nahaq* and *Romeo and Juliet* as *Bazm-e-Fani*. These were followed over the next 3-4 years by two more adaptations: *Twelfth Night* as *Bhool Bhulaiyan* and *The Merchant of Venice* as *Dilfarosh*. According to Somnath Gupt, and Nami, Ahsan also adapted *Othello* under the title *Shaheed-e-Wafa* which could not be staged. However, in the absence of any corroborating evidence or source, Gupt's claim cannot be verified.

Khoon-e-Nahaq (1898, *Hamlet*)

As far as I know, Ahsan's *Khoon-e-Nahaq* was the earliest professionally staged Urdu adaptation of a Shakespearean tragedy. Regarding the genesis of this play, Ardeshar Dadabhai Thoonthi says that Ahsan first wrote it under the title of *Jahangir* for Badri Prasad's Lucknow-based jubilee Theatrical Company of which Thoonthi was the manager. This was in late 1896 or early 97, during which the company was going through a grave financial crisis and Thoonthi had resigned his job and was replaced by Cowasji Palanji Khatau. Initially, Badri Prasad was hopeful that the company would overcome the crisis but the losses were so huge that the company was finally closed down. Following the closure of the company, Cowasji returned to Bombay and, on establishing a company of his own staged *Jahangir* under the title, *Khun-e-Nahaq* in 1898. The play's popular success prompted him to bring Ahsan from Lucknow and, after appointing him the new company's official playwright, got Ahsan to make certain changes in the plot before staging it.

Khoon-e-Nahaq retains the central sequence of the *Hamlet* story, but, as Ahsan himself states, rewrites and rearranges large parts of Shakespeare's text. In accordance with the established Parsi theatre practice, he divides the play into three acts and each act into several scenes. The opening scene shows Prince Jahangir (Hamlet) frolicking with Meherbano (Ophelia), who he is in love with and whom he promises to marry on ascending the throne. The scene ends with a duet sung by the two lovers. It is only in the second scene that his father, the Badshah (the old Hamlet) is killed. In terms of the action that it dramatises, this second scene is both invented and borrowed. In Shakespeare the details of how exactly the Old Hamlet was murdered is revealed to us only in the third Act (iii, ii) through the dumb-show performed by the travelling players. While Ahsan reproduces players' mute performance quite faithfully in the last scene of his play, he also directly dramatises the action of the old king's murder in this early scene. He even fleshes it out with interpolations of a number of new motifs and details. Set in the royal garden and opening with a song by *ramishgaran*, the scene reveals that Badshah is worried because of an astrologer's prediction that he would die that day. He is anxious about the Queen's fate after him. However, the Queen (Gertrude), declaring her undying love for him, says she could not survive without him. She gets him to lie down and rest. As he lies down, she, like a devoted Indian wife, presses his feet and sings a soothing song till he falls asleep. The king's brother Farukh (Claudius) enters and is egged on by the queen to go ahead and kill the sleeping monarch. When he shows signs of inner conflict and reluctance to commit this "unjust murder" ("khoon-e-nahaq"), she encourages him and and gives him the vial of poison. It is interesting that the main responsibility for the murder is thus laid on the queen while Farukh's hesitation here as well as his anxiety in a subsequent scene somewhat mitigates his role. It is entirely possible that this part of the scene was inspired by the example of Lady Macbeth's encouragement to her reluctant husband to go ahead and kill Duncan (I:vii).

After another scene in which the Prince laments his father's death in a song and is consoled by friend Akhtar (Horatio), Ahsan picks up the thread of the plot again. Farukh is worried about his own fate if Jahangir, the true successor to the throne, becomes the king and decides to avenge his father's death. The queen offers to find a solution to the problem with the help of Humayun (Polonius). This is exactly what she does in the subsequent scene. Humayun initially refuses out of loyalty to the late king but the threats and offers of a reward makes him fall in line and he agrees to assist in the conspiracy to deprive Jahangir of his rightful claim and install Farrukh on the throne.

The next two scenes are largely, although not entirely, made up of interpolated matter. In one, Jahangir laments his father's death and the mother's haste in remarrying and is quizzed by Humayun about the reason for his pensiveness. The other scene has Meherbano with companions (Rehana and Farzana) talking about love and singing several romantic songs (mostly in folk language and style), while Jahangir enters looking thoughtful and worried. On Meherbano questioning him about the reason, he, in an echo of Hamlet, only expresses bewilderment at the lack of loyalty and fidelity in the world, particularly in women. The play reconnects with the original once again in the next scene which parallels Shakespeare's rampart sequence. Jahangir meets the spirit of his father who reveals the details of his murder. As in Hamlet, the spirit asks Jahangir to avenge his death.This scene concludes Act One of Ahsan's text.

Fidelity to Shakespeare's text continues in the opening scene of Act Two. Humayun informs King Farrukh that the cause of Jahangir's strange behaviour is his love for his daughter, Meherbano. As an evidence of this, Humayun presents a letter from the Prince addressed to her. Farrukh wishes to see and hear it himself and Humayun promises to arrange such an opportunity. In the scenes that follows this fidelity to the original text is broken again and what we are offered is a sequence which has no parallel in Shakespeare. Mansoor, a courtier's son, who too is in love with Meherbano, enters singing a song, and, after a frolicsome repartee in verse with Rehana and Farzana, enlists their assistance in uniting him with their mistress. This is followed by a scene in which Jahangir's servant, Suleman, informs Akhtar about his master's strange and frightening behaviour. As Jahangir enters talking madly, Akhtar insistently inquires about the reason for this condition. The Prince confides in him that he is playing mad as he is trying to keep something hidden from others. He divulges it to his friend only after, following the Ghost's injunction, he gets the friend to promise that he will keep it to himself.

The subsequent scene is a long one. It consists of several sequences, most of them interpolated and replete with love songs and poetic, playful repartees by and between Meherbano and her female companions. In a playful exchange in verse and rhymed prose, Rehana and Farzana quiz their mistress about her restlessness and try to disabuse her of her love for Jahangir and instead plead in favour of Mansoor. A little later, Mansoor himself enters and tries to woo Meherbano. Finding her unmoved he even threatens her with revenge. Jahangir enters and in a partly mad and partly sane exchange tries to dissuade Meherbano from attaching herself to him. On the latter's producing the handkerchief which Jahangir had given her as a token of his love, he slips into mad talk again.

This last sequence has a distant echo of "get thee to a nunnery" scene in Shakespeare 3:1. There is a rejection of Meherbano and an assertion of unreliability of marriages as in *Hamlet*. Jahangir asks about Meherbano's father as Hamlet asks Ophelia about Polonious. The reference to the handkerchief is also reminiscent of Ophelia's reference to "rememberances".

The scene that follows is entirely an Ahsan invention. It is marked by a profusion of songs and has no parallel in Shakespeare. Mansoor tries to lure Sulaiman to kill Jahangir in return for a lot of money. At first ready to do anything for riches, Sulaiman declines the offer on hearing the name of the person he is supposed to kill. He says he cannot be disloyal to his master who is a good and innocent man. However, on learning of Mansoor's love for Meherbano, he agrees to help him meet the lady and tells him that the young lady is scheduled to visit the graveyard that evening and Mansoor could meet her there.

The next scene combines events from Shakespeare's 2:2 and 3:4 and thus offers a number of textual parallels. Alone and thoughtful, Jahangir is met by Humayun who quizzes him about his state. He answers darkly but with oblique references to adultery, infidelity, and treachery. He also refers to Humayun's daughter repeatedly. Humayun informs the prince that his mother is worried about him and would like to speak to him. The Queen arrives and when the son speaks to her threateningly about her unfaithfulness and treachery, she is frightened and begins to scream. Humayun, who was listening to all this from behind a curtains, makes a noise and Jahangir kills him. The ghost of the old king appears and admonishes the prince about his promise to avenge his murder. The ghost also tells him to spare the mother. Jahangir lets the Queen go after admonishing her to purge her life of sinfulness. The scene ends with Akhtar announcing the arrival of the players.

The next scene takes place in a graveyard. There is no clear reason for Ahsan choosing this particular setting except that Shakespeare too has a graveyard scene. What happens in *Hamlet* and in this scene have no correspondence at all. Meherbano arrives at the graveyard at night accompanied by Sulaiman. Frightened of the nature of the place and the darkness of the night, she sings a song and asks Sulaiman why he has brought her there. She is told that Jahangir wanted to meet her there and will be coming shortly. On hearing the footsteps of someone approaching, Sulaiman leaves. The one who comes is not Jahangir but Mansoor, who tries to force her to commit herself to him. On her persistent refusal to do so, he prepares to kill her. Jahangir arrives in the nick of time and shoots Mansoor dead. Meherbano, relieved and happy, offers to take Jahangir to her father and ask his permission for them to be married. But the prince informs her that her father is now dead and is in no position to offer or deny permission. He says that he himself is not likely to live much longer.

Ahsan's Act III opens with a scene which again has no equivalent in Shakespeare. The Queen laments the outcome of her evil deed in a song. Farukh is also troubled and the Queen informs him of Humayun's death. Faramarz enters bewailing the death of his son, Mansoor, at the hands of Jahangir, and appeals for justice. The King sympathises with him and tells him of the scheme to poison Jahangir during the ensuing play. The King's advice to Faramarz echo Claudius's advice to Laertes in 4:7.

The next scene closely parallels the early part of Shakespeare's play-within-the-play scene (III, ii). Like Hamlet's instruction to Horatio, Jahangir tells Akhtar that the forthcoming performance would reflect the death of his own father and asks him to observe Farukh's reaction during the play. Again like Hamlet's advice to the actors, Jahangir, just before the commencement of the play, warns the players against exaggerated, hyperbolic acting. When the royal couple enters, the Queen wants her son to sit with her but Jahangir (like Hamlet) prefers to sit with Meherbano. The scene changes and the Badshah's murder is re-enacted as a dumb show by the players. There are several parallels here with Shakespeare. Even some of the lines are textually close to the original. However, Ahsan has also grafted material from Shakespeare's last scene into this scene and made it the concluding scene of his text. The poisoned drink and sword are both there. As in Shakespeare, the queen is killed, as is Jahangir. Akhtar, unlike his Elizabethan counterpart Horatio, dies too. Just as Hamlet, before dying, kills Claudius, Jahangir shoots Farukh before succumbing to the poison. Unable to bear the death of his friend and despite Jahangir's attempts to dissuade him, Akhtar too drinks the remaining drops of the poisoned wine and dies, as does Meherbano.

Thus, in Ahsan's adaptation of *Hamlet*, like in Randhelia-Murad's adaptation of *Pericles*, the main events of Shakespeare's plot are retained with the usual abridgements, modifications, and deletions of events and sequences. One example of this kind of abridgement and modification can be seen in the fact that, unlike his Elizabethan prototype, Prince Jahangir has not returned to the kingdom after a long absence but is very much there when his father dies and his mother marries his uncle. However, there is also a difference between *Khoon-e-Nahaq* and the Randhelia-Murad model. Ahsan's text includes several significant additions not only of songs and dances but also of characters and scenes. Among the interpolated characters are those of Mansoor, a rival to Jahangir for Meherbano's love and his father, Faramarz, who, like Humayun (Polonious) is a minister in the royal court. In addition to Rehana and Farzana, *saheliyan* (companions) of Meherbano, Ahsan also added to Shakespeare's text another character called Sulaiman, Prince Jahangir's servant who is a strange combination of a clown and a crook.

There are certain deletions as well. The more notable among these are Rosencrantz and Guildenstern, Laertes, the Clown, and Fortinbras. Along with these characters, the roles as well as the sequences associated with them are also jettisoned or reallocated. For instance, while the roles of Fortinbras and Rosencrantz and Guildenstern are entirely deleted, some of Laertes's role is redistributed among two interpolated characters. A significant part of it is given to Mansoor's father, Faramarz. In a scene possibly inspired by the graveyard scene in which Hamlet challenges Laertes over Ophelia's love, Mansoor is shot dead by Jahangir when he is trying to kill Meherbano after surprising her in a graveyard where she had come to meet Jahangir. In Shakespeare, Leartes is distraught by the deaths of his father and sister, and is clamouring for revenge.

However, he is persuaded by Claudius to wait till the treacherously rigged fencing match which, as we know, forms the material of the last scene of *Hamlet*. Interestingly, this part of Laertes's role is given to Mansoor's father. However, while Laertes dies in the end, Faramarz survives.

Ahsan's other Shakespearean Adaptations

Ahsan's next Shakespearean adaptation was *Bazm-e-Fani* (*Romeo and Juliet*), also known as *Gulnar-Feroz*. Unfortunately, I was not able to locate a copy of this play anywhere. All I could find was a brief reference to the play in some secondary sources. Like his adaptation of *Hamlet*, Ahsan's *Bazm-e-Fani* too seems to have adhered closely to the basic plot outline of the Shakespearean original. Somnath Gupt summarises this outline thus: "Ahsan has developed the plot in his own fashion. He shows that Ghafur ud-Daula and Zahur ud-Daula are both respectable citizens of Firozabad. Feroz (Romeo) is Ghafur's son...whereas Gulnar (Juliet) is Zahur's daughter.... The most significant characters retained by Ahsan include the king, his minister, Zarif (the king's jester), Masud and Anjaam (Firoz's companions), Mirza (Zahur's nephew) and Musharraf (Gulnar's fiancé)." The play ends with Feroz killing Musharraf in a fight and marrying Gulnar (Gupt, 91–92).[9]

Khoon-e-Nahaq was not only Ahsan's first Shakespeare adaptation, but, as I have already mentioned, also the very first Urdu adaptation of a tragedy to be staged by a professional Parsi theatre company. It also has the distinction of being the only adaptation of a tragedy which conformed to Shakespeare's ending. His adaptation of *Romeo and Juliet* came within a year after his *Hamlet* adaptation, and, judging from the brief synopsis of *Bazm-e-Fani* by Somnath Gupt, we find that Ahsan has changed the ending into a happy one, thereby conforming to a mandatory requirement in Parsi theatre plays.

After *Bazm-e-Fani*, Ahsan's next play was a comedy titled *Dilfarosh* (1900), an adaptation of The *Merchant of Venice*. This Shakespearean text seems to have been a great favourite of Indian writers of that period. In Urdu alone, I have identified at least five published translations before Ahsan's *Dilfarosh* which was written in 1900. A probable reason for the play's popularity is its fascinating story and the fact that, if one did not concern oneself with the subtle nuances of Shakespeare's text, it is relatively easier to translate or adapt. However, its popularity with earlier writers notwithstanding, *The Merchant of Venice* was never turned into a stage production in Urdu language till Ahsan's *Dilfarosh*.

Ahsan's adaptation reproduces the main events of Shakespeare's story but alters several of its details. As in the Elizabethan play, a kindhearted wealthy man, Zar, takes a loan from a Jewish money lender on the extraordinary condition that if he did not repay on time he would give a portion of his flesh to him. The way the story develops and concludes is the same as in Shakespeare. However, there is one significant interpolation. Ahsan has created a new villainous character called Mahmood, who is brother of Zar's friend Quasim. Quasim loves a woman called Shirin, and it is for his sake that Zar borrows the money. It is Mahmood who cheats Zar of all his wealth and renders him incapable of repaying the loan. Furthermore, Ahsan jettisons the entire casket sequence with various suitors and, instead, makes Mahmood present himself as a suitor to his own brother's beloved Shirin.

Ahsan's 1905 play, *Bhool Bhulaiyan*, was his last Shakespearean adaptation. Like his other adaptations, it too reproduces the main plot of *Twelfth Night*. The identical twins, Jafar and Dilara, are separated by an accident. By sheer coincidence, they end up in the same kingdom, although they remain unaware of one another's whereabouts till the end. In order to conceal their true identities, both disguise themselves and operate under assumed names. As in Shakespeare, the female protagonist, Dilara, takes on the name and appearance of a man. A number of complications follow as a result of mistaken identities, till everything is clarified. The twins are reunited and each also finds a partner to love and marry.

This sequence of events clearly parallels the plot trajectory in Shakespeare's original. However, there are several variations and interpolations as well. For instance, an interesting change that Ahsan makes to the original is in relation to the subplot. He jettisons Shakespeare's witty and humorous sequences involving Malvolio, Sir Andrew Aguecheek, and Maria, and replaces it with a crude comedy of adultery, greed, cheating, and thievery. Another alteration is to the manner in which the twins are separated. In the original this happens when the ship that they were travelling in capsizes. In Ahsan, they lose one another after the train they were in is struck by lightning during a stormy night. This alteration allows Ahsan to interpolate a whole scene depicting a railway platform in stormy, rainy conditions with a train about to take off. The scene tries to reproduce the confusion and the noise of an Indian railway platform. It dramatises an argument between a railway guard and two passengers which turns abusive, compelling a senior officer to intervene to restrain the guard. This enables the playwright to bring in a discourse on the value of good and benevolent governance. The senior officer tells his junior in English that it is important to treat the natives with kindness and civility because that will prompt them to uphold the British government with all their might. Eventually, the train leaves. The porter sings a song about the moving trains. The scene ends with the porter's comments about the hard life that workers like him lead.

Ahsan was the first Parsi theatre playwright to make an adaptation of Shakespeare presumably from the plot summaries of the original texts. Murad, as we noted, adapted his *Khudadad* from an already existing Gujarati adaptation. Ahsan was very proud of his Shakespearean adaptations. Writing more than two decades after his *Khoon-e-Nahaq*, he boasted that what he had produced became the model for all future plays of Parsi theatre. "It was my humble pen," he proudly declared, "that gave to the Indian stage a new dramatic style. It was my *Khoon-e-Nahaq* which brought about this great revolution. 1898 was the year of radical transformation in playwriting. The work of subsequent years merely followed and built upon this model." About his approach to Shakespeare's plays, he says, "My plays contain more verse than prose, and my poems deal with various subjects, such as the transience of the world, love and romance, union and separation, betrayal, heroism, historical events, sincerity, matters of the heart, etc. Instead of drawing upon

Shakespeare's poetic imagination, I have tried to fashion a style of my own. I jettisoned aspects of Shakespeare that I thought were not appropriate for the Indian stage and made modifications that were in keeping with our times. To list and describe all the changes and interventions that I made in Shakespeare would be a very long story. Even the plots have been completely overhauled. I have not made these modifications because I wanted to demonstrate my superiority over him but because I felt that they were needed. I have followed the dictates of my own sensibility.Whether it is good or bad, is another matter" (Rahmani, 186).

It cannot be doubted that Ahsan's adaptations, including *Khoon-e-Nahaq*, did contribute significantly towards making Shakespeare acceptable to the popular Indian audiences of the Parsi theatre during its more developed, more commercial phase. He achieved this largely by interpolating a variety of distinctly Indian motifs and sequences, such as the *ramishgarans* and their songs and dances into the original plot, and thereby desi-fying or nativising the Elizabethan Bard more thoroughly. Nonetheless, compared to subsequent adaptations, particularly those by Hashr, Ahsan's work is not without flaws. Somnath Gupt says that Ahsan's writing, despite its forcefulness and poetic richness, lacks depth. He concerns himself with "the superficial aspects of society", perhaps in keeping with his audience's expectations. His patrons were also only interested in making money. Thus he could not give us drama which would have a durable value(92). However, to be fair to Ahsan, the same could be said about all Parsi theatre playwrights, including Hashr during its more advanced, more commercialised phase. Many of the features that Gupt faults Ahsan for were integral to the Parsi theatre style and were introduced, as Gupt himself suggests, at the behest of the owners and directors who commissioned the plays.

In my judgement the main flaw of Ahsan's playwriting was his inadequate grip on the dramatic form. He was more of a poet than a playwright. His interest seems to be so focused on songs and poetry that *Khoon-e-Nahaq* can be described as a musical which also has a story rather than a play with songs and poetry. The play has at least 63 instances where songs are indicated in the text. Ahsan seems concerned chiefly to charm his audience by demonstrating his skills as a poet and song writer. His dialogue lacks that resounding and declamatory quality which gives Hashr's plays their dramatic quality and impact in performance. He often missed out on the little nuances that could enhance the dramatic power of a scene. The graveyard scene in *Khoon-e-Nahaq* is an example of his weak sense of drama. In this scene, the information of Humayun's murder is offered quite casually and Meherbano also receives it somewhat casually without showing much shock or grief at the news of her father's sudden death. Songs and verbal repartees too are often quite inappropriate to the occasion. Meherbano, for example, sings a song when Mansoor draws his sword and is about to kill her. The songs as well as the versified exchanges between him and her often sound like ludicrous love play and do not reflect the seriousness or the menacing aspect of the moment.

Furthermore, it will not be incorrect to describe *Khoon-e-Nahaq* as *Hamlet* without the state of Denmark (or, for that matter, any other state), because that political dimension which gives Shakespeare's *Hamlet* its cognitive richness and depth is missing from Ahsan's play. In addition to jettisoning the characters and sequences listed above, the playwright also excluded anything that could give his play a political meaning.

However, this rejection of the political, too, is not peculiar to Ahsan. Parsi theatre plays carefully excluded everything and anything that could be construed as an anti-Empire. This can be witnessed also in that very first Urdu language play, *Khurshid*, which takes from Shakespeare the story of Imogen but leaves out the entire story of King Cymbeline's anti-imperialist battle against the Romans. It is in keeping with the character of the Parsi stage, which, like all commercial forms, was a conformist theatre and did not aim at anything more than entertainment of a more or less superficial kind. It admitted motifs of treachery, adultery, intrigue, jealousy and so on, but not anything suggesting an opposition to an established political order. It did not wish to rock any boats. The British were in power and the plays that Parsi theatre companies offered could not be allowed to include any critical political reference or possess any dimension of meaning that could be even remotely interpreted as anti-establishment. A rare, though very minor, exception to this general rule is found in Hashr's *Mureed-e-Shak* (an adaptation of *Winter's Tale*) wherein a character, when told that he had become a slave to a woman, retorts in an aside:

Aurat ka Ghulam to Sara jahan ho raha hai
Europe ka chhota bhai Hindustan ho raha hai
(The entire world is now slave to woman
Even India, Europe's junior cousin.)

This reference to Queen Victoria's rule disguised as a witty, throw-away aside by a villainous character is the closest that the commercial Parsi stage could allow itself to come to making a political comment.

Agha Hashr Kashmiri: *Mureed-e-Shak* (1898, *Winter's Tale*)

Ahsan had begun with adaptations of tragedies and had moved on to comedies, Hashr began with a romance play, followed by a comedy and finally a tragedy. His first play, *Mureed-e-Shak*, an adaptation of Shakespeare's *Winter's Tale*, written in 1898, was staged within a year after Ahsan's *Khoon-e-Nahaq*. He wrote it for a Parsi theatre company after he moved from Banaras to Bombay and was employed as the resident paywright of Caoosji Palanji Khatau's Alfred Theatrical Company. The play was also performed under the title *Jangal ki Rani* and *Jangal ki Shahzadi*. Like Ahsan, Hashr too set out to Indianise the Elizabethan text. Just as Ahsan had jettisoned aspects of Shakespeare that he thought were "not appropriate for the Indian stage", Hashr, too, declared that he had recast "this foreign beloved with Asian dress and Indian humour", and thereby transformed her into "a lovely bride"who on her public appearance is sure to steal all hearts" (103–04). Hashr was right. The play proved to be immensely popular and was staged more than 60 times in the space of 9 months.

On the whole, Hashr's *Mureed-e-Shak* is relatively more faithful to the plot of *Winter's Tale* than Ahsan's adaptation of *Hamlet.*

The latter, as we saw, is full of interpolations not only of songs but also of whole scenes and characters. Ahsan has even somewhat altered the story by inventing a rival (Mansoor) to Hamlet for Ophelia's love. Although Hashr's play, too, is not entirely free from interpolations and amendments either, they are fewer and relatively minor. There is, of course, a farcical plot which has no connection with the main story and runs parallel to it. But practice of including a crudely humorous and farcical subplot to alternate with the main plot, probably Hashr's own original contribution to the standard formula, was an almost mandatory component of Parsi theatre plays to ensure their success at the box office. Hashr used it in his plays, including in all his Shakespearean adaptations. We find this extraneous farcical component in *Mureed-e-Shak* and *Shaheed-e-Naaz* (*Measure for Measure*) as also in *Safed Khoon* (*King Lear*). Interestingly, in Shaeed-*e-Naaz*, Hasr even jettisons Shakespeare's own original comedy involving the bawds (Pompey and Mistress Overdone), as well as the chief executioner and the hardened criminal Bernadine. In its place, he inserts a comic subplot of his own which has no connection at all with the main story.

Perhaps the most significant alteration in *Mureed-e-Shak* is found in the character called Toofan, a courtier, who has no exact parallel in *Winter's Tale*. On the one hand, one part of him stands for Shakespeare's Antigonus and subsumes the main functions of his role in the play. On the other hand, his deliberate malignity sets him quite apart from his Elizabethan original. The play opens with a short scene which is entirely a Hashr innovation and contains a brief soliloquy by Toofan. In this speech, he, right at the outset of the play, declares his intention to harm queen Husnara. He hates her because he suspects that she was responsible for destroying his chances of rising to the top in the hierarchy at the royal court. In the scene that follows, he begins to put his villainous project into action. He plants the suspicion in the mind of the King that his friend and guest, King Humayun, is in an adulterous relationship with the queen.

A conjectural explanation for this could be that Hashr wanted to underplay the King's responsibility in behaving so ignobly towards his chaste queen and his loyal friend. It is not unlikely that, Hashr was inspired in this by another Shakespeare play, *Othello,* in which the protagonist comes across more as a victim of Iago's villainy than an evil man who unjustly suspects and kills his chaste wife, Desdemona. Hashr's Toofan, thus, can be said to embody a bit of Antigonus combined with a bit of Iago.

Modifications like this and a few others apart, *Mureed-e-Shak* reproduces Shakespeare's main sequence of events quite faithfully. King Sikandar Jah, instigated, as we saw, by the villainous courtier Toofan, wrongly suspects his friend and guest King Humayun of an illicit relationship with Queen Husnara, and plans to kill him. Alerted by Koshish, Sikandar Jah's noble-hearted courtier, Humayun quietly flees to his own kingdom. Unwilling to serve an evil master, Koshish too leaves with him. Accusing the queen of adultery, Sikandar Jah orders her to be imprisoned. When, as in the original, the courtiers intercede and urge him to be merciful, he reluctantly agrees to allow them to consult the city's revered sage (Hashr's equivalent of Apollo's Oracle) about the queen's character. At this point the play makes a sudden, although momentary, departure from the original. Provoked by the queen's composure and dignified attitude, the king lunges at her with a dagger. While his courtier tries to restrain him, in a typical Parsi theatre style the queen sings a song, written in folk style and language, about the pain of loving an unjust and heartless man.

In prison, Husnara gives birth to a daughter. When the child is brought to him, the king, still blind with jealousy, orders Toofan to take the infant somewhere else and kill her. But as Toofan reaches a forest, he himself is killed by a tiger. Interestingly in this very brief scene the few lines that Toofan speaks while abandoning the baby in the forest reproduces the sense of guilt and remorse that is found in Antigonus. These are not consistent with Toofan's own otherwise diabolic character in the play. As in Shakespeare, the baby herself is saved and adopted by a family of farmers where she eventually grows into a beautiful young maiden and falls in love with King Humayun's son. Meanwhile, the verdict of the revered sage vindicates the queen's honour and declares the king to be a tyrant. But the king refuses to countenance this verdict till, shocked by the news of his only son's death and seeing in it a sign of divine retribution, he repents. However, by the time he is prepared to make amends, the queen is reported to have died.

Sixteen years go by. Interestingly, this passage of time is indicated by a placard reading, "16 years later", instead of the figure of Time announcing it as in Shakespeare. Prince Feroz runs into Gulnar who turns out to be the farmer Prabhu Singh's daughter. They fall in love, and Feroz, without disclosing his identity as the prince of the realm, approaches the farmer with a marriage proposal and obtains his consent. As the two lovers are about to be married, they are surprised by the sudden arrival of Feroz's enraged father, King Humayun. Koshish, who is about to sail in a boat to return to his former master, saves them from Humayun's wrath by taking them along.

A notable feature of this scene is the use of a stage spectacle. The escape of the farmer's family with Koshish is visualised by what the script refers to as a "plot". This drop scene at the back of the stage shows Koshish, Prabhu's family and the young lovers boarding a ship. Spectacles like this were an important part of the commercially successful formula that the Parsi theatre employed in its productions. We saw above how, in *Bhool bhulaiyan,* Ahsan interpolated a whole new scene into Shakespeare's original in order to employ a spectacle depicting a railway platform with a train about to leave.We also mentioned above how the spectacle of a ship on waters was first used in *Khusro na Khavind Khuda* in 1870 and was sought to be repeated two decades later in *Badshah Khudadad.* Its use again in *Mureed-e-Shak* indicates that the Parsi directors were so enamoured of it and impressed by its popularity that they tended to use it whenever they could.

In the third act, the fugitive family and the lovers arrive at Sikandar Jah's court. Gulnar is recognised as the abandoned princess. This mollifies the angry King Humayun and makes her marriage to Prince Feroz possible. General reunion and celebrations follow. Sikandar Jah apologises to Humayun and rejoices at the fact that his daughter is going to marry Firoz. A cleverly crafted statue of Husnara is unveiled. Sikandar Jah and Gulnar are amazed at the likeness and its life-like smile. Hameeda, the loyal maid of the "dead" queen, claims that she can make the statue move. Husnara comes down the pedestal and discloses that she never died. Hameeda apologises to the king for concealing the fact for sixteen years. The queen embraces her husband and Gulnar, and joins the hands of the young lovers to formalise their relationship. The play ends with general rejoicing followed by a celebratory chorus by women.

Thus, certain alterations and interpolations notwithstanding, Hashr's *Mureed-e-Shak* reproduces the main sequence of events that make up the plot of Shakespeare's *Winter's Tale*. As we shall see below, it was the same with his next adaptation of a Shakespeare play.

Shaheed-e-Naaz (1898, *Measure for Measure*)

It was a standard practice in Parsi theatre to append at the beginning of every play a song and dance sequence. Invariably, every stage production opened and usually even closed with some kind of a festive, musical scene. Adaptations of Shakespeare, whether tragedy, romance or comedy, were not exempted from this convention either, as we saw in the case of Ahsan's *Khoon-e-Nahaq*. However, Hashr's *Mureed-e-Shak* was a rare, perhaps the only, exception to this rule.As I pointed out above the main plot of this play, unlike Ahsan's adaptation of *Hamlet*, was not allowed to be overwhelmed by a profusion of musical sequences. It did not open with a song and dance number as did Ahsan's play. Instead, it began with a soliloquy by Toofan which was followed by a court scene with which the play's story begins to unfold as it does in Shakespeare. But, presumably to accommodate the demands of his profit conscious company directors, Hashr changed his style in subsequent adaptations. For example, in his second Shakespearean adaptation, *Shaheed-e-Naaz* (written in 1898 and reprinted with some changes in 1922), Hashr modified his style. The play has a leisurely beginning with courtesans dancing and singing, followed by an exchange of erotic jokes and playful bantering between the courtiers and courtesans. The main story begins only in Act 1, Scene 3.

It is with the subsequent scene that the play begins to follow the Elizabethan original and, a few variations notwithstanding, does so quite faithfully. Jahandar expresses his wish to travel out of the kingdom and requests Safdarjang to manage the affairs of the state in his absence and gives him his signet ring. In the 1922 version, the scene ends with a soliloquy by Jahandar in which he reveals that he does not plan to go anywhere but stay on in disguise in order to observe how his deputy rules. In the first version this fact is revealed to the audience later. As the play progresses, Jahandaar Shah, disguised as a fakir, witnesses his deputy's abuse of power and like his Shakespearean counterpart, the Duke, even intervenes in the events by advising the tyrant's victims. The play ends with Jahandar Shah, taking off his Fakir's disguise and confronting Safdarjang and other wrongdoers with their crimes. Responding to Saida's plea on behalf of Safdarjang's virtuous wife, he pardons him. Like *Measure for Measure*, the play ends happily, with multiple reunions and a celebratory song about the beginning of a new age of happiness and justice.

Safed Khoon (1906, *King Lear*)

Agha Hashr's next play *Safed Khoon*, an adaptation of *King Lear*, was written for Adesar Bhai Thoonthi's company. He wrote it in 1906 or 1907. Following the established Parsi theatre practice, he reduced the five acts of Shakespeare's text to three acts, comprising seventeen scenes, of which one scene in each act deals with the interpolated comic subplot.

This abridgement of the original play is achieved as usual by excluding or bunching together several scenes. There are also numerous instances of modifying or even rewriting Shakespeare's original scenes. For example, Sadan (Gloucester) is not blinded but beheaded along with Akram (Cornwall) whose role itself has been altered from that of Gloucester's attacker to his protector. Shakespeare's Fool is jettisoned and, in some places, whole episodes are excluded. For example, in the scene which dramatises Khaquan's (Lear's) visit to Dilara's palace and reproduces the main events of *Lear*'s Act 2 Scene 4, the entire episode of the confrontation between Kent and Oswald leading to Kent been put in stocks II:2, is deleted.

Another notable change in the original plot is that it does not end in the death of the old king and his youngest daughter. Instead, in accordance with the standard Parsi theatre practice, and unlike Ahsan's *Khoon-e-Nahaq*, Hashr ends his adaptation happily. All bad characters are killed at the end. Khaquan and Zara (Cordelia) survive and the latter is invited by the father to ascend the throne.

Despite these and other such modifications, the significant features of the main plot relating to the story of Lear and his daughters and those of the parallel subplot relating to Gloucester and his sons are retained. For example, although, unlike Shakespeare's Edmund, Bahram is not an illegitimate son but simply an evil and villainous person, a malcontent, the main events in the story of his treachery against his own father and brother are nevertheless kept intact. Another example is that of Arsalan (Kent). Although, unlike his Elizabethan counterpart, this honest and loyal courtier is not banished from the kingdom, he, like Kent, continues to serve Khaquan ardently to the end, albeit without any need to disguise himself. Furthermore, again like his Elizabethan prototype, Arsalan's moral and philosophical comments tend to highlight the larger, universal meaning of the Lear story.

The play opens and closes with a leisurely and festive note with song and dance. It begins with a chorus of three or four songs interspersed with 'dohas' (couplets), praising the beauty and colourfulness of springtime. The last song and dance overlaps with the king's ceremonial entry accompanied by his ministers and courtiers. As Khaquan mounts the throne, in yet another chorus, a group of young dancers sing in praise of love and happiness. Like its opening, and in keeping with the happy conclusion of the plot, the play's ending too is musical and celebratory. The last scene begins with the courtiers singing a joyful song about the world in the spring season, etc. Zara invites her father to resume royal power but he declines and says that it is Zara who deserves it better. He offers her the crown and, in three rhymed couplets, blesses her. He also expresses gratitude to Sadan for his dedication and selfless service. The scene ends with courtiers singing another joyful song: "aao mil kar shaadi rachayen", which means "Come, let us rejoice together".

It is not just the opening and the closing parts, but almost every scene is adorned with poetry and songs. For instance, when Khaquan is being made to wait at Dilara's gate, Arsalan enters speaking philosophically about life and death in rhymed prose and then bursts into a song about the futility of greed and lust for power and wealth. He follows this with a ghazal on the subject. Similarly, in a scene which parallels Shakespeare's Heath scene, Parvez (Edgar) sings two songs, one after another: the first about the inseparability of pain and life, and the other about a world being a temporary stop for travellers. In a short scene in the third act, during the raging war between Zara's army and the evil forces of Mahpara and Dilara, Bahram (Edmund) leads a group of soldiers across the stage singing a marching war song. Although, *Safed Khoon* cannot match the record of Ahsan's *Khoon-e-Nahaq* in this respect, there is certainly a good deal more singing in this play of Hashr's than in his *Mureed-e-Shak*. However, it must also be noted that the songs here are much more apt and therefore possess greater dramatic value than the songs in Ahsan's adaptation of *Hamlet.*

Although often abridged, re-arranged, and rewritten, the sequences of events correspond quite closely to the order in which the plot unfolds in Shakespeare's play. They parallel the action in Shakespeare and even the drift of speeches and, sometimes, even their texts come close to his lines. The story begins with King Khaquan, like Lear, announcing his resolve to step down and live a retired life. To this end, he decides to divide the kingdom equally among his three daughters. However, before parcelling out the kingdom he wants to hear from each of his daughters how much she loves him: the elder sisters, Mahapara and Dildara, flatter him by declaring that their love for him is boundless, the youngest, Zara refuses to flatter him and merely says that she loves him as much as a daughter should love her father, no more and no less. A lengthy exchange of words between an angry Khaquan and an unrelentingly truthful Zara follows. Enraged by what he considers Zara's ingratitude and rudeness, Khaquan disowns her and excludes her from any share in the kingdom. Arsalaan (Kent) tries to intervene on Zara's behalf but is angrily silenced and banished from the court.

As the play progresses, Khaquan, now relieved of the responsibilities of a king, visits each of his two elder daughters, hoping to find a warm and affectionate welcome for himself and his companions. But to his grief and despair, they humiliate him and turn him away. Realising how wrong he was in his assessment of the true nature of his daughters, he, like his Shakespearean counterpart, curses Mahpara and Dilara profusely. Without power, without home, and without family, he learns to identify with the poor, unsheltered humanity. Interestingly, compared to Lear, Khaquan receives this enlightenment about the equality of the world much earlier in the play–that is soon after his disappointment at Dilara's door. In comparison, his Shakespearean counterpart attains this awareness only during his madness in the storm scenes.

Shattered and distraught, Lear roams madly in the wilderness. He is looked after by his loyal courtiers and well-wishers, such as Arsalan and Parvez (Sadaan's good son), till Zara, the youngest daughter whom he had disowned for refusing to flatter him, and her husband arrive with their army to attack his enemies and rescue him. The evil daughters, Mahpara and Dilara, their accomplice Bahram (Sadan's evil son), who had been trying hard to harm Lear and his friends, are killed.

Along with the Lear story, the sequences relating to Edgar's treachery and intrigue against his own father, Gloucester, and brother, Edmond, are also paralleled in the events relating to Bahram's villainous conspiracy to deceive his father, Sadan, and brother Parvez. Like the Shakespearean counterpart, Bahram cleverly uses a fake letter, purportedly written by Parvez. disclosing the writer's plans to have his own father murdered and arranges for that letter to fall into Sadan's hands. He also misleads Parvez into believing that their father is very angry with him and makes him run away. With the younger brother out of the way, Bahram, now in close political as well as sexual liason with Mahapara and Dilara, continues to betray his father as well as the hapless king.

Interestingly, in reproducing the Edmond-Gloucester story Hashr invents and interpolates an entirely new scene which, in terms of its action, replaces *King Lear*'s Act II, Scene 1 by not only modifying its contents but also its style of representation. In Shakespeare, Edmond stages and manipulates a situation so as to make it serve his dual purpose: to turn Gloucester against Edgar and to frighten Edgar into fleeing from home. Hashr takes the central idea of this scene and visualises it differently as a wordless mime or a dumb show. Bahram is seen quietly leading a hired murderer at night to Sadan's bedroom. At the last moment, the assassin is surprised by a noise within the house and flees. On his way out he kills the doorman who was guarding Sadan's room. Parvez is roused by the commotion. He rushes in and sees the slain guard. He is standing by the body, looking at it in puzzlement, when from afar Bahram signals to Sadan and points to Parvez. This dumbshow confirms Sadan in his suspicion of Parvez and creates a situation which causes the latter to flee.

This is an example of how skilfully Hashr abridges the Lear story and quickens its pace in *Safed Khoon*. Several such instances can be found throughout the play. Remarkably, each such abridgement seems to have been done thoughtfully so as not to distort or significantly alter the main story. For example, *Lear's* Act 1, Scene 3 begins with a conversation between Goneril and Oswald followed by the meeting between disguised Kent and Lear in Scene 4. Both the scenes are jettisoned in Hashr but part of Goneril's complaint about the rowdiness of Lear's courtiers has been incorporated within Mahapara's speech to Khaquan. The exchange between Lear and Fool is removed in Hashr. The motif of Goneril's letter to Regan found recurrently in Act 1 Scene 3 to Act 2, Scene 1 is also skipped. So Hashr's Act I, Scene, 3 stands for Shakespeare's Act I, Scenes 3, 4 and 5. Likewise, the fact that Sadan is beheaded, not blinded, eliminates the need for the scene in which Edgar pretends to help blind Gloucester commit suicide by jumping from a high cliff. Examples like these show that Hashr took care in order not to lose the significant details of the story while abridging the plot.

The scene corresponding to Shakespeare's heath scene is somewhat messy. Materials from several other scenes are bunched together and condensed in it somewhat implausibly and confusingly. As a whole, this scene merges and modifies the material particularly from Act 3, Scenes 1 to 4 of *King Lear*. It begins with a speech by Parvez, who is disguised as a homeless poor man. This speech approximates Edgar's speech in *Lear* Act 2, Scene 3 wherein he declares his resolve to disguise himself as a poor, naked man in order to escape detection by those who wish to harm him. In addition, Parvez sings a song about inseparability of pain and life and expresses his resolve to help Khaquan who is also homeless by remaining in his service till he is able to prove his own innocence. Before exiting, he sings another sad song about the world being a temporary stop for the traveller. Sadan as well as Arsalan and disguised Parvez are all moved by pity for Khaquan on a cold, stormy night. Sadan's message to the two daughters through Bahram, urging them to come and see their father's miserable condition yields no fruit. He is informed by his duplicitous son, how hard-hearted the response of the two sisters was. Next, we see Khaquan raving madly and tearing his robe into shreds. Eventually, in a complete departure from Shakespeare's storm scene, Mahapara arrives with her husband. Sadan tries to make her show pity towards her father but she obstinately remains unmoved. The sequence ends in an exchange of angry words between Sadan and Mahapara. This leads to a heated exchange between her and Sadan. Subsequently, Bahram and Mahapara talk in confidence and reveal their love for one another. Her husband overhears them. The two men fight. The scene ends with Mahapara urging her lover Bahram to kill her husband.

This is followed by another scene which is an equally condensed and modified collection of at least three discrete episodes. In the first, Saadan (Gloucester), unaware of Bahram's villainy, entrusts him with the information that Zara and her husband have arrived with their troupes and asks him to mobilise support for Zara and Khaquan and gives him a letter for the "Sipah Saalar" (army chief). Bahram in an aside declares that he has no intention of taking the letter anywhere but to Mahapara and Dilara. He follows this with a song in which he boasts about being the worls's greatest villain. In the subsequent episode, Khaquan who has escaped from Zara's camp, appears on the scene with Parvez and Arsalan following him. On his request, Arsalan sings an elegiac song about life. Arsalan's sad song is interspersed by Khaquan's mad ravings against the two elder daughters. In the third episode, Zara arrives with her husband and others. Despite Khaquan's mad resistance she and husband take him back into the safety of the fort. This makes Shakespeare's Act 4, Scenes 3 and 4 unnecessary. Zara's husband declares his firm resolve to fight for justice against villains and defeat them. The scene ends with Arsalan singing a short song lamenting the duplicity of some people.

The next scene (Hashr's Act 2, Scene 4), which takes place in Dilara's palace, is a variation on Shakespeare's Act 3, Scene 7. In certain ways the scene is radically modified or rewritten. Its central concern remains as in *Lear*. Dilara learns of Sadan's "treachery"from his letter to Zara. A departure from *Lear* is made when, right at the beginning of the scene, Dilara tells Bahram of her love for him. Unlike *Lear*, Dilara's husband Akram (Cornwall) arrives in the scene only at the end. In another modification, instead of blinding him the two sisters wish to have him beheaded. However, the most radical departure is that Akram arrives in the nick of time and saves Sadan by killing the executioners. As already mentioned, this is a reversal of Cornwall's role in Shakespeare where he in fact attacks Gloucester, not saves him, and dies as a result of an injury from the sword of a servant who was trying to protect Gloucester. It may also be noted that the sympathetic attitude of Akram parallels the attitude of Albany to Gloucester in Act 4, Scene 2. However, in *Lear* Albany survives and in Hashr husbands of both the elder sisters are killed, as Mahapara and Dilara turn on Akram and get him beheaded along with Sadan. This also makes Shakespeare's Act 4, Scenes 1 and 2 unnecessary.

After Zara and Khaquan are arrested by Bahram, we have a scene which shows us Mahapara and Bahram in dalliance, being entertained by singers and dancers. Bahram weaves a plot with Mahapara for killing Zara and Khaquan in jail. He also prejudices her against her sister, Dilara, by planting a suspicion in her mind. This scene, with its sequence of song and dance and erotic repartee in rhymed verse between Mahapara and Bahram, has no direct equivalent in *Lear*. Here as well as in the subsequent scene, Hashr draws upon the original and reworks the relevant motifs (particularly from *Lear*, Act 5, Scenes 2 and 3). The scene reveals the diabolic and debauched character of Bahram. Mahpara's husband has been killed by him and Dilara's husband was beheaded. So, with the intention of becoming the king, he has conceived an elaborate conspiracy to get Mahapara and Dilara as well as Zara and Khaquan also out of the way. He instigates each of the two sisters against Khaquan and Zara, and against one another. The scene parallels *Lear:* Act 4, Scene 5, particularly in Cordelia's words of pity about Lear's condition.

The subsequent scene shows Zara and Khaquan in prison as two killers approach the old king and take him away, despite Zara's appeals to them. On hearing Mahapara enter, Zara hides. Implausibly, through all this, Dilara has been sleeping in a bed, Mahapara mistakes her for Zara and stabs her. Bahram's treachery and duplicity is exposed in a conversation between Mahapara and the dying Dilara. Bahram tries to flee but is killed by Mahapara. Mahapara, in turn, is shot by the dying Bahram. It is not logically conceivable that there should be a bed in a prison cell and that Dilara, a princess, should be lying in it. But the Parsi stage never concerned itself with such minute details. With all the villainous characters killed this scene virtually ends the story. All that remains to be shown is the fate of the old king. This is taken care of in the subsequent scene which is yet another dumb show in the play. It depicts two executioners, about to kill Khaquan, being shot dead by Zara's husband.

Thus, unlike Shakespeare's *King Lear*, Hashr's *Safed Khoon* is not a tragedy but a happy melodrama which begins and ends on a joyful and celebratory note with song-and-dance sequences which includes a totally unconnected farcical subplot; and, above all, in which Lear and Cordelia survive and Cordelia ascends the throne. It thus represents another step towards refashioning Shakespeare's plays in accordance with the popular Indian taste in stage entertainment.

In addition to the adaptations discussed above, Hashr also continued the tradition of Khori's remarkable talent of skilfully grafting parts of Shakespearean texts onto an overarching traditional Indian or oriental tale. The practice of incorporating Shakespeare's plot ideas into plays which are not direct adaptations, as we saw in the examples of *Khurshid*, *Hatimtai*, and *Noorjahan*, can also be evidenced in Hashr's *Khwab-e-Hasti*, where one of the main characters is Abbasi, an evil and wicked woman who instigates a young man to murder his own father in order to inherit his wealth. The play clearly derives its basic plot idea from *Macbeth* and even incorporates Lady Macbeth's sleep walking scene and her speech 'Out, damned spot.' Similarly, in *Said-e-Hawas,* written around the same time as *Khwab-e-Hasti* (1907–08), Hashr built upon the plot ideas drawn from two different history plays: *King John* and *Richard III*.

By the early years of the 20th century, Hashr had become the most popular playwright in India. His adaptations of Shakespeare were so well regarded that he was widely referred to as Shakespeare-e-Hind (Shakespeare of India). By that time the Parsi theatre productions, too, had acquired a distinct form and style based on a commercially successful formula. Hashr's works helped significantly towards the development of this formula.

Parsi Playwriting and Performance Style

At some point during the process of becoming a full-fledged commercial theatre, the Parsi stage had begun to follow the stage and dramaturgic conventions of 19th century Europe. Among other things, it accepted the Victorian practice of dividing a play into three acts as the norm and applied it even to their Shakespeare adaptations. *Khurshid* was an exception and we do not know how Randhelia's Gujarati version of *Pericles* was structured. But Murad's Urdu version of it is divided into three acts, with each act subdivided into several scenes. By the time Ahsan and Hashr entered the scene, this practice was already well established as an unshakeable convention, and every Parsi stage adaptation of Shakespeare was structured on this three-act division. This was true of Ahsan's *Khoon-e-Nahaq* and his other adaptations as well as those by Hashr in the subsequent years.

Much like today's commercial Hindi cinema, a typical Parsi theatre play, in its construction, was a mixture of something like the Victorian melodrama and indigenous popular *sangeet natak* (operatic) forms like the *nautanki* or the *tamasha*. They used intricate plots with pronounced emphasis on intrigue, conflict, suspense, and sudden reversals in the protagonist's fortune that one usually associates with the plays of Scribe and Sardou. At the same time, the Parsi theatre plays, like those in the tradition of *Indersabha*, *nautanki* or *tamasha*, were operatic in style and everything was oriented towards a loud and immediate audience response. Its target audience was as much the gentry in the five rupee enclosures as the common people in the cheaper classes. Everything–the text, the music, and the spectacle–appears to have been pitched at the level of both these sections. Narrative situations and even characters were often so conceived as to give the play an appearance of a more profound, a seemingly philosophical or moral dimension. The dialogue in rhymed verse and rhythmic prose, underscored by loud music, and a dramatic roll of percussion sounds were employed to enhance a play's immediate impact and to provoke applause and cries of 'encore' from the galleries. Songs, too, with their catchy traditional Indian tunes and often accompanied by gay dances had a similar effect. No opportunity was ever missed to introduce a song, or dance, or an appropriate *sher* (couplet) or ghazal.

A commercialised and box-office driven entertainment industry almost invariably requires its artists to make major compromises with their art, and Parsi theatre companies were no exception to this rule. The playwrights employed in those companies were required to write according to the standard formula for a successful stage play. The more sensitive ones among these writers, such as Ahsan and Hashr, were not happy with this infringement of their creative freedom and, sometimes even expressed their sense of frustration in their notes and comments, as evidenced in Ahsan's *Nama* that we quoted above. Nonetheless, whether they liked it or not, they had no option but to write according to their employers' wishes and embellish their scripts with anything and everything that would appeal to popular audiences. As we saw above, adaptations of Shakespeare, too, had to conform to the requirements of a commercial stage.

The use of songs in a play was not by itself a new trend on the Parsi stage. From the beginning, Parsi theatre was characterised by a profusion of songs. But, in contrast to the dominant style of later, more commercialised era, the early plays, such as those by Khori, Aaram, and even Murad, tended to combine poetic-musical interest with an equal attention to the dramatic interest and focus in the speeches of characters. Songs, usually in the form of ghazals, were not superfluous, add-on embellishments to the text but an integral part of the dramatic speech. In other words, characters often spoke to one another in sung verses. This also meant that an actor's ability to sing was an important consideration while casting a play. For example, while casting for *Khurshid*, Dadabhai Patel wanted Jahangir Khambata to play the main male role of Ferozshah and Khambata too was keen to get that role, However, he could not be chosen precisely because that role included several songs and Khambata could not sing (Taj, 75).

However, as far as the requirement of including as many songs and dances as possible in every stage play is concerned, it might not have bothered Urdu playwrights much. There are two possible reasons for this. One, these writers, particularly those who hailed from the land of Avadh, were accustomed to the performance traditions in which songs, dance, and poetry were usually strung together by a thin story line. Writers like Murad, Ahsan and Hashr were familiar with the famous examples of Wajid Ali Shah's *Radha Kanhaiya* and Amanat's *Indersabha*, as well as the popular traditions of the *Raasleela* and the *Nautanki*. Moreover, these playwrights were also accomplished poets in their own right and were very proud of their poetic talent. It is reasonable to conclude, therefore, that they saw this preference for song-and-dance format as a welcome opportunity to demonstrate their poetic skills on a public stage and gladly conformed to it in their plays.

This tradition of characters speaking rhymed verse as well as frequently singing was retained in the stage productions throughout the Parsi theatre's existence. Directors continued to prefer actors who could sing as well as act. However, a new feature was added to the Parsi plays of the later period. As we saw above in the case of Ahsan and Hashr's adaptations of Shakespeare, most plays now included the role of what was identified as *ramishgaran* who had little function in the play other than to sing and dance. There is an instance or two of *ramishgaran* appearing in *Khurshid* but the playwright had taken some care to make such examples appropriate to the plot situation. The frequency and indiscriminate ways in which this role is used in later plays is not found in either Khori or Murad-Randhelia. Later plays tended to use songs and sometimes even dances as a separate component of the text, in other words as autonomous musical interludes. Frequently, plays not only began and concluded with a series of songs and dances but often included them in between as well. Any excuse, no matter how flimsy, was enough to bring in *ramishgaran* or *saheliyan* (friends of the female protagonist) who sang and even danced to denote a joyful or festive situation in the plot.

Like the use of song, dance,and poetry, the mandatory happy ending was also not an unfamiliar rule for Urdu playwrights. Unlike the Greek and Elizabethan traditions, Indian aesthetics does not recognise tragedy and comedy as two distinct, mutually exclusive forms. What we have is a strong tradition of sentimental, even melodramatic, stories which could have tense and sad moments within it but which musst invariably end happily. Parsi theatre directors probably chose Shakespearean tragedies like *Hamlet*, *Romeo and Juliet*, and *King Lear*, not for their tragic form but because they offered gripping tales of selfless love, betrayal, intrigue, treachery, and violent conflict. There was an almost non-negotiable insistence that a play's conclusion be a happy one. This is why, with the sole exception of Ahsan's adaptation of *Hamlet*, no Parsi stage adaptation of a Shakespearean tragedy conformed to the original tragic ending. Clearly, this requirement, too, had to do with the demands of a commercial theatre as well as with Indian taste and tradition. In other words, the box office logic of a vernacular, commercial stage required it and the Indian aesthetic tradition favoured it.

An equally indispensable component of the Parsi theatre formula was the use of comic scenes, usually whole comic subplots. Every play had to include them and, as we saw above, adaptations of Shakespeare were no exception. Every adaptation, whether of a romance, tragedy, or comedy, had to have a comic story criss-crossing through the main plot, with which it usually had no connection at all. Comedies were not spared presumably because subtler and relatively wittier aspects of Shakespeare's humour, even with all its bawdiness, was not considered hilarious enough for the general Indian public. Consequently, playwrights were required to provide loud and raucous hilarity by interpolating jokes and comic scenes of a crudely farcical nature. Thus, in addition to the over-abundance of songs, low and crude, and often unnecessary, jokes, puns, and innuendoes became an essential feature of plays. No play was considered complete without a generous helping of these.

We noted above that songs, dances, comic scenes, etc. were like autonomous units of entertainment. The connection between these micro performances and the main action was at best tenuous. They embellished a play and enhanced its popular appeal. A significant consequence of this was that every play became a mixed bag in terms of its literary and intellectual value. For, poetry of impressive quality as well as features of skilful and imaginative adaptation of a foreign text coexisted (and aesthetically clashed) with these sequences of relatively less sophisticated and, if you like, vulgar pieces of writing. It was this combination of high art and low art within a single play which enable Parsi theatre to appeal to all sections of society and become, interestingly much like the Elizabethan theatre itself, a truly popular form of entertainment.

Summing Up

My endeavour throughout this chapter has been to demonstrate how the Parsi theatre directors and playwrights, including the early college-educated ones like Khori, treated the English Bard as little more than a treasure-house of interesting, melodramatic stories and characters. They were originally trained to regard Shakespeare as a universal, timeless icon of high culture but, in adapting him for the vernacular public stage, they overcame all inhibitions of awe and reverence and allowed themselves to be guided almost entirely by the pragmatic logic of that stage. They took from Shakespeare what they wanted and refashioned it according to the dramaturgic and performative formula that suited the Indian taste and the commercial interests of a profit-driven theatre. In making the Elizabethan texts acceptable to the Indian public, they usually transformed him quite radically.

NOTES

1. Parts of this chapter have been offered before as seminar papers at different universities in India and abroad. An earlier version of it appeared in *Theatre India*, published by the National School of Drama (New Delhi). A version of the section relating to the play *Khurshid* was published in Poonam Trivedi and Denis Bartholomeusz, eds., *India's Shakespeare*, University of Delaware Press, Newark, 2005.
2. This and all subsequent quotations from Urdu texts in this essay have been translated into English by me. It is interesting to note that, in contrast to the landed *bhadralok* sections of Calcutta, upper class and caste Maharashtrians and the wealthy Parsi traders and business men of Bombay, the Urdu-speaking gentry of the north seem to have been somewhat less enthusiastic in responding to English Studies and even to Shakespeare. The earliest literary (as against, performable) Urdu translation that I have come across is Mohammed Fateh Ali Nazar's *Tajir-e-Venice* which is dated 1884 and was, significantly, dedicated to 'His Excellency the Right Honourable Sir James Fergusson, Governor of Bombay.' This was followed in 1887 by *Venice ka Saudagar*, another Urdu translation of the same Shakespearean text, by Babu Baleshwar Prasad, B.A., who was the Principal of the Normal School in Banaras and went on to become the town's Deputy Collector.
3. The people mentioned by Khambata were obviously students at the time of the production. The official designations that he attaches to some names obviously refer to the positions that these men occupied later in life.
4. It would be interesting to make a comparative study of the Parsi theatre Shakespeare and the Vaudeville style representations of

Shakespeare's scenes and characters popular in the US during most of the 19th century. Lawrence W. Levine discusses this in his *Highbrow Lowbrow: The Emergence of Cultural Hierarchy in America*, Harvard University Press, 1990. But such a comparative study will have to wait for another time and another paper.

5. The Urdu text in Gujarati script was published by Behramji Firdunji Company, Bombay in 1871. A copy of this edition exists in the India Office Library, London. It was this text that was transcribed into Arabic script and reprinted, under the editorship of Imtiaz Ali Taj in 1969. All quotations from the play in this paper are from the Taj's edition.
6. Act 1 has four scenes; Act 2, five scenes; Act 3, six scenes; Act 4, five scenes; and Act 5, five scenes.
7. All quotations from Shakespeare in this paper are from Alfred Harbage ed. *William Shakespeare: The Complete Works.*
8. In those competitive times, plagiarism was very common. Parsi theatre writers, particularly the lesser ones, freely stole from each other. Sometimes, a writer would pick up a popular play by someone else, slightly modify its title, add a couplet or two of his own to the text and give it out under his own name. Given the cut throat competition among the companies, it is likely that it was actually the companies that encouraged plagiarism and commissioned the lesser writers to steal from the more successful ones. However, since the Parsi company owners somehow did not follow the practice of publishing authentic versions of the texts commissioned and staged by them, one cannot but feel grateful to these plagiarists for preserving some of those texts, in however impure a form, for posterity.
9. As I said, I could not find a copy of *Bazm-e-Fani*. I did find, however, in the collection of Khudabaksh Library (Patna), an ostensibly different adaptation of *Romeo and Juliet*, titled *Firoz Laqua urf Gulnar Seer* by one Mirza Nazir Beg of Akbarabad. There is a strong probability that this text, which carries 1905 as its date of publication, is nothing but a rehash of Ahsan's play of 1898. Such plagiarism was very common in those days. Although some characters' names have been altered, the names of the main characters–particularly, Romeo as Firoz and Juliet as

Gulnar–are the same as in Ahsan's play. The sequence of events also corresponds to the one found in Ahsan. Furthermore, Beg's text is replete with songs (in folk dialect) and dance. These too could have been plagiarized from Ahsan whose style, as we saw in the case of his adaptation of *Hamlet*, had a preponderance of songs, poetry and dance.

WORKS CITED

Azad Kakorwi, Mohammed Athar Ali. 1902. *Jaam-e-Ulfat* (a 1902 translation of *A Midsummer Night's Dream*) Riazul Akhbar Press, Gorakhpur.

Faridi, Quamarulhuda. 1991. *Urdu Dastaan: Tahquique aur Tanquid* (Enquiry and Criticism) Patna: n. d.

Gupt, Somnath. 2005. *The Parsi Theatre: Its Origins and Development*. Trans. and ed. by Kathryn Hansen. Seagull Books, Calcutta.

Hansen, Kathryn. 1998. *"The Migration of a Text: the Indar Sabha in Print and Performance." Sangeet Natak*, No. 127-28.

Harbage, Alfreded. 1969. *William Shakespeare: The Complete Works.* Baltimore: Pelican Books.

Hashr, Agha. 2004. *Kulliyat-e-Agha Hashr Kashmiri*, Vol. 1. Eds. Agha Jameel Kashmiri and Yaquoob Yawar. New Delhi: National Council for Promotion of Urdu, 2004.

Khambata, Janhangir. 1914. *Maro Nataki Anubhav* (My Theatre Experience). Mumbai.

McManaway, James. 19689. "Introduction to *Pericles, Prince of Tyre*" in Alfred Harbage ed., *William Shakespeare: The Complete Works.* Baltimore: Pelican Books.

Mehta, Kumudini. 1960. *English Drama on the Bombay Stage in the Late Eighteenth and the Nineteenth Century.* PhD Diss., University of Bombay.

Nami, Abdul Aleem. 1962. *Urdu Theatre*: Vol. 2. Karachi: Anjuman Taraqqui-e-Urdu.

Rahmani, Ishrat. 2006. *Urdu Drame ka Irtiqua.* Aligarh: Educational Book House.

Taj, Imtiaz Ali 1969. "Introduction to *Khurshid*", Lahore: Majlis-e-Taraqqui-e-Adab.

Wells, Stanley. 1966. "Shakespeare and Romance," in John Russell Brown and Bernard Harris, ed. *Later Shakespeare*, Stratford-Upon-Avon Studies 8. London: Edward Arnold Ltd.

3

Refashioning Modernity: Habib Tanvir and His Naya Theatre[1]

Habib Tanvir (1926-2009) ranks among the foremost theatre directors of post-independence India. Working mainly with mostly illiterate folk and tribal actors, who did not have any formal theatre training, he developed a distinct form of contemporary Indian theatre. He and Moneeka Misra, his partner in life as well as in theatre, founded in 1959 a professional company called Naya Theatre which exists to this day although in a much devitalised form. As the director of the group for five decades, Tanvir produced a number of masterpieces which are now widely recognised as classics of the contemporary Indian stage. Tanvir had an iconic presence in the country's theatre scene and came to be widely recognised as a legend in his own lifetime.

The Folk and the Modern

In the popular mind, the name of Habib Tanvir is inextricably linked with the idea of the folk and his theatre is often mistaken to be a variety of folk drama. This misconception is understandable. For, Tanvir worked almost exclusively with village actors who brought with them their traditional style of acting. In fact, it was precisely the immense energy and enthralling quality of their performance which attracted Tanvir to them and made him develop his unique style of theatre in partnership with them. His productions not only used traditional performers but also made abundant use of folk music and musicians. Moreover, the language of his plays was also in large part the folk dialect of Chhattisgarh. In short, his work possessed a very close proximity to the traditions of folk performance in India in general and in Chhattisgarh in particular.

However, besides its indebtedness to traditional forms and conventions, there was another, and equally significant, current that ran through all Tanvir's work and gave it an unmistakable dimension of modernity. It is the robustly democratic and contemporary consciousness, which was the result of his lifelong and strong, though informal, association, with left-wing politics which permeated all his work in the theatre. It could be witnessed in each of his plays from the early *Agra Bazaar* to his last production, *Rajrakt*. In other words, his stage creations, their strong and unmistakable folk flavor notwithstanding, did not offer traditional folk drama in its pure or unmediated form but represented a specific and distinctively Indian folk-based version of contemporary theatre. His was an incisive theatre which raised and interrogated major issues and concerns of the time. It was a measure of the political poignancy of his theatre that he was repeatedly attacked by rightwing (mainly Hindutva) forces.

Tanvir became involved in Communist politics in his post-university years during the 1940s in Bombay. Although he never formally joined the party, he worked close to it and, for many years, was an active member of its cultural wings–particularly, the Progressive Writers' Association (PWA) and the Indian People's Theatre Association (IPTA). It was in this crucible of radical politics that his social consciousness was tempered. This radical influence of his youth never left him.

The fact that Tanvir remained not only politically alert but also politically involved throughout his life can be most clearly evidenced in what may be called his activist work in the theatre. Works like *Ponga Pandit*[2] (A Fake Priest), *Zehreeli Hawa*, *Sadak*, *Kushtia ka Chaprasi*, and even the controversial *Indira Loksabha*, are examples of how Tanvir used his art as a weapon in order to intervene in an immediate socio-political situation or movement. *Ponga Pandit*, an old Chhattisgarhi farcical skit ridiculed caste prejudice and untouchability. *Sadak* was a comic skit which depicted a people's view of the idea of development which only serves the rapacious interests of the capitalist class. *Kushtia ka Chaprasi* (Peon of Kushtia) was a hilarious farce created and performed in support of the erstwhile East Pakistan's war of liberation. *Indira Lok Sabha* was Tanvir's theatrical intervention in favour of secularism against sectarian communalism in an electoral contest between the Congress Party and the Hindu-rightwing Party (Jana Sangha, precursor of today's BJP) during the general elections of 1972. Similarly, *Zehreeli Hawa* (Poisonous Air), scripted by Rahul Varma, dealt with the deadly effects of the industrial disaster of Bhopal of 1984 and treachery and dishonesty of Union Carbide in dealing with the victims of that lethal gas leak.

These two dimensions of Tanvir's work–i.e. his predilection for the folk and his modern and democratic consciousness–as we shall see below, are not two separate currents or aspects of his theatre. On the contrary, they are closely interconnected or intertwined as defining strands in the colourful and vibrant tapestry of his work. He combined and interwove them into a style of theatre which was unique in the sense that it neither followed the European model nor did it blindly copy any traditional Indian form. His approach to folk cultural forms was neither revivalist nor antiquarian. He did not romanticise them. He knew quite well the debasement and devitalisation that the traditional forms had suffered due to rapid urbanisation and the homogenising influence of films and TV. He was also aware of the severe ideological limitations underlying the simple approach to issues and problems that one found in traditional forms of folk culture. However, this did not prevent him from recognising that there were skills and energies that still existed in our folk traditions which could be harnessed to forge a new, truly indigenous performance idiom. So, what he did was to draw upon these energies and strengths of traditional performances in order to fashion an artistically exciting and cognitively enriching kind of theatre which was specifically contemporary or non-traditional in both its outlook and its form–that is to say, in what it said and even in how it said it.

In doing this, Tanvir was not only evolving a new style and idiom for his own work, he was also, in some ways, redefining the very concept of modernity, particularly in relation to Indian theatre. He was against the post-colonial project of modernity which tended to exclude from the focus of its attention large areas and large sections of ordinary Indians who lived outside metropolitan centres. This modernity, he recognised, was flawed. It failed to give adequate attention or importance to India's regional languages, cultural forms, traditions, and lifestyles. In the name of nation and nationality, markers of regional identities were often swept under the carpet and even sought to be bulldozed into one homogeneous phenomenon, by introducing centralised policies and establishing "national" institutions for implementation of those policies.

Thus, just as Tanvir did not sentimentalise or romanticise the folk or the traditional, he did not uncritically reject the modern either. He opposed the colonial model of modernity for its ruthless and insensitive approach to urbanisation and its idea of progress which paid no or scant attention to the interests and concerns of ordinary people. But, at the same time, he cherished a rational and scientific approach and a historical perspective on life and issues. In other words, what Tanvir's work implied was, on the one hand, a more sensitive and more imaginative approach to traditions and, on the other, a more inclusive, just and equitable concept of modernity. It is this complex blend of tradition and modernity that defined Tanvir's theatre and gave form to his plays. While the connection between Tanvir's work and folk theatre traditions, particularly Chhattisgarh's *nacha*, is widely recognised, what is not fully appreciated is this distinctiveness of his approach to "the folk" as well as "the modern" which clearly set him apart from his contemporaries.

Engaging with the Folk Heritage

As I point out elsewhere in this book the origins of what is generally understood by the term modern theatre in India are closely bound with our colonial past.[3] Establishment of colleges imparting modern education to their Indian pupils with drama in general and Shakespeare in particular, comprising the central component of its curriculum. Along with this the enthusiasm for theatre that was instilled in the young undergraduates–combined to inspire amateur and professional theatre groups to emerge first in Calcutta and then in Bombay. This tradition has a long and undeniably rich history which includes the first anti-colonial political plays of Bengal and the massively popular phenomenon of subcontinental proportions called the Parsi theatre as well as the work of the Indian People's Theatre Association (IPTA), Prithvi Theatre, the productions of the National School of Drama under Ebrahim Alkazi, and the work of myriad other amateur and semi-professional theatre groups. However, although this history is quite varied, it is also united in the fact that, by and large, it continued to look to European theatre for inspiration and a role model till well after India's independence from British rule.

Combined with extensive social changes, (steady urbanisation and the rise of a more or less educated middle class) this "modern" theatre tradition, with possible exceptions of some specific examples of the work done by IPTA, had the effect of marginalising the native or conventional forms of theatre. From the beginning, new city-based social groups, despite their social and economic links with the countryside, consciously endeavoured to distance themselves from their rural cultural roots and even scoff at them. As years went by, patronising or doing Western style theatre became the dominant fashion with the urban elite. In any case, the European example presented theatre with a regular and daily form of entertainment or activity, whereas the traditional performances took place only seasonally or on specific occasions. A consequence of this neglect and lack of patronage was that, although, the local forms and traditions did not entirely disappear, they gradually and over several decades, began to dwindle and lose their social and artistic vitality. By the time India attained freedom from British rule, whatever traditional forms survived did so in a more or less moribund condition.

Thus, when Tanvir began his career, "folk" was neither the fashion nor the passion of India's contemporary stage. Far from being an all-inspiring catchword that it later became in Indian theatre, it was a neglected and greatly devitalised category. Tanvir was one of those who pioneered the revival of interest in folk performance traditions and made it into a significant and influential category in regard to contemporary theatre practice in India. Tanvir began in 1958 following his return after training in England and travelling extensively through Europe. He spent several years researching and studying folk traditions in drama, storytelling, music, and dance. He frequently and widely wandered through the interiors of Chhattisgarh, meeting and spending time with local performers and often watching their nightlong performances. Incidentally, in the course of his sustained engagement with the cultural heritage of the region, Tanvir was also able to bring a number of hitherto unrecognized fork form and styles (such as, *Chandaini*, *Pandvani*, and *Nacha*) from the remote tribal areas of Chhattisgarh into national focus. Today some of them -especially, *Pandvani*–are known and appreciated internationally.

Early Years

Raipur, where Tanvir was born and brought up, was, during his childhood, a small town which was not only surrounded on all sides by miles and miles of villages but where the lines between town and country were far from being clearly defined. You just had to walk a few steps, as it were, before you found yourself in some village. The life of the townsfolk was closely and inseparably enmeshed with rural life and agrarian occupations. The interaction between the Raipurians and their country neighbours was regular and sustained. Men and women selling milk, curds, vegetables, eggs, fruit, etc. came from villages and visited private homes to sell their products. This relationship often grew very close and friendly through generations of daily interaction. The townspeople too had reasons to frequent villages because many of them either owned agricultural land or had relatives who were zamindars.[4] Although Tanvir's own immediate family did not have a direct connection with the countryside, several of his uncles and grand uncles did. It was through these that he had his first exposure to the rural life and its songs and music. As he himself recalled in 1995 in a conversation with me, "As a child, I had often accompanied my uncles to villages in Chhattisgarh. I used to listen to their songs and music. I had even learnt many of these songs, some had stayed in my memory automatically and some I made an effort to learn because I liked them and wanted to know them" (Tanvir 1995, 103).

Tanvir completed his schooling in Raipur and moved to Nagpur for a BA degree. After graduation, he went on to enrol in a Master's programme at Aligarh Muslim University, but abandoned it half way. The reason was that, while his excellent performance in matriculation had encouraged him to try for a career in the civil service, a decline in his grades during the college years made him change his mind. He began to explore alternative career options. Among the interests that Tanvir had nurtured since childhood was an interest in acting. During his school years in Raipur, he had watched many plays and acted in school productions and won prizes for the excellence of his performance. He was also an avid movie watcher and his passion for cinema had remained with him throughout. So, having abandoned the idea of the civil service, he was now keen to go to Bombay with the intention of becoming a film actor (Tanvir 1996b, 123-41).

Tanvir arrived in Bombay in 1944-45, and lived there for nearly a decade before shifting to Delhi. During those years, he tried various career options. He worked as a film journalist, gave radio programmes, and also organised literary events. He even managed to obtain small roles in a few films. But perhaps the most significant development of that period in his life was the deep and permanent influence of leftwing politics. The political environment at the time was infectiously throbbing with radical passion and activity. Besides, Tanvir was a sensitive young man in his early twenties and, like so many others of his generation, he too was drawn towards the radical politics of the Communist Party of India. As I have already mentioned above, he did not formally join the Party but closely associated himself with the activities of its various literary and cultural organisations. He became an active member of PWA and IPTA and thus began an association which stayed with him to the end. During 1948–50, when there was a crackdown against the communists and IPTA's office bearers were arrested, Tanvir was obliged to run the Bombay chapter of IPTA singlehandedly and functioned as its organiser, secretary, playwright, actor and director.

When IPTA became dysfunctional, Tanvir left Bombay and went to Delhi. The reason that he cites for this move is that he wanted to get out of the way of the temptation to act in films. "Because by then I had come to the conclusion that in the cinema of those days there was no autonomy for the artist–you could not act the way you wanted, nor direct the way you wanted. The producer, who had no artistic sense, who was only a money bag, a financier, would meddle in the work of the director, actor, writer, everyone... Anyhow, right or wrong, I was convinced that I had something to say. And for what I had to say, in aesthetics, in the performing arts, as well as what I had to say socially, politically–the medium was not the cinema, it was the theatre. This was a very clear realisation in the early fifties which brought me to Delhi" (Tanvir 1996b, 134–35). In Delhi, Tanvir began working with school children, writing and staging plays for and with them, before producing his first major play *Agra Bazaar*.

Seeking a Career in Theatre

When Tanvir arrived in Delhi, the city's stage scene was dominated by amateur and collegiate drama groups which offered English plays in English, or in vernacular translation, to a socially restricted section of the city's anglophone elite. As mentioned above, these groups, as also the National School of Drama a decade later under Ebrahim Alkazi, derived their concept of theatre, their standards of acting, staging, and direction, from the European models of the later 19th and early 20th centuries.There was little effort to link theatre work to the indigenous traditions of performance, or even to say anything of immediate value and interest to an Indian audience.

It is likely that, given his background in left-wing cultural movements, the kind of theatre Tanvir had in mind even that early was in complete contrast to this. He probably wanted plays to offer a socially poignant experience, radically different, both in form and content, from anything that Delhi's theatre-goers were accustomed to. Tanvir's active involvement with IPTA in the 1940s had not only renewed his early interest in folk culture but also given it a new political significance and dimension. IPTA's slogan "People's theatre stars the people" prompted many to link their art to plebeian cultural forms and traditions as opposed to the culture of the ruling classes. It had inspired Tanvir, too, to return to his native region where he began to collect Chhattisgarhi folk songs in earnest. "I must have got the inspiration from my IPTA background in Bombay. I worked in the Hindi group but we were also surrounded by the Gujarati, Marathi and Konkani groups. Each group had a music squad. These were strong music squads and some of the great figures in the world of music were associated with them. For example, the Marathi squad included stalwarts like Annabhau Sathe and Amar Sheikh.They drew upon the folk traditions like the *burrakatha* and *pawara*.... That was the time, in the 1940s, that I got interested in my own background.... After my association with the IPTA, I collected more songs consciously" (Tanvir 1995, 103).

Besides music, Tanvir also possessed a strong interest in poetry. An avid student of literature, he had been writing poetry ever since his student days at the Aligarh Muslim University. In Bombay, when he became part of the progressive writers' movement, he started writing poetry of radical social and political import. As a writer, Tanvir was interested also in the way languages are produced and used. He shared with many others the aversion to the artificially created, stilted, official Hindi or Urdu. In an interview with Anjum Katiyal, he said that it was his "literary interest" which enabled him to recognise the amazing richness and creativity in the way ordinary people coined and used new words and expressions. "My literary interest brought me... to the dialects," he said, "because I considered that to be the source for all great literature. Tulsidas, Mirabai,

Kabir–all derived such strength from the people's dialects." Citing the example of how the coolies referred to a train's airconditioned coach, not by its official Hindi name, but simply as '*thandi gaadi*', he goes on to observe, "Language is constantly getting coined by people who use it, who need it, who make their living off it. For words connected with horse and saddle, every part has a name, but who has given the names? Those who make those things. You go to the ironsmith, he'll give you all the names connected to the horse's hooves. Our scholars have taken recourse to books to coin words, an artificial, arduous and futile process, instead of going to the people and learning. I am mentioning all this because it became the basis of my theatre." (Tanvir 1996b, 6)

It is this complex of a democratic bias in favour of the common people, an interest in music, and passion for poetry which lies at the basis of the entire corpus of his work in the theatre. It is evident in all his plays from the first major production, *Agra Bazaar*, which he wrote and produced, albeit in its initial, severely truncated form, soon after moving to Delhi in 1954, to his last production *Rajrakt*, an adaptation that derives from a combination of two stories by Rabindranath Tagore.

Producing *Agra Bazaar*

Agra Bazaar, which dramatises the work, life and times of a very unusual 18th century Urdu poet, Nazir Akbarabadi, was written in response to an invitation by an old friend, Athar Parvez, who was associated with the Jamia Millia chapter of the Progressive Writers' Association. In early 1954, Parvez asked Tanvir if he could help prepare a play to be staged on the occasion of "Nazir Day" that the Jamia was planning to observe later that year. Although Tanvir was familiar with Nazir's work and had found it interesting, he had never actually thought of writing a play about him or his poetry. The invitation from Jamia prompted him to start thinking of writing one. With this idea in mind, he began to study Nazir and related literature about him and his times in earnest. The result was *Agra Bazaar*. It was first performed on March 14, 1954 in the Okhla campus of Jamia Millia with members of the university community and ordinary men and women from the neighbouring villages of Okhla and Tughlakabad comprising the audience as well as the huge caste of 75 people. The production, thus, not only marked Tanvir's permanent relocation to Delhi but also his debut as a playwright-director on the theatre scene.

In the course of his research into the life and work of this poet, Tanvir discovered that Nazir's uniqueness as a poet lay largely in what may be described as his "democratic" outlook and in his strong predilection for popular culture and colloquial idiom. He recognised that these qualities, which were akin to Tanvir's own socio-aesthetic predilections, were in sharp contrast to the classical elitist tradition of Urdu poetry and set this poet apart from the more famous and iconised poets of his time. Later, in his preface to the first published edition, he recalled that in Nazir's poetry he heard "echoes of optimism and social relevance." He argued that Nazir's voice was "not only different from any other poet's but was also the voice of humanity and no one else could achieve this all-embracing quality" (Tanvir 2006, 1). The fact, that Nazir lived and wrote at a time when major cultural and political changes which had a profound impact on the professions of writing and publishing were taking place, helped Tanvir give his play stronger historical moorings.

Nazir died in the early 19th century after living for nearly a hundred years. He finds no or at best marginal mention in the histories of Urdu literature. In Tanvir's words, this "undoubtedly Urdu's most Hindustani poet", from whose "poetry one can still learn how to use people's language," was also the most neglected of Urdu poets. Ignored by critics and historians, his poetry was kept alive for over two hundred years by mendicants, vendors and others in streets and bazaars. It was with this awareness that Tanvir decided to locate the action of his play in a market or bazaar and to make ordinary people, played largely by his group of village actors (each of whom could sing as well as dance) virtually its protagonist.

From its first abbreviated version, *Agra Bazaar* gradually grew into a full-length play which is so structured that, although Nazir himself never appears on stage, his presence is felt palpably throughout the play. His personality and poetry are made the pivotal centre around which every conversation and action in the play revolves. The frequent friendly and unfriendly references to him and his work, stories and anecdotes about him, as well as the large number of his poems set to music and sung–these virtually make him come alive vividly as a poet, who not only wrote about ordinary people and their everyday concerns but frequently wrote for them. We also see how, despite being derided and ignored by the literary establishment, he continued to be popular with the plebeian masses. Tanvir's abundant use of songs also makes us see how richly variegated Nazir's range is in both style and subject matter.

Today *Agra Bazaar* is unanimously acclaimed as a masterpiece of modern Indian theatre. Cherished by critics and audience alike, it went on to become one of the most loved plays of our time. It was loved not only for Nazir's poetry, but also for its music and songs, its humour and wit, as well as the amazing quality of the performance by its cast of folk actors. But, its enormous popularity and its subsequent inclusion into the ranks of modern classics notwithstanding, the initial critical response to the play was not favourable. At the time of its first staging, there was, among critics and commentators, a sense of bewilderment at something so different from anything they had seen before. They found it difficult to accept as a stage play, a free-wheeling, episodic and musical composition, which was something so completely lacking in the Aristotelian prerequisites of character, plot, and conflict.

However, it was not long before this bewilderment gave way to a better appreciation of the novelty and richness of Tanvir's approach. It was eventually recognised that what Tanvir, using a mix of educated, middle-class urban actors and more or less illiterate folk and street artists, in a highly innovative, and, for its time, revolutionary strategy, had put on stage was not the socially and architecturally walled-in space of a private dwelling with its emotional or psychological conflict, but a bazaar–a marketplace with all its noise and bustle, its instances of solidarity and antagonism, and above all, its sharp social, economic and cultural polarities.

Incidentally, the idea of locating his play's action in a bazaar was also partly inspired by a book titled *Dilli ki Awazein*, (literally, the sounds of Delhi) that Tanvir had recently read. Although the play has been significantly modified since its first performance in Jamia Millia, it retains its sharply polarised structure and dramaturgic and stage design to this day.

In *Agra Bazaar*, the societal and cultural distinction is not only evident in its verbal text but is also unmistakably manifest in the physical arrangement of the stage, which is pointedly divided into two distinct socio-cultural realms. Downstage, on the left hand corner, is a bookstore where traditional and conservative writers, publishers and critics gather and discuss literature. Their class and cultural bias is evident throughout in their conversation which is replete with scornful remarks and expressions of disgust at the sight or mention of the poorer, less fortunate class of persons. They deride Nazir, both for the way he lives and the way he writes. They admire high traditions of classical poetry and although Nazir could, and did, write in that lofty style too, he is never mentioned except disparagingly. They are full of praise only for great canonical poets like Mir and Insha. The promising quality of an emergent 12-year-old Ghalib, too, finds a favourable mention in their conversation. This discussion of poetry is led by a veteran literary scholar who frequents the bookstore and and who everyone, most of all the bookseller himself, looks up to. Such is this white-bearded critic's dislike of Nazir that he walks off in a huff when he learns that the ghazal that he had been admiring with such gusto so far was in fact by Nazir. Although this causes great consternation among those present at the bookstore, it reveals the hypocrisy of that much revered literary scholar to the audience. Interestingly, these characters and their exchanges are also used by Tanvir to frame the play's action in history. They are literate and therefore well aware of the new developments such as the introduction of English education, arrival of newspapers, and the ongoing work of compilation and publication at the Fort Williams College. Troubled by widespread economic difficulties, they see new possibilities in these developments.

The kite shop on the opposite corner of the stage functions as the societal and cultural counterpoint to the elitist space of the bookstore. It is owned by an ardent Nazir fan who consciously posits himself in opposition to the bookseller. He describes himself as a selfless and passionate lover of poetry, while the bookseller, he says, is one who merely trades in it. In contrast to the predominantly anti-Nazir congregation at the bookstore, the kite shop is patronised by the poet's friends and admirers, the conversation relates to Nazir's goodness as a person: his loyalty to friends, his aversion to money, his generosity and sense of fairness, etc. Nazir's poetry, too, is favourably discussed, quoted, and recited. Anecdotes about Nazir and recitals of his poems attract poor, toiling street vendors who crowd around the kite shop on all such occasions.

Between these two poles downstage and the row of a few small shops and a courtesan's chamber that line the back of the stage lies the open space of the Bazaar street. This is a public thoroughfare. vendors selling a variety of items squat there. Itinerant hawkers pass through announcing their respective wares. It is frequented by public processions, fakirs, beggars, *hijras* (transvestites), street performers (such as acrobats), a bear tamer, and madaari with performing monkeys, corrupt policemen, a love-smitten young Romeo, besides struggling poets and ordinary passersby. In other words, a whole bazaar. A significant part of the play's action takes place in this middle space or street. Every character–whether the courtesan, shopkeepers, vendors, *hijras* or the beggar–sings a Nazir poem at some point. The only exception to this is the members of the conservative group at the bookstore. The two fakirs who, as the play's chorus, enter the stage repeatedly, sing some of the most remarkable compositions of the poet on a variety of topics including poverty, money, bread, death, etc. These fakirs open the play with Nazir's poem about Agra in the grip of severe economic distress.

My words no longer have their usual grip
My speech has begun to falter and trip
I am always in a sad thoughtfulness caught
And my poetry has virtually come to a halt.

> Why shouldn't my tongue lose its eloquence and my words retreat
> When everyone in Agra finds it hard to make two ends meet.

The play ends with the Fakirs' chorus about Man and many different forms and shades in which his humanity and inhumanity are manifested. One of the stanzas read:

> Here, a man is willing to give his life for another,
> He too is man who kills and commits murder,
> It's man who betrays and humiliates his brother,
> It's man who calls for help and succour to another,
> The one who rushes out to help too is man.
>
> (Tanvir 2006, 4 and 88)

Thus, Tanvir's play and the bazaar that he puts on stage vibrate throughout with the sound of Nazir's poetry. The kite shop becomes the nodal centre which attracts all those who love and cherish the poet's work. Among those who gather to listen to the stories about Nazir and to recitations of his poetry are the hopelessly impoverished street vendors. They listen with rapt attention to everything that is said about this people-friendly poet. What they hear gives one of them (and gradually to others) the idea that if they could persuade Nazir to pen a few lines for their respective merchandise, they could use them to attract customers. The play ends with the jubilant vendors returning from the poet's house with a song and a jig, and finding brisk business. In this way, the play foregrounds a poetry that takes the people, and their everyday struggles as its inspiration, its subject, as well as its addressee. It uses the example of Nazir's poetry and his plebeian appeal to challenge orthodox, elitist literary canons. This makes the play a joyful celebration of what the Russian literary theorist Mikhail Bakhtin called 'the culture of the marketplace.'

Thus in *Agra Bazaar*, two major emphases that characterise Tanvir's work in the theatre–one, an artistic and ideological predilection for the plebeian, popular culture; and, two, a penchant for employing music and poetry in plays not as superfluous embellishment but, much like Brecht, as an integral part of the action–had their first and one of the finest expressions.

In Delhi, Tanvir came in contact with a number of important persons, some of whom helped him significantly in furthering his career in the theatre. One such person was Begum Qudsia Zaidi, who was as resourceful and influential as she was culturally accomplished. She was married to Colonel B.H. Zaidi, former Prime Minister of the princely state of Rampur and a member of parliament. Begum Zaidi had a wide network of friends and acquaintances among the political and cultural circles of Delhi. Impressed by Tanvir's work, particularly with his success in *Agra Bazaar*, and his commitment to socially meaningful theatre, she took him, as it were, under her wing and virtually became his patron saint during the middle years of the 1950s. A dream that was very close to Tanvir's heart those days was to have a professional theatre of his own. In Jamia, he had set up a group called the Okhla Theatre, but the mistrust and hostility of a section of the faculty obliged him to wind it up. But he did not give up his desire to establish a professional theatre company. Instead, he continued ardently to explore ways and means to achieve his goal. It was Begum Qudsia Zaidi who was his main source of support and strength in this pursuit.

European Experience

In 1955, Tanvir went to England on a British Council scholarship for theatre training at the Royal Academy of Dramatic Arts (RADA). It was a two-year programme. But no sooner had he got there than he wanted to get out. He realised that he was wasting his time. He recognised that the kind of training that RADA provided, would be of no use to him in India. The main focus of the training seems to have been on movement and speech. He feared that this training would make him "stilted" as an actor. Because, as he puts it, "language is connected with speech, which is connected with movement and therefore, quite simply, a change of language makes a change of movement and character and cultural ethos" (Tanvir 1996, 12). Although the rules of his scholarship did not allow one to opt out, he continued to insist on the complete futility of staying on. Finally, a more understanding woman officer in the British Council drama cell intervened in his favour and arranged for him to be transferred to another, a more acceptable theatre training programme at the Bristol Old Vic.

Thus Tanvir moved out of RADA half-way through his course and completed the second year of his training at the Bristol Old Vic Theatre School. He was happy with this new place and what it taught him. Instead of movement and speech as in RADA, the students here were taught various skills and crafts connected with play production and direction, such as making masks, stagecraft, playwriting, and designing stage production. He found the experience remarkably enriching. He was particularly impressed with one of the teachers, Duncan Ross, whom he describes as "a very good producer, a very articulate man and a great teacher." Tanvir often recalled how Ross once told them, "succinctly, in a very lucid, terse language", that "production is telling a story". This virtually became a mantra for Tanvir. "To this day I quote it and I believe it couldn't have been put more simply...Telling the story is all the game in production. If it falters, it means the production is faulty, you fail to tell the story. If anything is coming in the way–costume, light, décor, anything–you've failed to tell the story" (Tanvir 1996, 12).

After the Old Vic, Tanvir spent a year travelling through the length and breadth of Europe. He had started from England with the express purpose of going to Germany to meet Bertolt Brecht and see his work. But it was quite a while before he reached Berlin. He zigzagged his way to Germany through almost every other country and major city of Europe watching plays and meeting local theatre persons. His first port of call was Paris, where he met the famous actor-director, Jean Vilar, the founder of the Avignon Theatre Festival and the Theatre National Populaire, and saw some of his work. An ongoing theatre festival took him to Avignon, where he picked grapes to support himself. This gave him enough money to travel to Madrid and Barcelona and thence to Nice, Trieste, Zagreb, Belgrade, Budapest, and so on. He supported himself by writing for radio and newspapers and singing and performing in night clubs.

Unfortunately, when he finally arrived in Berlin, Brecht had died. However, his productions were there in the repertoire of the Berliner Ensemble. Tanvir spent eight months there and saw every play. This was his first encounter with the work of this great playwright-director. He also sat in on their rehearsals and had long discussions with members of the group in their canteen. Among those he met were, Helena Weigel, Elizabeth Hauptmann, and Ekkehard (Brecht's actor son-in-law).This experience had a profound and lasting influence on Tanvir and his subsequent work as a playwright-director. For, as Tanvir never failed to emphasise in all his interviews and writings, he learnt a great deal more from watching theatre of different countries than from his training in England. In fact, on returning to India, he quickly began to unlearn much of what he was taught during training and thus followed a trajectory diametrically opposite to that followed by other foreign-trained Indian directors of his time. He now felt reconfirmed in the belief acquired from the IPTA days: that one must work close to and in tandem with one's cultural roots. "I thought you could do nothing worthwhile unless you went to your roots and tried to reinterpret traditions and used traditions as a vehicle for transmitting the most modern and contemporary messages which means intervening in the tradition creatively." (Tanvir 1995, 104).

Thus, Tanvir was now doubly convinced that no truly worthwhile theatre–that is, no socially meaningful and artistically interesting theatre–was possible unless one worked within one's own cultural traditions and context. The result of this enhanced awareness was, that disregarding the colonial mindset that dominated the theatre scene at the time, Tanvir began his long quest for an indigenous performance idiom. This quest went through various stages before he arrived at the form and style which became the hallmark of his work in theatre.

The Dream of a Professional Repertory Company

As we noted above, ever since the 1950s, when he left Bombay and moved to Delhi, Tanvir had been passionately nursing his dream of having a theatre group of his own. His earlier attempt with Okhla

Theatre had failed but he had not given up. On the contrary, his subsequent European experience, particularly the examples of Jean Vilar's Theatre National Populaire and Bertolt Brecht's Berliner Ensemble, reinforced his resolve and helped him develop it further. He was now doubly confirmed in his belief that, in order to put his own ideas and inclinations about a truly Indian theatre into practice, a full-time repertory company was a prerequisite.

He had been sharing his thoughts on the matter with Begum Zaidi with whom he was in regular correspondence during his travels in Europe. She was very supportive. She approved of the idea of a professional company and offered to find the necessary resources for setting it up. As she was well connected and knew many influential people, she managed to collect an initial corpus of funds. Furthermore, she herself translated the twelve odd plays, suggested by Tanvir, which, he said, were required to make up the repertoire. These included three Sanskrit classics (*Mrichchakatikam*, *Mudra Rakshasa*, *Uttar Ramcharit*), some plays by Brecht, Ibsen, and Shaw. So at the end of two years, she wrote to him, saying, ".... we have twelve plays, 2-3 lakhs of rupees for the organisation called Hindustani Theatre and you must come. Two years are over. It must start." (Tanvir 1996b, 13).

Tanvir was still travelling through Europe and it was another year before he returned to India. Meanwhile, Begum Zaidi went ahead with activating Hindustani Theatre, and appointed as its director, Moneeka Misra who had a Master's degree in theatre from the US and had worked for some time with Kamaladevi Chattopadhyaya in Bombay. The theatre opened with its first production of *Khalid ki Khala*, Begum Zaidi's own Hindustani adaptation of *Charlie's Aunt*. Eventually, when Tanvir returned he took over as the artistic head of Hindustani Theatre, thus ousting Moneeka Misra, who he later fell in love with and married. The first production that he mounted after taking over was Begum Zaidi's translation of Shudraka's *Mrichchakatikam*, titled *Mitti ki Gaadi*. He included six folk actors from Chhattisgarh in the cast. This was his first production from a professional stage and also his first experience of working with folk actors.

Mitti ki Gaadi—Preparation and First Production

Before he began work on the production, Tanvir went to visit his mother in Raipur where he also happened to watch a performance of traditional Chhattisgarhi skits. Impressed by the skill and energy of those village performers he invited five of them—Madan Lal, Thakur Ram, Babu Das, Bhulwa, and the clarinet player, Jagmohan—to come to Delhi and work with him in theatre. He was also invited by the Rajnandgaon branch of the Indo-Soviet Cultural Society to talk about his visit to the USSR. In the course of his talk, he mentioned how he supported himself by singing Chhattisgarhi folk songs in Hungarian night clubs and illustrated this by singing one of the songs. At the end of the meeting, "a dark man with squint eyes and a short grisly beard" approached him and invited him to his house. Tanvir went and they ended up spending the entire night sharing ganja and folk songs. This was Laluram. Tanvir found him to be "one of the best singers in Chhattisgarh, a glorious voice," and enlisted him as the sixth folk artist to come to Delhi and work in *Mitti ki Gaadi*.

If there was one Indian play that had taken a firm hold of Tanvir's imagination and to which he constantly returned throughout his stay abroad it was this Sanskrit masterpiece. In his own words, "...in all these travels I was pursuing one aim apart from looking at theatre. I was trying to produce *Mritchchakatika* ... I had tried to sell the idea in Belgium, in Germany, and also Poland..." Tanvir goes on to describe how he, at one point, teamed up with a local theatre person, Kristina Skuszhanka, the head of a "very good" Polish theatre group, and decided to produce the play. They even got a new Polish translation done. However, the project fell through because the translator, who was not a theatre person, became greedy and tried to shortchange them. "But I did produce a small scene from *The Little Clay Cart* for television in Warsaw."

Tanvir also recalled that, during his European travels, he was constantly trying in his mind and on paper to design the stage for a possible production of *Mitti ki Gaadi*. Influenced by what he had learnt from Duncan Ross, he was looking for a way of making the story flow continuously without any obstructions. "I must have produced on paper something like twelve sets at least, drawings." But he could not make the performance flow without frequent interruptions for scene changes. He noticed that when he read the play this did not happen and the story just flowed without any break, each scene smoothly blending into the next.

After mulling over the problem for months, Tanvir realised that he was making the mistake of visualising the production on stage in terms of discrete scenes, each scene requiring a specific set and therefore each change in scene needing a change in the physical features on the stage. It occurred to him that there was a fundamental flaw in this approach. It envisaged the play in terms of the Aristotelian dramatic tradition which was alien to the classical Sanskrit playwrights. The tradition that these writers followed was not concerned with the unities of time, place and action.He noticed that this error also underlay much of the existing scholarship on Sanskrit drama. Western scholars, although praising the poetic quality and literary richness of the classical Sanskrit drama, seemed to fault these playwrights for what they thought was an ignorance of the rules of playwriting. What was worse, according to Tanvir, was that similar views were echoed by Indian scholars and commentators who, in his own words, "For all their knowledge of Sanskrit grammar and language... had no clue as to what was going on, because they had no contact with theatre" (Tanvir 1996b, 16).

Convinced that classical Indian drama was based on a different aesthetic principle and therefore required a different performative strategy, Tanvir began to prune his drawings and designs of all unnecessary features and eventually arrived at a very simple, austere stage design with just a circular platform, which was one foot high and about 12 feet in diameter, placed in the middle of the stage. This platform and the area around it provided enough space for the action to move freely to and fro between indoor and outdoor scenes without any interruption. "And the play just flowed. I did not have to explain the scene changes" (17).

At the beginning, Tanvir, probably influenced by the example of the Brechtian theatre, experimented for some time with banners dropping from above to communicate information about the locale. Later he removed that too. He thought it was unnecessarily "fussy". He also felt that "the description of the Sanskrit poets who wrote these plays are so vivid, and so beautiful, so graphic, that in your imagination, before your mind's eye, any kind of picture of which you are capable can be thrown up. One differing from the other, in the auditorium, in the audience. Now that liberty, that faculty, will not be given full play if you paint the scenery on the stage. I find it presumptuous to paint, to translate the words in terms of paint... So going by Duncan Ross, going by the internal evidence and the reading, I arrived at the conclusion that there were neither curtains, nor machinery, nor a revolving theatre in the classical theatre days. There was utter simplicity–it was an actor's theatre" (17).

It was clearly a while before Tanvir arrived at this idea of a bare and simple stage for *Mitti ki Gaadi.* It is entirely possible that, on returning to India, his initial inclination was further reinforced by an exposure to and experiments with folk performers and their styles. His penchant for the folk was already evident in his production of *Mitti ki Gaadi.* As mentioned, the cast of the play included five folk performers and a folk musician. In subsequent years many more village performers and artists were to join Tanvir's troupe. Many of these actors were to achieve great fame and acclaim in India and abroad on the basis of their amazing performance skills.

Tanvir's connection with the folk went beyond the use of folk actors, folk music, and folk dialect. He saw in the folk tradition a key to the classical theatre and even to Bharat Muni's *Natya Shastra*. *Mitti ki Gaadi* convinced him that the style and techniques of the folk theatre are akin to the ones implied in the dramaturgy of the Sanskrit playwrights. He believed that the theatrical style of the latter can be accessed through folk traditions. This view was contrary to the traditional approach which insisted on an irreconcilable dichotomy between *shastra dharmi* and *natya dharmi*, that is, between the classical and the popular. Tanvir argued against this orthodox position and eventually convinced, even the conservative Sanskrit pandits of the validity of his approach to the classical tradition. Later, he did this also by staging other Sanskrit classics, *Veni Sambaar* and *Mudra Rakshasa.* As in all Naya Theatre productions, these classics too were played by the group's repertory of folk actors in their inimitable mesmerising style. Like his other plays, these too employed stage conventions of folk performance.

It is difficult to tell if Tanvir was actually aware of it or not, but, in seeing a connection between the folk and the classical, he was on firm ground. European scholars from George Thompson to Robert Weimann have also posited similar connections between the Western canonical (or classical) and popular traditions.[5] Tanvir argued that the imaginative flexibility and simplicity with which the classical playwrights establish and shift the time and place of action in a play can be found in abundance in our folk performances. *Mitti ki Gaadi*, as well as *Veni Sambaar* and *Mudrarakshasa*, were practical demonstrations of this fact. For example, changes in time and locale in these productions are suggested through dialogues and movements without formally interrupting the performance. To quote just one instance from *Mitti ki Gaadi*, when a judge orders his subordinate to go to the garden and see if there is the body of a woman there, the subordinate simply runs around the stage once and returns with the answer, 'I went to the garden and found that there is a woman's body there'.

Tanvir's production of *Mitti ki Gaadi* is also memorable for its haunting music and songs most of which were written in Urdu by the rebel communist poet Niaz Haider. However, even at that early stage of his engagement with the Chhattisgarhi folk, Tanvir got Niaz Baba (as he was popularly called) to fit his words to specific Chhattisgarhi tunes. The remarkable thing was that the poet not only did this but did it so well that it even allowed the use of refrains from the original folk song to be retained. Several years later, after founding a theatre of his own, when Tanvir revived this play in a radically new version with Chhattisgarhi dialogues and a fully folk cast, he did not jettison the old songs, but added several others of his own. The play ends with a song of unmistakable political import. Interestingly, the song which announces the arrival of "a new dawn," was given the tune of a militant peasant song from Tanvir's IPTA days. Another thing that he did was to further improve his use of the conventions and techniques of the folk stage, thus enhancing the production's distinctly Indian form and style. Through the subsequent decades of its active existence, the production remained in the repertoire of Naya Theatre. It continues to be widely regarded as one of the best modern renderings of a Sanskrit classic.

A Company of His Own—The Naya Theatre

Soon after his first production of *Mitti ki Gaadi*, Tanvir lost his job in Hindustani Theatre. By that time, he and Moneeka Misra had become friends. In 1959, they joined hands and, keen to have a company of their own, together founded Naya Theatre. They found a garage in central Delhi and used it as their office. The first production that Naya theatre mounted was a triple-bill with three short plays by Tanvir himself: *Saat Paise* (based on a Czech short story about poverty and deprivation), *Jaalidar Parde*, and *Tambakoo ke Nuksanat*. Staged first in Delhi's YMCA and then in the barracks called Theatre Communications Building (located in the centre of Connaught Place, exactly where Palika Bazar stands today), it went through several shows and even helped the group to raise money for the Kashmir Relief Fund. After this production, which did not include any folk actor, Naya Theatre, funded only by personal contributions, could not go on and had to be virtually folded up. It remained more or less dysfunctional throughout the 1960s till it was revived as a professional theatre company with salaried actors in the early 70s.

The 1960s were difficult years for Tanvir. Moneeka and he were now married and lived in a small rented apartment in the Karol Bagh area of New Delhi. A daughter, Nageen, was born to them in 1965. They had no steady funding for theatre work and Tanvir was obliged to earn his living by means other than theatre. He took up an editorial job with the *Soviet Land*, a periodical that the Information Department of the Soviet embassy in India used to publish in the country's various languages. He also worked as a freelance film and TV critic and wrote for various newspapers and periodicals. Occasionally Moneeka or he was invited by colleges and amateur groups to direct plays or conduct theatre workshops. Most of these productions were in English. They included *Good Woman of Schezuan*, *Taming of the Shrew*, *Shoemaker's Prodigious Wife*, *Servant of Two Masters*, and *Lady Windermere's Fan*. This was also the period when he acted in a play produced by the United States Information Service (USIS) in New Delhi. The play was Sherwood Anderson's *Abe Lincoln in Illinois*. It was directed by the head of Cultural Affairs in the USIS, Tom Noonan, and Tanvir was cast in the lead role of Abraham Lincoln. The production was toured for many months and visited numerous towns and cities in different parts of India. Later, Tanvir was awarded a fellowship and visited the US for a year.

From time to time during that period, Tanvir also teamed up with one group or another in order to direct and stage plays. For instance, in 1960, he staged *Mirza Shohrat* for Little Theatre Group (LTG). This was his first adaptation of Moliere's *Le Bourgeois Gentilhomme*. Years later, he created a new version and titled it *Lala Shohrat Rai*, which became part of the permanent repertoire of his group. Tanvir's next production in 1960 was Agha Hashr Kashmiri's *Rustam Sohrab*, also staged by LTG. In 1968, on the occasion of the death centenary of Mirza Ghalib, he wrote and, in association with friends, staged *Mere Baad* in which he himself played the role of the iconic Urdu poet. During the same year, Tanvir worked with another group and produced *The Signet Ring*, an English translation of Vishakhadatta's *Mudra Rakshasa*. This was followed in 1969 by *Shatranj ke Mohre*, based on Premchand's famous story.

Although Tanvir continued to be active in Delhi's theatre through the 1960s, he did not have the time or the opportunity to pursue his interest in traditional forms of theatre in a sustained way and, for most part of the decade, his quest for a truly indigenous yet modern form of theatre remained virtually on hold. Naya Theatre was now defunct and he had no troupe of his own. Understandably, this lack of time and adequate funding had an adverse effect on his ability to do independent work. However, it must also be mentioned that he did not entirely abandon his interest in folk traditions. For example, he had used three folk actors from Chhattisgarh in *Mirza Shohrat* in 1960, and in 1968, besides using the *kuchipudi* curtain (a traditional stage device) in his production of *Mudra Rakshasa*, he brought to Delhi, for the first time, a traditional Pandavani singer Poonaram from Chhattisgarh, who gave a rendering of the Mahabharata story of *Urubhangam*. Barring this occasional engagement, his contact with folk artists and their work was not as regular or as sustained as he desired.

The situation changed drastically in the 1970s, the most crucial decade in Tanvir's development, during which he finally succeeded in discovering the form and style that he had been searching for. The decade opened with the Sangeet Natak Akademi honouring him with a national award for his work in the theatre. As part of this award, the Akademi commissioned a number of shows of *Agra Bazaar* to be staged in different places from Delhi to Srinagar. This was a turning point in Tanvir's career. It gave him an opportunity to bring back all his folk performers and to revive Naya Theatre. The group which had started with just six folk artists now consisted entirely of them. After that, there was no looking back for Tanvir or his Naya Theatre. From then on, his theatre drew upon the folk traditions not only in terms of actors, music, dances, and sometimes even the plots, but the basic grammar of performance and conventions of staging too were distinctly and unmistakably refashioned from traditional material. This is how the Naya Theatre's productions came to possess all their outstanding energy and liveliness (such as, physical vigour, raciness, and humour) that one associates with folk performances.

The Breakthrough

However, as indicated above, this distinctive style and form was not achieved overnight but evolved gradually over several years of exploration and experimentation. Through the early years of the 1970s, alongside his explorations in various traditional forms from temple rituals to forms of storytelling (*pandavani*, *chandaini*, etc.), as well as in folk forms and traditions of different regions such as Haryana and Odisha, Tanvir continued to work with the village actors from Chhattisgarh. Nonetheless, he was not entirely satisfied with the way things were going. What bothered him was that the folk actors who demonstrated such incredible energy, skill and creativity on the traditional *nacha* stage seemed strangely awkward and inept in his own productions. After mulling over this for some time, Tanvir recognised two 'faults' (as he called them) in his own approach. One, he realised that it was not correct to fix the performance rather rigidly in advance by blocking movements and arranging lighting on paper. This, he felt, did not work with the rural artists who could not read or write and could not even remember which way and on what line they should move. The second difficulty was that, by doing plays in standard Hindi or Hindustani, he was making these actors speak in a language they were not accustomed to. This had the effect of making them work with a severe handicap and thus of inhibiting the full and free expression of their creativity in performance.

Having identified the flaws in his approach, Tanvir began to rid his style of work of them. He started using improvisation instead of orthodox or textbook methods of preparing a production. He also allowed the folk actors to speak in their native Chhattisgarhi dialect, thus giving them back what he usually referred to as "their autonomy". As mentioned, 1970–73 was an experimental phase for him. During this period, he worked intensively with rural performers in their native language and style of performance. He allowed them to do their own traditional pieces mostly in their own way, merely editing and touching them up here and there to make them more stage worthy. It was during this period that he also tried many other traditional forms, such as temple rituals, *pandavani*, and stock skits.

Another major breakthrough came during a *nacha* workshop that Tanvir conducted in Raipur in 1972. In addition to several scholars, experts, and observers from different urban centres across the country, more than a hundred folk artists from different parts of Chhattisgarh participated. The exercise lasted for one whole month. In the course of daily sessions, they presented their traditional skits, songs, and dances, and demonstrated their ways of doing make up and selecting costumes and jewellery. They listened to Tanvir explain to them how things (such as lighting and costumes) were done on the modern stage, and so on. During the workshop, three different comic sketches from the stock *nacha* repertoire were selected and more or less dovetailed into one another to make it look like a compact, full length play. A few short scenes were improvised and inserted to loosely link them up into a story which depicted a wealthy old man, desirous of marrying a very young woman, cheated out of the promised bride so that she could be united with her young lover. A number of traditional songs, which had never before been brought on stage were also included. The production which was thus created was a delightful blend of stock comic skits and gags, traditional songs, dances and temple rituals. It was titled *Gaon ka Naam Sasural, Mor Naam Damaad,* an almost wholly improvised stage play which was not only remarkable for its hilarity but also for the rare treasure of delightful Chhattisgarhi folk music and dances that it offered. Tanvir first tried it out before a large gathering of local villagers and found that it worked.

The workshop also brought a number of new folk artists into Tanvir's theatre. Till then he had been working with a mixed cast in which urban actors mingled with the six Chhattisgarhi artists, who were the nucleus of Naya Theatre. Among the new folk performers discovered during the workshop was Fida Bai, who came to be recognised as one of the finest actors of the contemporary Indian stage. A performer of immense power and skill, she not only played the main female role in *Sasural* but remained the leading actress of Naya Theatre till a tragic event made it impossible for her to act in plays.

The workshop was followed by a week long festival which too was held in an open ground and showcased tribal dancers from Raigarh and Bastar, and several *Nacha* parties performed their own songs and comic skits. A huge audience watched these shows, which included *Sasural*, and made the festival a great success. *Sasural* must have been quite a novel experience for the traditional performers as well as their customary spectators. For, the improvised skit, although based on traditional story elements and music, was at the same time quite different from the traditional *nacha* performance. For example, in Tanvir's production costumes and jewellery were carefully selected, a practice not found among traditional *nacha* groups which, according to Tanvir,"wouldn't care for this sort of thing, basically, they would give you any kind of costume, out of necessity, not design–any old coat, hat, jacket, sometimes not so good, sometimes fantastic....[In their contemporary debased and impure state] they wouldn't have Chhattisgarhi tunes either. They would mostly have film tunes and hybrid things... [The songs were there, nonetheless, and could be found] in the fields, at harvesting time, in the mandir, during rituals, in childbirth, good, authentic songs, death songs, marriage songs, all these existed in society, but on the rustic stage little of it was reflected" (Tanvir 1996b, 25).

The play was brought to Delhi where it played to packed houses for nearly two weeks. Its success was a great relief for Tanvir who was somewhat anxious about how Delhi's metropolitan audience would respond to a play so steeped in Chhattisgarhi folk and tribal cultural traditions and dialects. Describing his experience, he recalled that the play's success indicated that his theatre had transcended the language barrier. "People came again and again for the wonderful musical quality of the play and for the clarity of expression we had gained by the first time, despite the fact that it is a specially difficult play in terms of dialogue, full of improvisation.... I realised that the Delhi audience had accepted us" (25).

Sasural thus was a significant landmark in the development of Tanvir's theatre. It proved that it was possible to do a modern play in Chhattisgarhi dialect and with a cast entirely made up of folk actors. He felt that, with this production, he had broken new ground, and that he had found the form and style that he had been searching for ever since the 1950s. After the 1973 workshop, it became easier for him to go on with the construction and casting of a play through improvisations--a method that he continued to use till the end. It had the effect of preparing the way for all Tanvir's subsequent work, including the celebrated play *Charandas Chor*.

Charandas Chor

Tanvir's *Charandas Chor* is today the best known of all his productions. It is also his most frequently performed and most widely travelled play. In more than four decades since its creation, the play has had hundreds of performances in scores of places in India and Europe. It is regarded as a masterpiece, indeed a classic, of contemporary Indian theatre. It is also one of the best examples of the kind of theatre Tanvir has been practising and which I have tried to describe above. The play had a long and interesting genesis, involving a protracted process, lasting nearly two years of work on and around its story, before it reached its final shape in 1975. How it evolved over this long period of intermittent experimentation and improvisation is worth recording here.

Tanvir first heard the story in 1973 from the well-known Hindi writer-folklorist Vijay Dan Detha, who had, in turn, recorded it from the oral tradition of Rajasthan. Later that year, Tanvir tried to use the story during a khayal workshop with Rajasthani folk artists. It did not work and he was forced to abandon the idea at the time. However, the story stayed in his mind and he decided to give it another try—this time with Chhattisgarhi folk actors. Towards the end of 1974, he held another month-long workshop in Bhilai. During the workshop they prepared six short skits. However, towards the end of the workshop, in a purely exploratory and tentative move, Tanvir gave them the *Chor* story and asked them to work on it. After four days of improvisations they had a rough sketch.

This elementary and raw sketch was then presented to a large gathering during an all-night programme in a sprawling open field known as Bhilai Maidan. It was the annual event of the Satnamis, a community of low caste people who are often treated as "untouchable" by the orthodox upper caste Hindus. They are spread throughout India. Thousands of Satnamis had congregated in the Bhilai maidan to participate in the nightlong cultural programme which consisted of skits, songs, and dances, both devotional and simply entertaining. Tanvir too was there with his group of artists who presented the skits produced during the workshop. While watching and listening to the Satnamis, it occurred to Tanvir that he should try out the improvised thief story. The basic tenet of the Satnami creed is : Truth is God, God is Truth. Therefore a story about a truthful thief, he thought, would be appropriate for the occasion. So, at about 6 o'clock in the morning, Tanvir decided to give his stage adaptation of this Rajasthani folk tale a public trial. Despite all its incompleteness, the sketch was received well. In Tanvir's own words, "It was a very rough version. It ran for about 40 minutes. We called it *Chor Chor*. For songs I had this Satnami book with me and I just improvised by singing and asking them to repeat. And there was a big response for this rough, *kachha* (raw) thing" (Tanvir 1996b, 26).

This then was the first dry run of what was to eventually grow into a full-length play called *Charandas Chor*. Encouraged by the enthusiastic audience response, Tanvir continued to work on this first embryonic version. During subsequent months, he wrote new scenes to flesh out the basic plot of the story. During the process, he also modified the original ending slightly. In Detha's version, the thief is killed for his vows and the queen's offer is accepted by the guru who becomes the king. Tanvir's play departs from this. While he ends the story itself with the dramatic highpoint of the thief's execution (leaving out the guru's opportunism), he prolongs the play by adding a sequence which, accompanied by a chorus in praise of Truth, shows the thief's posthumous deification by the people. Through this and the last chorus, he brings the performance to an anti-climactic conclusion. Tanvir's deviation from the conclusion of the original story in Vijay Dan Detha's version was deliberate and of significance. During a conversation with me, he recalled: "Detha was not very happy with this alteration in the story. But, being a very cultivated and open-minded man, accepted it as *my* version without any argument. He merely said: 'Your end is the end of evil, mine is a continuation of evil.' And, of course, he had a point there" (Tanvir 1995, 113).

In the course of rehearsals, Tanvir also strengthened the play's Satnami connection by introducing into it several specifically Satnami motifs. He brought in as the opening song the words of the basic article of their faith: "God is truth, Truth is God." The play opens with the chorus crooning precisely these words in Hindi. He also introduced the motif of the white flag with which the Satnamis traditionally mark their places of worship. It is at this white flag mounted on a pedestal that the people offer floral tributes to their newly deified "guru" in the last scene.

Another interesting Satnami feature that Tanvir brought into the play was the introduction of the *panthi* dancers, who were not a permanent part of the Naya Theatre troupe but were commissioned for specific performances from time to time. The *panthis* are a group of muscular, bare-chested young Satnami men who perform a vigorous and masculine dance which combines rhythmic footwork with spectacular demonstrations of acrobatic feats. It is accompanied by a choric song, more in the way of rhythmic chanting than singing, and loud beating of drums. Besides reinforcing the Satnami connection, these dancers invariably had a spellbinding effect on the audience.

Songs are a major element in *Charandas Chor*, as they indeed are in every Tanvir production. Tanvir worked closely with some Chhattisgarhi folk poets for the compositions. They possess a certain simplicity of style and expression which comes from the folk tradition. They are set to delightful tunes and contribute immensely towards enhancing the play's pleasure ability in performance. However, in a style reminiscent of Brecht, Tanvir also uses them to comment on an action and to elucidate and underline its larger moral and social significance. In some cases, they reflect a certain complexity of articulation and consciousness which is obviously Tanvir's contribution. For example, the refrain in the *panthi* song in the second act, 'Oh, Charandas, don't try to rob Death of his due,' was deliberately added because Tanvir wanted it to work on the audience's mind subliminally, preparing them for the death that comes at the end of the play. Similarly, the last chorus, 'an ordinary thief is now a famous man,' which comments on Charandas's fate and articulates its significance, was almost half written by him using the simplicity of Nazir Akbarabadi's poetry.

In the case of the *Panthi* dancers, just as he retouched the choreography, Tanvir also got the folk poets to write what he refers to as "my type of song to go with the dance." The original composition was simplistic and, in a reformist vein, saying lying is bad like drinking and gambling. Tanvir got the folk poets Ganga Ram Sakhet and Swaran Kumar to reverse this proposition and say that speaking truth is an addiction like gambling and drinking and therefore difficult to give up. Thus revised, the song became wittier and a more poignant comment on the thief story (Tanvir 1996b, 26).

The production also broke new ground in terms of staging. Its simple, bare stage design was arrived at after a number of experiments, during which several things (including a long, painted curtain for the backdrop) were tried out. The design that was finally arrived at was austere in its simplicity and very effective in functional terms. All that it required was a stage and, mounted on that stage, a rectangular platform which was 9 inches high, 6 feet wide and 12 feet long, with just foliage or a leafy branch of a tree behind it. The spaces created by this austere architectural design were used in different ways throughout the production. For the opening scene between the policeman and the thief, only the forestage was used. But in the *guru dakshina* scene, the entire stage came into use, with the guru and some of his followers sitting on the platform and the rest scattered all over the stage. It was the same in the next scene where the landlord and his store of food grains were on the platform, but the peasants, Charandas and, finally, the Raut dancers used the fore stage. In an innovative and visually pleasing strategy, the platform on the stage was approached sometimes in a rectilinear fashion (as, for example, in the *guru dakshina* scene where the guru sits facing the audience), and sometimes diagonally (as in the temple scene where the idol is placed downstage left and congregation stands facing it). This created an interesting variation in the spectator's perception of the stage, which appeared physically altered, although in reality it was not.

Stage props were kept to the minimum–only objects which are actually used in the action, such as the treasure chest or the idol or the sacks of rice–and no elaborate lighting was required. Change in the locale was suggested almost entirely through changing the grouping and not by any physical rearrangement of the stage. During the early scenes, the stage is quite flexible and informal. But after the first half of the play, it suddenly takes on a formal and sharply defined quality in order to present the royal treasury, the queen's court and her bed chamber. The grouping is also significantly more formal in these last scenes.

The Spartan stage design, used in several subsequent productions (including *Mitti ki Gaadi*) as well, also allowed the actors and their performances to be foregrounded. This was important since a great deal of the play's appeal and strength in performance depended on the remarkable quality of Tanvir's folk actors. The uncluttered performance space brought the amazing dexterity and skill of the actors and their various antics into sharper focus. Further, this minimalist stage design reinforced the sense of openness that lies at the heart of the play's story. Unhampered by any physical changes in the scene, the action unfolded briskly and grippingly from one scene to another, like a tale of adventure or a fairytale (which, on one level, is what this story about an honest thief really is), till the last episode when its serious import suddenly bursts into focus.

In Tanvir's major productions the real protagonist, almost invariably, is the ordinary people. We saw this above in the case of his very first major production, *Agra Bazaar*. It continued to be so in subsequent plays as well. This protagonist is sometimes latent, operating on the deeper, subtextual level (or, if you like, in the interstices of the episodic structure), and sometimes quite apparent (as in *Agra Bazaar* or *Gaon ka Naam Sasural*). In either case, it is almost always there somewhere. This collective subject of the dramatic action points to a tendency towards what may be described as a utopian horizon-akin to what the German philosopher, Ernst Bloch, refers to as 'the hope principle.' It signifies a desired, but empirically unavailable, state of happiness, the idea of an egalitarian rearrangement of society which critically reflects on and offers a radical alternative to the prevailing social order.

This utopian dimension is particularly strong in *Charandas Chor*. It is explicit in the scene where the hoarded rice is cunningly liberated from the clutches of a cruel and avaricious landlord and redistributed among the starving peasants. But it also underlies the rest of the play. The central character, Charandas, himself implies it. He is a figure of the common man who is capable of virtues rare in an unjust, class-based society. He rises from the status of a petty, village thief to that of a popular hero. He had come from among the ordinary people and to them he returns after death. Significantly, the exact moment of this transformation of his image coincides in the play with his redistribution of the hoarded food amongst the poor. The moment is sharply focused by the Chorus announcing that 'Charandas is not a thief, not a thief, no way!' This chorus also underlines the contrast between Charandas's moral uprightness and benevolence and the injustices of a corrupt, anti-people system. It sings

> There are so many rogues about, who do not look like thieves
> Impressive turbans on their heads, softly shod their feet.
> But open up their safes and you will surely see
> Stolen goods, ill-gotten wealth, riches got for free.

Charandas, thus, can be said to stand for the ordinary toiling masses. He is conceived in terms of paradoxes and contradictions. He is a thief. Like any ordinary thief, he lives by duping and robbing people and dodging the law. But he is also an extraordinary man of principles. He is kind hearted and cannot bear to see a woman is distress. He has a strong sense of social justice and aids the poor against the rich. Above all, he is truthful and a man of his word. Caught in a critical situation, he had jokingly taken certain vows before a priest. Amazingly, he lives up to them and in the end actually dies for them.

Charandas Chor is constructed on the principle of carnivalesque reversal, the principle of a world turned upside down. There is a reversal of hierarchy, particularly on moral and ethical levels. Truthfulness, honesty, integrity, ethical values, and even professional efficiency are shown to belong exclusively to a thief, leaving the upper echelons of society devoid precisely of these values and virtues. Through his acts and deeds Charandas debunks religion, the state, and class economy. He shows up the existing social order as disorder. His integrity, uprightness, and professional efficiency are in direct contrast to the lack of these qualities in the policeman, the priest, the government official (*munim*), the wealthy landlord, and, finally, the queen. Interestingly a carnivalesque reversal of roles is also suggested when Charandas assumes the identity of the new minister to rob the royal treasury. His unshod feet, although, technically, a means through which his real identity is later recognised by the *munim*, seems symbolic of his earthiness and his link with the common (unshod) masses as against the exclusiveness and distance of the politician who is typically dressed in spotless white.

Furthermore, Tanvir's play does not allow the audience any monocular, cosy point of reference, Instead, it implies what has been termed in the context of Shakespeare, the principle of 'multiple consciousness' and which Brecht describes as 'complex seeing.' This principle designates a complex and dialectical process of presenting a thing in such a way that its underside also becomes visible. It has the effect of destabilising smug responses based on received, orthodox values and norms.

This can also be exemplified in the way religiosity, in its orthodox sense, is constantly undercut in the play through subversive comedy and juxtaposed with a secular, social viewpoint. There are three representations of religious ritual and practice in the play and in all of them this process of undercutting is evident. First, there is the *guru dakshina* scene. Although ostensibly a religious congregation, the song significantly deals not with religion or spirituality, but with the impossibility of salvation without first paying the guru in material terms. Also, the guru's ashram virtually becomes a hideout for drunkards, drug-addicts, gamblers, and thieves, and Charandas refers to the guru as one who robs people in broad daylight. In visual terms, too, the 'spirituality' of the scene is seriously undermined, on the one hand, by the constant in and out movements of the thief and the policeman, and, on the other hand, by the gambling and drinking that goes on merrily in a corner downstage.

The second instance occurs in the temple scene. The main action in this scene is the *aarti*, a traditional religious ritual before a deity. The song that is sung at length is also devotional in tone and content. But then this religiosity is again comically undercut by the actions of the thief and the policeman who, although pretending to be part of the congregation of worshippers, actually form a comic pair of the chaser and the chased. They constantly weave in and out of the line of devotees throughout the *aarti* which ends with Charandas making off with the jewels and even the idol itself.

In the third instance, which comes at the end of the play, Charandas is posthumously deified as a saint and people pay homage to him by worshipfully filing past his *samadhi* and placing flowers on it. There is no comedy there. The entire action–beginning from the ritual of lighting a lamp and breaking a coconut to the action of filing past–is performed with great reverence. Yet there is something which distances and differentiates it from the usual kind of religious experience. Undoubtedly we see, and are perhaps moved by, the people's worshipful attitude towards their 'saint.' But if we are alert to the context of the play as a whole, we also see that this saint did not drop out of the blue yonder. The play shows us the actual process through which a very ordinary man, indeed a thief, attains sainthood in the eyes of the common people and we recognise that the process is entirely this-worldly. In other words, we see the secular and historical stuff that saints are made of.

It is tempting to read this ritual of homage to a thief as an ironical comment. In some ways, the play is steeped in comic irony. The way in which Charandas is confronted with the choices that oblige him to live up to the pledges that he had jokingly taken; the very coexistence of honesty and integrity in a thief; the guru's acceptance of stolen goods as *guru dakshina*–these are some of the elements which contribute towards this irony. Nonetheless, in its totality, in terms of the overall mood and flavour, the play is more celebratory than ironical. In this context, the last popular homage scene, too, becomes a celebration of a popular hero, and, by that token, a celebration of the people and their desire for truth and justice.

With *Charandas Chor*, the form and style of Tanvir's theatre had reached a significant level of perfection. His Naya Theatre now worked almost exclusively with folk actors. Even his occasional productions with urban actors and for groups other than Naya Theatre–such as, *Dushman* (Gorky's *Enemies*, 1990) directed for the National School of Drama Repertory Company, or his powerfully moving production of Asghar Wajahat's play on communal bigotry and violence, *Jis Lahore Nai Dekhya Wo Jamyai Nai* (He *Who Hasn't Seen Lahore Has Seen Nothing*, 1991), for the Sri Ram Centre Repertory Company–were marked by the style that he had developed through his work with folk artists.

We saw how a political undercurrent questioning, challenging, or subverting the established social or moral order can be witnessed in all his plays. In the half century of his career as a theatre director, Tanvir wrote and staged many original plays, offered improvisations from the traditional repertoire, produced Sanskrit classics as well as translations/adaptations of Shakespeare, Moliere and Brecht. He held workshops in different parts of the country, worked with various urban and folk theatre groups, and scripted and produced what may be called community dramas on issues of immediate social and political relevance. An overview of his oeuvre in all its aspects reveals a sustained endeavour on his part to develop and perfect a style of theatre which is both 'traditional' in the sense of being oriented towards folk and popular forms, and 'modern' in the sense of being alert to the major issues and concerns of our time.

These concerns may be cultural, as in *Agra Bazaar* which focuses primarily on the conflict between elitist mores and a robustly plebeian concept of culture and literature. Or psychological, as in *Bahadur Kalarin*, an Oedipal folktale dealing with a son's incestuous disposition towards his mother. Or philosophical, as in *Dekh Rahein Hain Nain*, a play freely adapted from Stefan Zweig's short story titled *Eyes of My Brother*, which explores the questions of action and its consequence in terms of human suffering. Or expressly political, as in *Hirma Ki Amar Kahani*, which foregrounds and critically interrogates the issues of development and centralisation of political power. But no matter what the theme, and how traditional the basic plot, Tanvir had a way of imbuing his work with a socio-political dimension. He weaves into any material that he worked with certain elements (such as choric comments and sequences of action) which unmistakably point to the play's political import and emphasise the harsh reality of the everyday life of the people. For example, when Tanvir took up *Mricchakatikam* for staging, he not only sharpened the political theme already present in the original, but also gave it a subtle plebeian bias by foregrounding, as a prominent cognitive concern, the vision of a longed for just, happy, alternative to an oppressive and tyrannical social order. Similar inflection towards a liberatory horizon is unmistakable in the ironies that *Charandas Chor* abounds in, particularly in the irony of a dreaded thief being an honest, truthful, kind and benevolent person.

Summing Up

In conclusion, I must return to the point with which I began and which I have tried to develop throughout this chapter. For all its involvement with traditional music, actors, and styles of performance, the theatre that Tanvir developed was not a "folk theatre" in the strictest sense of the term. His interest in folk culture and his decision to work with and in terms of traditional styles of performance was an ideological choice as much as an aesthetic one, whether Tanvir himself was fully conscious of it as such or not. There is a close connection between his predilection for popular traditions and his left-wing disposition. His involvement with the left-wing cultural movement, an association which he maintained (no matter how loosely) to his last days, already meant a commitment to the common people and their causes. His work in the theatre, in style as well as in content, reflected this commitment and can be seen as part of a larger (socialist) project of empowerment of the people.

As I have already pointed out, Tanvir's fascination with the "folk" was not motivated by a revivalist or an antiquarian impulse.

It was prompted, instead, by an awareness of the tremendous creative possibilities and artistic energies inherent in these traditions. He did not hesitate to borrow themes, techniques, and music from them, but he also desisted from the impossible task of trying to resurrect old traditions in their original form and also from presenting them as stuffed museum pieces. Notwithstanding a popular misconception, his theatre does not belong within any one form or tradition in its entirety or purity. In fact, as he often pointed out, he never ran after "folk forms as such at all but only after folk performers who brought their own forms and styles with them." The performance style of his actors is, no doubt, rooted in their traditional *nacha* background, but, as mentioned above, his plays are not authentic *nacha* productions. For one thing, while the number of actual actors in a play in this Chhattisgarhi folk tradition is usually restricted to two or three, the rest being stop-gap singers and dancers, Tanvir's production involved a full cast of actors, some of whom also sang and danced. More significantly, his plays have a structural coherence and complexity, which one does not usually associate with the "simple" form of the *nacha*. Another important difference is that while in the nacha songs and dances are used largely as autonomous musical interludes, in Tanvir's plays they are neither purely ornamental in function nor are they formally autonomous units inserted into a loose collection of separate skits. On the contrary, they are closely woven into the fabric of the action and function as an important part of the total thematic and artistic structure of the play.

In other words, Tanvir did not approach the 'folk' uncritically and a historically. He was aware of their historical and cognitive limitations and did not hesitate to intervene in them and allow his own modern consciousness and political understanding to interact with the traditional energies and skills of his performers. His project, from the beginning of his career, had been to harness elements of the folk traditions as "a vehicle and make them yield new, contemporary meanings and to produce a theatre which has a touch of the soil about it." This rich interaction–indeed, this partnership–between Tanvir's urban, modern consciousness, on the one hand, and the folk styles and forms, on the other, is perhaps best exemplified by the songs in his plays. For example, Tanvir's excellent adaptations of *A Midsummer's Night Dream (Kamdeo Ka Apna, Basant Ritu Ka Sapna*) and *The Good Woman of Szechwan (Shahjapur ki Shantibai)* as well as his complex philosophical play, *Dekh Rahe Hain Nain*, could not be possible without this collaboration. In the first two, Tanvir beautifully blended a fidelity to the original foreign texts, the authenticity and freshness of poetic expression, and native folk tunes. In *Nain*, he successfully represented an intellectually complicated theme employing the full range of the resources and energies of the folk stage.

However, Tanvir was careful not to create a hierarchy by privileging, in any absolute and extrinsic way, his own educated consciousness as poet-cum-playwright-cum-director over the unschooled creativity of his actors. In his work, the two usually met and interpenetrated, as it were, as equal partners in a collective, collaborative endeavour in which each gave and took from, and thus enriched, the other. An excellent example of this non-exploitative approach, as we saw above, is the way Tanvir often fitted and blended his poetry to the traditional folk and tribal music, allowing the former to retain its own imaginative and rhetorical power and socio-political import, but without in any way devaluing or destroying the latter. Yet another example can be seen in the way he allowed his actors and their skills to be foregrounded by eschewing all temptations to use elaborate or clever stage design and complicated lighting.

Thus in contrast to the fashionable, folksy kind of drama on the one hand and the revivalist and archaic kind of 'traditional' theatre on the other, Tanvir's theatre, with its incisive blend of tradition and contemporaneity, folk creativity and modern critical consciousness, offered a new and more inclusive model of modernity in Indian theatre. It is this rich and enriching blend which makes his work so unique and memorable.

NOTES

1. An earlier version of this essay appeared in *Theatre India* (New Delhi) and also in Neeraj Malik and Javed Malick ed. *Habib Tanvir* (Sahmat, New Delhi).
2. Despite the slanderous propaganda of the rightwing Hindutva brigade, *Ponga Pandit* was neither written nor directed by Tanvir. The play was originally written by two Dalit writers of Chhattisgarh in 1935 and Tanvir's actors merely reproduced it. However, the decision to perform this anti-caste play on various politically significant occasions was Tanvir's.
3. See chapter, "Decolonialising a Colonial Icon".
4. I am drawing upon my own experience here. Like Tanvir, I too was born in Raipur and spent the first eighteen years of my life there. The Raipur of Tanvir's early years must have been even closer to the countryside than it was during my time
5. See George Thompson's seminal work *Aeschylus and Athens,* and Robert Weimann's *Shakespeare and the Popular Tradition in the Theatre.*

WORKS CITED

Tanvir, Habib. 2010. In conversation with Javed Malick. In *Habib Tanvir: Reflections and Reminiscences.* Eds. Neeraj Malik and Javed Malick. New Delhi: Safdar Hashmi Memorial Trust.

____.1996a. *Charandas Chor.* Trans. Anjum Katyal. Kolkata: Seagull Books.

____. 1996b. In conversation with Anjum Katyal. *Seagull Theatre Quarterly* (STQ No. 10).

____. 2006. *Agra Bazaar.* Trans. Javed Malick. Kolkata: Seagull Books.

4

Trapped in Infinity: Beckett's *Waiting for Godot*[1]

Samuel Beckett, who died in 1989 at the venerable age of 86, was an iconic and one of the most written about *avant-garde* writers of the 20th century. The body of critical scholarship on him is as diverse in approach as it is enormous in size. During his lifetime itself, he was described variously: as a formalist, a modernist, a post-modernist, an existentialist, an Absurdist, and so on. Psychoanalytical critics had their own take on him as did the theological ones who saw strong and persistent Christian motifs in his writings. More recently, a French scholar, Pascale Casanova, has come up with an interesting thesis suggesting that Beckett strove to achieve in literature the kind of abstraction that is found in avant-garde painting and music. The remarkable thing is that Beckett's work lends itself readily to all these diverse readings.

Born in the town of Foxcock near Dublin, Ireland, Beckett was the younger of two sons of an affluent bourgeois family. His father, William Beckett, was a successful businessman and an active sportsman. Beckett's mother, May, was a fiercely independent woman whose main passions were animals and gardening. Beckett himself said: "I had a happy childhood...although I had little talent for happiness. My parents did everything they could to make a child happy. But I was often lonely."[2] Free from any intellectual aspirations, the parents wanted the children to join the family business after the university, a fate that Beckett managed to escape with some difficulty.

At Trinity, Dublin: Formative Years

After finishing school, Beckett joined the programme in Modern European Languages at Trinity College, Dublin, and obtained his BA in 1927 and MA in 1931. In the early years of his education, Beckett seemed to have little interest in studies. He had inherited his father's interest in sports and spent much time pursuing it. He excelled in cricket, rugby and tennis at school as well as at Trinity. He even played first class cricket before becoming a famous, Nobel Prize winning writer. But, in the early years of his education, his academic performance was poor. It was only during his third year at Trinity that Beckett underwent a sea change and became a keen student, taking courses in Italian and French. He felt especially attracted to French which was taught by Thomas B. Rudmose-Brown, an authority on Racine and Corneille and a great enthusiast of contemporary French poetry. Critics think that it was perhaps Rudmose-Brown who rekindled a serious literary interest in him. Thus, while continuing to excel in sports (which pleased his father more), Beckett became one of the most serious students in his class.

Towards the end of his university life, Beckett also developed a keenness for theatre. There was a marked resurgence of theatrical activity in Dublin at the time and enthusiasm for drama–both Irish and European–was widespread. While the Irish theatre was energised by a nationalist (Gaelic) spirit (exemplified particularly by Yeats, Synge, and O'Casey), its continental counterpart was known for its experimental boldness and intellectual non-conformism. There were several theatres in Dublin specialising in different kinds of drama. The Abbey Theatre, which was the centre of Irish-nationalist drama, presented the works of Sean O'Casey, Lady Gregory, Lenox Robinson and Denis Johnston, among others. The Gaiety Theatre specialised in the experimental plays of contemporary European writers like Pirandello. In addition to these, the Queen Theatre concentrated on melodrama while the Theatre Royal and the Olympia Theatre presented popular vaudeville shows.

Beckett saw most of these plays. He showed more interest in the formal aspects of a play than its content. He admired the realistic comedies of writers like Sean O'Casey, but was more attracted to the bold experimentalism of the modernist writers of Europe. This early predilection for a post-First World War current in European art and literature–which came to be known as 'modernism' and which was based on anti-realism and an exaggerated concern with formal criteria–was to grow further and deeply influence Beckett's own later work. During this period, he also developed a great fascination for the knock-about comedy which he witnessed not only in O'Casey's plays and the music-hall entertainments, but also in the movies of Charlie Chaplin and Laurel and Hardy. Meanwhile, Beckett had grown into an avid reader. During this period, he read, among others, Descartes, Dante, and modern French poetry–particularly Rimbaud, Baudelaire, and Apollinaire. His academic performance was now excellent and he was awarded a BA with honours, as well as a two-year fellowship to the famous Ecole Normale Superieure in Paris.

Paris Years: Exploring Career Options

The years in Paris had a formative influence on Beckett's development. Paris at that time was the intellectual and cultural capital of Europe. It was the home of the avant-garde in art and literature, and attracted ambitious young men and women. Writers, artists, and students gravitated towards Paris from either side of the Atlantic in search of artistic stimulation and freedom. In the Irish mind, Paris was also linked with James Joyce who lived there in exile. During his stay there, Beckett came in contact with a number of writers and critics, read European literature and philosophy and produced his first serious writings.

Beckett was introduced to Joyce soon after his arrival in Paris and became a member of a small group of friends and admirers whom Joyce loved to have around him. This association, which has been the subject of a good deal of critical interest, was to last despite setbacks till Joyce's death in 1941. When Beckett first met him, the author of *Ulysses* was already famous as an uncompromisingly modernist writer, while Beckett, only twenty-two at that time, had yet to establish himself in any specific profession. So Joyce, for whom he had admiration verging on awe, became his model. In his own early writings, Beckett tried to imitate the famous novelist's 'seemingly casual style' but found it frustratingly difficult. However, this initial difficulty notwithstanding, something of what he admired in the fellow Irishman and his work stayed with him and influenced his development.

Beckett was not yet sure of his vocation. He wrote in several genres: fiction, poetry and criticism. During these years, Beckett was still trying to situate himself within what Pascale Casanova refers to as"the Irish literary universe" (28). His most important and lasting work from this period, however, is in the area of criticism. He wrote an essay on Joyce in which he dealt with the latter's relationship to Dante, Bruno and Vico. It was published as the opening essay in a volume of studies on Joyce's *Work in Progress*, later titled *Finnegan's Wake*. He also wrote a full length study of Proust, which is generally regarded as his first systematic attempt to formulate the ideas that were to shape his mature work several years later.

Returning to Dublin in 1930, Beckett took up a teaching position at Trinity. Having spent two years in the cosmopolitan atmosphere of Paris, he found life in Dublin provincial and repressive. He found the Catholic censorship of arts and morals unacceptable and was disgusted by the Irish insularity to what he considered the liberating influences of Continental experimentalism. He did not like teaching and spent his time largely reading and brooding (often undergoing long periods of acute depression). Finally, he could not take it any more and resigned his job at the end of 1931 and left Ireland. For the next six years, he wandered in exile from place to place–London, Paris, Germany–in search of a home and a vocation. At one time, he even contemplated going to Moscow to study cinema under Eisenstein and Pudovkin.

These were difficult years for Beckett, psychologically and physically (he had not been keeping good health) as well as financially. However, he continued to write. In 1934 he published a collection of short stories under the title *More Pricks Than Kicks*. The book was banned in Ireland because its title–from Christ's statement: 'I am Jesus whom thou persecutest: it is hard for thee to kick against the pricks' (*Acts of the Apostles* 9:5)–was considered blasphemous. The story relates the adventures of the protagonist, Belacqua Shuah, in and around Dublin. In this anti-heroic protagonist, whose name derives from the Fourth Canto of Dante's *Purgatorio*, we can see 'a first sketch of the heroes of Beckett's mature fiction, bumping around in a cosmos where nothing synchronises nor harmonises' (Kenner, 1973, 51).

Although, a year later, he published a collection of poems, *Echo's Bones*, Beckett's main endeavour was to write in the novel form. His first attempt at extended fiction produced the unsatisfactory *Dream of Fair to Middling Women*. It was only towards the end of his vagabond period that Beckett succeeded in writing his first proper novel, *Murphy*. Set in London, the novel focused on what was to become one of the most persistent preoccupations of his work–namely, the Cartesian duality between the mind and the body.

In 1937, after extensive travel through Germany, Beckett gave up his wandering and settled down in Paris where he lived for the rest of his life. He started writing in French as well as English–a fact that Hugh Kenner attributes to a schizophrenic division in Beckett's temperament between 'the gentle comedian', who is prominently present in his early fiction and 'the morbid solipsist', who becomes dominant in his mature French fiction of the post-war years.[3] During the next two years, he wrote several poems in French and made his first (unsuccessful) attempt at writing a play in English.[4] With a few publications to his credit, Beckett was more settled. He was now resolved to make a career of writing. Also, he had found a companion in a young French pianist, Suzanne Dumesnil, whom he later married.

Worsening Political Climate and Beckett's Indifference

While Beckett was busy sorting out his life, the political situation in Europe had deteriorated alarmingly. Memories of the First War and the Great Depression were still strong when the danger of the second large-scale conflict became imminent following the rise of

Hitler in Germany, fascism in Italy, and the civil war in Spain. These developments agitated most minds. Social awareness and political activity pervaded not only personal conversations and actions but also writing and publishing. But Beckett tried to be completely apolitical, in life as well as in his writings. He carefully avoided all political discussions and sought to eliminate or suppress all social references from his work. He believed that "artists had no business concerning themselves with anything but art, and politics–an anathema to him–was the least of his concerns" (Bair, 133). His view of art itself, as expressed in his book on Proust, was consciously subjectivist and anti-realist: 'For the artist, the only possible hierarchy in the world of objective phenomenon is represented by a table of their coefficients of penetration, that is to say, in terms of the subject." His mature writing was concerned, not with the larger, shared experiences of men and women in society but rather with the inner experiences of the unassimilated, and unassimilable, individual.

As mentioned above, before settling down in Paris, Beckett travelled through Germany for six months. He visited art galleries and met a number of people, many of them Jewish. It is a measure of Beckett's consciously cultivated quietism that although he must have noticed the Nazi persecution of the Jews, he did not express any outrage or made any critical reference to it in his public statements or writings of the period. "it is almost as though Beckett moved through a phantom country in which he was the only occupant, paintings were only objects, and museums and galleries the only buildings" (Bair, 133).

However, in the light of the new evidence brought forth by Knowlson, it appears that this unconcern was a deliberate public posture. It was not as if Beckett lacked humanity, or that he really did not care for or even register, all the suffering, misery and unfreedom that he encountered during his German tour. For, drawing upon Beckett's German diaries and notebook, Knowlson notes that Beckett was indeed saddened by what he saw and heard during his tour of Germany. According to Knowlson, Beckett was not interested in the political implications of Nazism, but he did feel disturbed by the "human injustices being perpetrated by the Nazi regime." His notations in the diaries reveal his disdain for what he mockingly referred to as the "interminable harangues" of Hitler, Goering and Goebbels, as well as his irritation at people constantly greeting one another with 'Heil Hitler'. His comments also reflect his concern for the constraints that the Jewish artists were forced to work under (Knowlson, 222-23).

There are also many instances of Beckett helping out friends and even strangers in financial or emotional distress. For example, Knowlson cites an interesting story of Beckett befriending an impoverished, out of work tailor in Germany and eventually allowing him to stitch him an evening suit at considerable cost, knowing full well that he was being taken for a ride. He wrote in his diary, "Curious that I can court a person that essentially I shudder away from. My need of the sick and evil." After much delay, when the requisitioned suit finally arrived, it was, in Beckett's own words, "of grotesque cut, coat too big, and trousers too short, but blue." Beckett wrote to the tailor saying, "the suit is lovely except that it doesn't fit anywhere" (Knowlson 236-37). Thus Beckett, it seems, combined two very distinct, almost mutually incompatible, identities as a person and as a writer. It is as if his personal life and his writings belonged in two mutually exclusive realms. Reading about him, one cannot help being struck by his humanity, compassion, generosity and kindness to others. At the same time, the figure behind his writings, the mind that defines and shapes his novels and plays, particularly since after the Second World War, comes across as fiercely private, entirely self-absorbed, self-enclosed, obstinately and systematically eschewing any reference or direct relation to the larger collective and rational world of society and history.

Joining the Resistance

When Beckett returned to Paris, the possibility of a war loomed large on Europe's political horizon. Writers and artists of various artistic and political persuasions were increasingly feeling compelled by the circumstances to take a position *vis-a-vis* the growing political turmoil. In the beginning, Beckett continued to maintain his characteristic posture of indifference. However, when Paris fell to the Nazis and the German forces occupied Paris in 1940, Beckett found it impossible to sit by idly while his close friends were being arrested or killed by the Gestapo. So he joined an underground resistance cell. According to Knowlson, Beckett did not need much persuasion to join the Resistance. "He had followed the rise of Nazism in the 1930s with fascination, growing disgust, and finally, horror. He had dipped with revulsion into Hitler's *Mein Kampf* and recognised the racial hatred at the roots of national socialism." (Knowlson, 278).

He and his partner, Suzanne, joined the cell called Gloria SMH. Beckett's role involved collating and typing information about the German troop movement brought to him on scraps of paper by many different secret informants. Beckett would then take it to a Greek photographer who turned the type sheets into microfilms to be smuggled to England to be used by the Allied forces (Knowlson, 282). In 1942, their underground group was busted and many of its members were arrested. He and Suzanne were forced to flee in a hurry and, after a few days of hiding at different places, left Paris and eventually settled in a small mountain village called Roussillon in unoccupied France. During their exile in that village, Beckett continued to help the resistance fighters by hiding weapons in his house. After the war was over his contribution was recognised and he was honoured with the Croix de Guerre. However, he never talked about his role in the Resistance and dismissed it as "boy scout stuff".[5] Nor did he allow any sense of political involvement to enter into his writings, which, in fact, became even more consciously apolitical and subjectivist than before.

Beckett spent two and a half terribly lonely and depressing years in Roussillon. He was trapped in a small place, away from friends and books, in a situation of terrifying uncertainty. He worked as a farmhand in a farmer's fields during the day and wrote during the evening. It is said that Beckett had a nervous breakdown soon after arriving in Roussillon. However, Knowlson finds these reports doubtful. "I have found no evidence at all to support such a claim from those who knew him well in Roussillon. But it would have certainly been surprising if he and Suzanne had not been subject to feelings of deep depression. After all, they had just come through an extremely traumatic series of events ..." (Knowlson, 294).

The result of Beckett's creative endeavour during the Roussillon years was his second novel, *Watt*, which also happens to be the last novel he wrote originally in English. The story of a solitary figure, *Watt* is more inward then *Murphy*. Beckett says that he wrote it as "a game, a means of staying sane, a way to keep my hand in." The novel, although it makes no direct use of the author's own experience, is nonetheless rooted in that experience insofar as it analyses what Kenner has described as 'the grim business of survival amidst uncertainties, ambiguities" (Kenner 1973, 73).

All that he went through since his return from Germany, including the terrifying experience of being incarcerated in a small village surrounded on all sides by a raging, brutal war, had a profound and lasting influence on all that Beckett wrote in the subsequent period. As Knowlson observes, it is difficult to imagine the work "he produced in the creative maelstrom of the immediate post-war period without the experiences of those five years. It was one thing to appreciate fear, danger, anxiety, and deprivation intellectually. It was quite another to live them himself, as he had done at the time he was stabbed or when he was in hiding or on the run. ... Many of the features of Beckett's later prose and plays arise directly from his experiences of radical uncertainty, disorientation, exile, hunger and need. Humour had proved, however, a strong lifeline many times before. And in occupied Paris, in Roussillon, and in St. Lo, it became–with an appreciation of life's simplest pleasures–one of the few things that made life at all tolerable" (318).

Returning to Paris

Returning to Paris shortly after the German surrender in 1945, Beckett virtually shut himself up in his apartment and devoted himself entirely to writing. The next four years was his most productive period. It was on the work of this period that his reputation today rests. Writing with ease and immense confidence, and exclusively in French, he produced in rapid succession four *novellas* (*The End*, *First Love*, *The Calmative*, and *The Expelled*), four novels (*Mercier and Camier*, *Molloy*, *Malone Dies*, and *The Unnamable*– the last three constituting a trilogy), two plays (*Eletburia* and *Waiting for Godot*), several poems, thirteen texts (later published under the title *Texts for Nothing*), and some art criticism.[6]

Soon after the war, Beckett had visited his mother in Ireland. During that visit, he had a "revelation" which is of crucial importance to a fuller understanding of his subsequent work. This revelation finds its way into the fragmentary recording of Krapp's "vision" in the 1957 play, *Krapp's Last Tape*: "...clear to me at last that the dark I have always struggled to keep under is in reality my most [Krapp curses, switches off, winds tape forward, switches on again]–unshatterable association until my dissolution of storm and night with the light of the understanding and the fire.", Darkness here means, explains Knowlson, "the darkness of an inner world... as extending to a whole zone of being..." Beckett's revelation also meant that "he would draw hence forward on his own inner world for his subjects; outside reality would be refracted through the filter of his own imagination...; rational contradictions would be allowed in; and the imagination would be allowed to create alternative worlds to those of conventional reality" (Knowlson, 319).

Critics have tended to regard this "vision" as some kind of a mystical or metaphysical experience–an almost divine revelation or epiphany. However, Casanova discounts this view of a sudden enlightenment and argues that "Beckett's 'vision' was at once the result of a very long process and the outline of a practical (one might almost say 'technical') solution to an aesthetic impulse. For him this unique moment, whose trace he wished to preserve ... unquestionably signalled a concrete way out of the literary aporia he was imprisoned in for many years. The solution hit upon was so satisfying that it enabled him to start work straight away. Accordingly, from this famous night in 1946 dates Beckett's first great creative period, which he called 'the siege in the room'" (78).

Beckett's post-war fiction marks a culmination of his development towards a fully interiorised and monologised form of the novel. Beckett decided at this time that the "dark he had struggled to keep under" should become the main inspiration and material of his writings. This had a two-fold implication: firstly, "that all his writings would henceforth begin from within himself", and secondly, "that no clearly defined fictional character would be needed to tell these stories, as no distancing is necessary between the teller and his tale" (Bair, 354). The result is a steady elimination of external reality from Beckett's fiction. The distinction between the external and the internal worlds, which characterised his early fiction, is thus abolished in the *nouvelles* and the trilogy by eliminating externalising details such as plot, character, and spatio-temporal setting. The third person, omniscient narrator of *More Pricks Than Kicks* and *Murphy* is abandoned in favour of the first person narrator, and the four *nouvelles* present a series of arbitrary, disjunctive memories, punctuated by an unnamed narrator's own commentaries. This already introspective form is accentuated in the trilogy, in which the first person narrator, or 'the narrator/narrated', as Beckett calls this new character, talks exclusively about himself. This narrator/narrated is not only nameless, but also timeless and placeless, and, as Ruby Cohn has observed, "he often feels languageless through all his talk" (Cohn 1973, 100).

The Unnamable, the last novel in the trilogy, has been described as a 'zero-book'–that is, a book about Nothing–and as 'really about the obsessive-compulsive need for words" (Kenner 1973, 112; Bair, 400). It ends in an impasse. 'I can't go on, I'll go on" are its last words. Several years later, Beckett remarked: 'At the end of my work, there's nothing but dust–the namable. In the last book, *L'Innomable*, there's complete disintegration. No "I", no "have", no "being", no nominative, no accusative, no verb. There's no way to go on.' Having arrived at this dead end he found it difficult for many years to write fiction and, instead, turned his attention to writing plays.

Beckett's first completed plays, the jettisoned *Eleutheria* and *Waiting for Godot*, were written between the three novels of the trilogy. *Eleutheria*, about a young man's revolt against his bourgeois family, was written between *Molloy* and *Malone Dies*, while *Waiting for Godot* was written between *Malone Dies* and *The Unnamable*. He wrote these plays, he said, as an interesting diversion from the 'awful depression the prose led me into'. But ironically, it was *Godot* that brought its middle-aged author an international reputation. Although Beckett, for a long time, saw himself as primarily a novelist who also wrote drama, he is better known today as a playwright who also wrote novels.

Beckett's drama followed the same trajectory of development as his prose fiction. The same process of increasing interiorisation becomes evident as one reads his plays in chronological order. In *Eleutheria* (the Greek word for 'freedom'), he had written a clumsy, conventional play about a young man's efforts to free himself from the constrictions and restraints of his bourgeois family. He used three acts, seventeen characters and three different sets to write it. In *Godot*, the process of dimunition and disintegration had already set in, as Beckett devised a circular, repetitive form to dramatise a static situation in two identical acts. However, despite long and frequent pauses and the local inconsequentiality of dialogue and activity, the play contains a great wealth of gestural and verbal energy which makes it an exciting theatrical experience. But as we move through his subsequent plays, *Endgame*, *Krapp's Last Tape* and *Happy Days*, to the later ones like *Not I*, *That Time* and *Play*, we find Beckett perfecting an increasingly monologic form. Instead of the so-called 'pseudo-couples', whose interdependence as well as the closed situation in which they were placed, provided key structural elements in *Godot* and *Endgame*, the latter plays highlight the nameless shadowy figure of the solitary and inward individual inhabiting the twilight realm between consciousness and oblivion. The figure's confrontation with its own consciousness, mind, or memory–externalised as 'voices' from the past, within or beyond–provides the mainspring of drama in these later plays. Consequently, there are no characters, no real dialogue, no setting, and no development in them–just an abstract and undefined subject confronting its own subjectivity.

Waiting for Godot: Form and Meaning

Waiting for Godot, which is now universally recognised as a contemporary classic, was written in 1948, and was first staged in a small theatre in Paris in 1953 where it ran for 400 performances and was later transferred to another theatre. Since then it has been translated into almost every language and has been performed at least once in every major country of the world.

The most striking thing about this play is its innovative formal design. From the beginning Beckett was fascinated by the modernist experiments in form and style. He was particularly impressed by what he regarded as the perfect fusion of structure and content in Proust and Joyce. He wrote admiringly of Joyce's *Work in Progress*: "Here form is content, content is form...His writing is not about something: it is that something itself". Beckett's own work can be regarded as a relentless quest for a form which would not merely incarnate the experience that he wished to express but would become that experience itself. This quest led him, in his mature fiction, to a style of writing which, deliberately and systematically eschewing all reference to the external world of social and historical experience, became increasingly interiorised and auto-referential.

Waiting for Godot was Beckett's first successful attempt at this kind of writing in drama. For all its apparent haphazardness, it is conceived with a great deal of attention to detail. Indeed, its very haphazardness, as also the utter simplicity and austerity of its basic situation and of the artistic means employed, are integral to its formal design. This design is conceived so as to be indistinguishable from the experience it embodies. The result is an extraordinarily powerful play whose power derives precisely from its skilful blending of form and meaning, dramaturgic structure and cognitive experience.

The play is formulated in such a way that, on the one hand, there is a certain emptiness precisely at those places–such as plot, character, dramatic speech, setting, etc.–where one would conventionally look for meaning, and, on the other, the cognitive emphasis moves from the immediate dramatic interest to some ultimate philosophical horizon beyond history and society. Two tramps of indefinite identity wait at an indefinite place for an uncertain appointment with somebody called Godot who never comes. His identity–indeed the very reality of his existence–is in serious doubt. In the course of the play, he is perceived in various ways: Saviour, God, a vindictive tyrant, a rich employer, somebody who has the tramps' 'future in his hand...at least [their] immediate future'. In their attempts to solve this mystery, critics have searched Beckett's own life, history, and etymology without being able to establish definitively who or what 'Godot' might mean. Beckett's own angry response to this has been that if he knew who Godot was he would have said so in the play.

Meanwhile, the play as well as the figure of Godot has been interpreted in different ways by different people. For example, a group of German prison inmates found a strong reflection of their own situation in the play. The prisoner who translated the play into German and produced it with and for his fellow inmates wrote to Beckett in a letter that he was writing from "a prison where so many thieves, forgers, toughs, homos, crazy men and killers spend this bitch of a life waiting...and waiting...and waiting. Waiting for what? Godot? Perhaps." He went on to explain that the prisoners saw themselves and their own individual predicaments echoed in Gogo and Didi's wait for something to come along to give their lives meaning. For him, the play offered a lesson in the value of human solidarity and brotherhood even in the direst of situations. "We are all waiting for Godot and do not know that he is already here. Yes, here. Godot is my neighbour in the cell next to mine. Let us do something to help him then, change the shoes that are hurting him!" (Quoted in Knowlson, 369).

It is in fact a measure of Beckett's masterly craftsmanship that, despite all its artistic simplicity and technical austerity, the play is so richly layered that it readily lends itself to very different interpretations. This is because Beckett has not allowed Godot to represent any one idea, ideal or person. Instead, he is made to come across as Absence itself. Like the 'boy' outside in *Endgame*, he is the absent figure whose non-presence is the play's centre. He is also the name for that emptiness which one finds at the heart of the play after cutting through all its immediate noise and activity. He is also, by analogy, that "dark", that "void" that Beckett found at the centre of human existence after it is stripped of all its social and historical specificities. This leaves people free to give whatever name or identity they like to this absent figure.

Significantly, even the tramps who wait for Godot as well as the wayfaring couple whom they encounter have no fixed individual identities, barring a few biological, temperamental, and situational traits. They are perceived "at this place, at this moment of time," not as four distinct personalities but as two radically truncated and grossly generalised images of all "mankind", which, in Lucky's phrase, is "seen to waste and pine, waste and pine". Incapable of any significant action or initiative, they imply an utterly pessimistic view of man as a helpless victim of his ontological fate.[7]

The play has a symmetrical structure like a mathematical formula in which one part balances the other. This symmetry is evident, first of all, in what may be called the device of coupling, of conceiving things in pairs. The play seems to have been constructed primarily on sets of binaries. It has two acts which purport to dramatise two consecutive evenings in the life of its central characters. It employs two sets of characters and each set is a pair. Interestingly, even the messenger boy has a brother.

The relationship between and within these pairs is not always one of identity and harmony but also one of opposition and tension. This generates a pattern of binary oppositions and arranges its emphases contrapuntally. Each of the two central couples in the play, for example, is conceived so indivisibly that it functions as a single agential unit: while Pozzo and Lucky are physically tied to each other, Vladimir and Estragon are unable to part company despite their frequently expressed wish. Thus the play has not four characters but two agential units. The two units are sharply in contrast to each other, each epitomising a mode of being which is counterposed to the other. The tramps are compelled to a futile and perpetual waiting and are imprisoned, as it were, in space, Pozzo and Lucky, on the other hand, are committed to an equally futile and perpetual wandering, and are confined within a temporal prison. Mutual love and care between the tramps is also in contrast to the exploitative relationship that the wayfarers symbolise.

What complicates this simple pattern of inter-couple contrasts is the further tension and contrast that is offered within each agential unit. Estragon's easy defeatism and despair (he seems to be waiting primarily for death) and his preoccupation with immediate physical needs (hunger, sleep) are contrasted to Vladimir's almost obstinate optimism and intellectual preoccupation with philosophical questions. This contrast makes them mutually complementary, but it also adds a contrapuntal dimension to their relationship. This becomes particularly evident in their exchanges which often take on the quality of a verbal ping-pong. The contrast within the other major couple is mainly situational. While Pozzo is a domineering, bullying master, Lucky is a treacherous but abjectly obedient slave. A similar situational contrast is offered between the boy who looks after the goats and is treated well and his brother who looks after the sheep and is often beaten.

The contrapuntal arrangement of emphases so pervades the play that the text itself alternates throughout between the opposite poles of the farcical and the tragic, routinised speech and ponderous silence, change and permanence, and, as we shall see later, between theatrical vitality and contemplative stasis. The binary opposition that underlines the play and organises all the other oppositions into a unified experience of absolute ambivalence is that between hope and despair. The play's shape seems to be based on Beckett's favourite quotation from St. Augustine: "Do not despair, one of the thieves was saved; do not presume, one of the thieves was damned." In this see-saw formulation, as also in the play, hope and despair, prospects of salvation and damnation, are held in an even balance, almost cancelling each other out. Right at the beginning of the play, Vladimir applies his thinking to the matter of the Biblical thieves. He tries to assess his and Gogo's prospects in the light of the information available on the thieves. The thought that one of the thieves was saved is found reassuring: "It's a reasonable percentage", he says.But as he goes on to examine this information in the light of certain other facts, he finds that, out of the four Evangelists present on the scene, "only one speaks of a thief being saved," another says that both of them abused Christ (thereby implying the possibility that both were damned), while the remaining do not mention any thieves at all. This shortness of the odds destabilises his hope, shakily propped up, as it was on a mere fifty per cent chance.

There is, however, a crucial difference between St. Augustine's theological formulation and Beckett's non-theological one. The former, while rejecting both presumption and despair, implicitly affirms a third alternative, that of faith in divine will and justice. No such positive alternative emerges in *Waiting for Godot*. Imprisoned within a closed situation, Didi and Gogo perpetually alternate between assurance and doubt: Are they at the right place? On the right day? Is the tree really a willow? Are the boots in the second act Estragon's? Is Pozzo Godot? Is Vladimir's name Mr. Albert? Almost everything in the play is in doubt, and nothing is conclusively resolved.

The sense of closure and nullity is reinforced further by the play's repetitive rhythm. The entire play, as Ruby Cohen observes, is "woven with repetition". (Cohn 1980, 98) Act Two is a repetition of Act One. In each act we are offered basically the same sequence: the tramps, reunite, wait, contrive ways of passing time, encounter Pozzo and Lucky, receive Godot's disappointing message, contemplate suicide, decide to leave and do not move. Some variations, particularly in regard to the tree and the physical condition of the wayfaring couple do occur, but they do not detract from our perception of the essential sameness and circularity of the situation. Even the routines with boots and hats, certain standard gestures like brooding, pacing and falling, and arguments about the correctness of place and time, identity of Pozzo and Lucky, events of the previous evening, etc. occur in both acts, as do Estragon's need for food and sleep and references to Vladimir's bladder problem. The play also contains a variety of verbal repetitions, the most important of which are 'Nothing to be done,' and 'We're waiting for Godot./Ah!' which recur throughout and function as refrains.

Beckett once said that he wrote the play in two acts because one act would have been too little and three acts too many. It is true that if the situation and sequence were dramatised only once it would not have had the same effect as its redramatisation in the second act. For, the presentation of the entire sequence twice and the repetitive character of the verbal and gestural activities within that sequence imply an endless and unchanging process–repetition ad infinitum. Besides, without any possibility of progress or break from this closed circularity, this process also becomes mechanical and meaningless–repetition ad absurdum. Epitomised in Vladimir's round song (at the beginning of Act Two) this meaningless, everlasting circularity intensifies the feeling of stasis and closure, which is reinforced by the play's spatio-temporal dimension.

Space and Time

Beckett's play is different from realist drama, where the locales are clearly established through solid sets and physical objects. It is also different from any non-realist or emblematic style of representation in which, although the stage remains bare, the physical environment of action can be imagined through verbal descriptions and gestures. In Beckett, the place where the tramps wait for Godot is totally without any markers of identity, verbal or physical. Beckett's stage direction identifies it as a "country road", but, barring a rather surrealistic tree, there is no other physical feature to evoke that identification in performance. Rather, the play's spatio-temporal location comes across, in Kenner's interesting phrase, as 'nowhere-nowhen.'

Such non-specific settings are a common feature of Beckett's drama. They 'enable him to isolate his characters from any social reality that might deflect attention from the generalised human situation he is portraying" (Duckworth, 47-79). What strikes the spectator foremost is the almost absolute barrenness of the stage-space. "It's indescribable. Its like nothing. There's nothing. There's a tree," says Vladimir looking around him. The strange happenings (sudden rise of the moon, sudden sprouting of leaves), strange characters and their frequently arbitrary and irrational behaviour further underscore the abstract quality of this setting. The text describes it as void or nothing. In answer to Vladimir's needling question: "And where were we yesterday according to you?", Estragon says: "How do I know? In another compartment. There's no lack of void". Similarly, trying to persuade Gogo that the opportunity of amusing themselves with Pozzo and Lucky should not be missed, Didi says: "In an instant all will vanish and we'll be alone once more, in the midst of nothingness".

What surrounds this lonely, empty space on all sides is further nothingness. This is perhaps why, strangely for a play so full of gestural energy, Estragon cannot be permitted any gesture while saying "Over there". This is also why there is nowhere for a terrified Estragon to hide in and his "only hope left is to disappear". And above all, this is precisely why the tramps say, "Let's go" and do not move at the end of each Act. They have nowhere to go. They are tied to this nothingness and embody it.

Nothingness, by definition, cannot be a place. Nor can it be likened to the mythical chaos out of which God is said to have created a universe. Rather, it is absolute emptiness, a vacuum, an absence. As such it is an abstract (philosophical) idea rather than a place. In *Godot*, this idea takes on the quality of a metaphysical or numinous place whose reigning deity is Godot or Absence. The central paradox of this space in this play is that it is perceived simultaneously as physically boundless–Estragon's gesture towards the universe is inclusive as is the tramps' frequent scanning of the horizon–and as psychologically and spiritually claustrophobic (because it is immutable and devoid of alternative possibilities).

The motif of being imprisoned in a vast or narrow space without complete freedom of movement is common to all of Beckett's plays. From the open, boundless space of *Godot*, through the enclosed shelter of *Endgame*, to the jars in *Play*, his characters are trapped within an increasingly narrow space and remain incapable of extended mobility which alone would have given them a chance to escape from their miserable situations. In *Godot*, we have come a long way from Shakespeare's Hamlet who could be "bounded in a nutshell" and count himself "king of infinite space" (*Hamlet*, I, ii, 258-59). Set adrift, as it were, in infinite space, the tramps feel trapped in infinity. They have full freedom to do whatever they like except one most crucial freedom: the freedom to leave. Throughout, they try desperately and ingeniously to give themselves the impression that they "exist" and are "inexhaustible". But, like Hamlet, though on an altogether different level, they have 'bad dreams', and after every burst of activity, always reach the point of complete exhaustion. At such moments, they realise the utter futility of their endeavours, and that it is pointless to 'struggle' or 'wriggle' because the 'essential does not change'.

In normal human experience, space and time are organically linked. They constitute a continuum. However, in Beckett's contrapuntal dramaturgy the two coordinates of human experience seem to be in tension. Time (the fourth dimension of space, as a famous definition describes it) seem to be virtually non-existent for the space-bound tramps. With only the haziest fragments of memory and no future prospects, they exist in a static, perpetual present: "They all change. Only we can't". Nonetheless, imprisoned as they are in a static situation, their immediate concern (as well as a central concern of the play as a whole) is Time, "that double-headed monster of salvation and damnation", as Beckett described it in *Proust.* They contrive various games and routines to experience the passage of time, they speculate about their chances of perdition or deliverance as they wait in anxiety and anguish for the night to fall so that they are released from their immediate misery, even if only temporarily.

Thus, time is the main source at once of the tramps' hope and despair. Their only certainty, as Vladimir says, "is that hours are long, under these conditions, and constrain us to beguile them with proceedings which...may at first sight seem reasonable, until they become a habit". In other words, time for them has become a habit, and habit, as we are told a little later, is a "great deadener". This time, like the tramps' improvised 'proceedings', is repetitive and cyclical–an existential prisonhouse from which there is no escape.

In Beckett's superb craftsmanship, the waiting and changelessness of Gogo and Didi are balanced against Pozzo and Lucky's wanderings and changeability. Just as the former are tied to space, the latter–with their compulsion to be constantly moving, with Pozzo's obsession with time and his cries of 'On!'– are inseparably linked to time. That is why time stagnates and becomes slothful when Gogo and Didi are alone on the stage, and it becomes energetic and moves when they are in the company of the wayfaring couple. The fact, that the night falls suddenly after each encounter between the two couples, also suggests a closer association between the wanderers and temporality.

Pozzo and Lucky incarnate time's twin qualities of change and changelessness. They are the only ones in the play who change. Pozzo changes from his "wonderful sight" to complete blindness, and Lucky–who has already undergone a drastic change when we first see him from a teacher of "beautiful things" to an incoherent babbler–changes from a speaking animal to a dumb automaton who cannot even groan. These changes signify concrete human time on the level of individual existence and experience. This time moves, but, in Beckett's perception of it, it moves inexorably towards loss, devitalisation, and death; life itself is devalued as a brief flash of light that "gleams an instant" between birth and death. Significantly, even on the historical level–that is, on the level of collective existence and experience–this human time is perceived as a devitalising process in which man continues to "waste and pine".

Time's changelessness, its cyclical stasis, is signified in Pozzo and Lucky's perpetual wanderings. Travelling has become a deadening habit with them. They feel they are going somewhere; Pozzo even says, in the First Act, that he is taking Lucky to the fair to sell him. But they are actually going round and round in a circle.[8] They are thus trapped in the circular time of the universe. Gogo and Didi too are trapped within this unchanging circularity of time in which day and night follow each other cyclically.

- But night doesn't fall.
- It'll fall all of a sudden, like yesterday.
- Then it'll be night.
- And we can go.
- Then it'll be day again. (Pause. Despairing.) What'll we do, what'll we do?

In the ultimate or philosophical framework of the play this temporal circularity is perceived as stasis, a meaningless and everlasting repetition of seasons, days and hours. Pozzo, after he has lost his sight, and, with it, his "notion of time", realises this in his last speech:" Have you not done tormenting me with your accursed time? One day, is that not enough for you, one day like any other day?... One day we were born, one day we shall die, the same day, the same second..."

Thus, time's changes in the play are experienced as a static circularity. In this, Beckett's time is like T.S. Eliot's metaphor of the wheel which turns yet remains "forever still."[9] But, in direct contrast to Eliot, in Beckett there is no possibility of a redemption through a direct or vertical intervention by some transcendental power–a God or a Godot. For, in Beckett, physical nature follows its own cyclical movement–man is born, grows old and dies; the sun rises and sets; bare trees sprout leaves and will be bare again–but Godot, the only but irredeemably absent possibility of escape from this existential trap, never comes. It is at this level of the idea of emptiness and meaninglessness that space and time are coordinated in the play and give it its philosophical setting of 'nowhere-nowhen.'

It would seem practically impossible to write a play which has the abstract philosophical idea of nothingness as its subject as well as setting. But Beckett, with his characteristic innovativeness, has solved this problem by coupling the nothingness of the philosophical framework with the concrete, material reality and specificity of the stage-space, that is, the space of the play's performance in theatre. The two kinds of space are diametrically opposed to each other. While the play's philosophical framework is characterised, as already suggested, by its absolute and cosmic dimensions in which all spaces and times are collapsed into one transcendental idea of the void (its 'nowhere-nowhen' is synonymous with 'allwhere-allwhen'), the stage space is characterised by its immediacy, its insistence on the dramatic 'here-and-now'. Furthermore, Beckett's philosophical space is a given and unalterable condition, within which man is a helpless prisoner and all human endeavours are devalued as mere meaningless routine. Contrary to this, the basic quality of the stage space is precisely its alterability and its potential to invest any action with significance. The theatrical space, moreover, implies an image of man as demiurge, an 'actor' who through his actions creates and recreates meaning.

These two kinds of space are juxtaposed in *Godot* and constitute yet another feature of the play's contrapuntal dramaturgy. The play's blatant theatricality enhances our perception of the immediacy and enormous possibilities of the stage-space. As characters repeatedly indulge in histrionics, we see how meaning (however fragmentary and peripheral to the totality of the play's cognitive experience) is produced on the immediate theatrical level of this ultimately (philosophically) 'meaningless' play.

Theatricality

The *sine qua non* of all dramatic writing is the theatre. Ever since the time of Aeschylus, plays are written with a view to putting them on stage, and their value is centrally linked to their stageability. It is important to remember this in 'reading' drama because a common flaw in the dominant critical approaches, particularly since the 19th century, is that they tend to treat drama primarily as literature or verbal text. Concentrating almost exclusively on dramatic speech, to the neglect of the other elements of theatre's composite language, these approaches provide an explanation which is often at variance with the experience a play actually communicates in performance.

Theatre's composite language employs a variety of means, or sign-systems, to signify or communicate meaning. It includes not only speech but also non-verbal elements such as setting, lighting, movement, gesture, etc. It is through a complex interaction of all these that meaning is produced in theatre. A more adequate reading of drama therefore, is one that remains constantly alert to this interaction, to the play's possibilities in performance. This approach is helped by the modern practice of including in the dramatic texts the parts known as 'stage-directions' which enable us to visualise a play's performance.[10]

Such an approach is particularly useful in dealing with a text like *Waiting for Godot*, in which the verbal text is relatively sparse and fragmentary, consisting largely of snatches of one line or one word exchanges, separated by long ponderous pauses. Much of the play's textual space is occupied by Beckett's stage directions which specify expressions, movements and gestures. The gestures and movements are often non-verbal pantomime. In actual performance, all these non-verbal activities take up a good deal of the play's duration and make it remarkably rich in theatrical energy.

The abundance of theatricality in *Godot* both results from and cleverly compensates for the plays' emptiness in other respects. Sent out on to an almost bare stage, without the conventionally available support from localised sets, handy objects, identity-fixing costumes, or even a logically developing plot or dialogue, Gogo and Didi (as well as the actors playing these parts) have no option but to draw upon their own ingenuity and resources–mainly bodies and voices–to keep themselves as well the spectators entertained. In doing this, they go through a whole range of dramatic postures, gestures and vocal modulations, often explicitly theatricalising themselves by assuming and playing different roles. Thus, from Vladimir's Chaplinesque gait at the beginning to the hilarious scene at the end when he and a trouserless Estragon pull at a chord to test its strength, from the tragicomic posture of standing motionless with drooping heads, dangling arms and sagging knees to running helter-skelter in panic, or from Gogo's 'feeble' appeal to Didi for help to his screaming 'at the top of his voice' for God's pity, the play demonstrates a richly varied repertory of actions which include standard vaudeville and circus items ranging from cringing, crouching, and huddling to staggering, tumbling, and falling limply.

All this has the effect of enhancing our perception of the play's theatricality, which is further strengthened by the improvisations and music-hall routines with which the tramps try to pass the time. Most of their verbal duets is sheer role-playing. Sometimes they seem to be enacting a conjugal situation: caring, nagging, arguing or simply getting bored with each other. Sometimes they assume the stock vaudeville roles of the 'straight man' and the 'comic man', made famous by Laurel and Hardy:

- Poor Pozzo.
- I knew it was him.
- Who
- Godot.
- But it's not Godot.
- It's not Godot?
- It's not Godot.
- Then who is it?
- It's Pozzo.

At one point, Vladimir suggests that he and Gogo "play at Pozzo and Lucky," and goes on to "do" Lucky. A little later they enact a series of situations beginning with polite formality ("No no, after you./ No no, you first"), then going through an argument turning abusive ("That's the idea, let's abuse each other"), and ending in reconciliation ("Now let's make up"). The play is so dense with these micro performances that sometimes it is difficult to tell if the tramps are 'playing' or in earnest. An example is the scene in Act Two when Lucky, Pozzo, Vladimir and Estragon fall down in a heap. They claim that they are unable to get up by themselves. However, a little later they get up quite easily and Gogo describes probably both the process of getting up as well as the act of collapsing in a heap as "Child's play".

Seemingly without fixed roles and fixed texts, Gogo and Didi feel compelled to improvise constantly and try a little bit of everything, at random. However, the most sustained example of histrionics in the play is offered by Pozzo and Lucky who are like the travelling players of old times. Their entry is heralded by a "terrible cry" off-stage and their exits are preceded by Pozzo's command of "On!" The tramps, who provide the immediate audience for their performances, themselves regard the experience as an interesting pastime. With his commanding presence, "terrifying voice," "enormous laugh," vapouriser, and declamatory style, Pozzo is an arch performer who pompously announces himself to his audience: "I present myself: Pozzo." Before beginning his act, he demands complete attention; "I am ready. Is everybody listening?".

After the performance he wants it rated: "How did you find me?... Good? Fair? Middling? Poor? Positively bad?" As Beckett's frequent stage-directions indicate, Pozzo's performances are packed with gestural energy. He puts on a variety of roles: slave-driving master, orator, bully, friend, tragic figure. He speaks in a variety of voices: terrifyingly, poetically, affably, sobbingly. He performs a number of actions from eating voraciously to tragically rolling on the ground and writhing in pain and grief. And he strikes a number of attitudes alternating between peremptory, ceremonious and magnanimous.

Besides being a performer, himself, Pozzo is also a whip-wielding ring-master who brings in a trained animal; (in this case a human one) on leash, whom Estragon later remembers as a "lunatic" who "played the fool." On his master's command, Lucky dances and performs his thinking act. Interestingly, during Lucky's excruciating thinking act, Didi, Gogo, and Pozzo himself as audience, go through four distinct stages of response, ending in a "general outcry." During all this we, the play's real audience, watch simultaneously the performers and the behaviour of their immediate onstage audience, thus becoming part of what Hugh Kenner has described as a "hierarchy of watchers and watched."

This theatrical vigour must have been a novel experience for the play's first audiences. For, in the West, such blatant theatricality, although quite common in the plebeian forms of theatre, had not been witnessed in serious drama for a long time. Ever since the rise of naturalism, in the mid-19th century the emphasis in dominant drama and theatre had been on illusionism: that is, on the practice of concealing the play's artfulness (or, more precisely, its *playfulness*, through the "pretence of unarranged and untheatrical actuality" (Fergusson, 191).[11]

The most fundamental convention of illusionism required that the spectators be treated as virtually absent, as the proverbial 'fourth wall' in order to communicate and sustain the illusion that the dramatised world–characters, situations, problems, physical environment–was 'real.' This had the effect of making the spectators identify themselves entirely and uncritically with the dramatised experience. It was in conscious opposition to this illusionism of the dominant tradition in Western drama, best exemplified by Ibsen, that the German playwright, Bertolt Brecht developed the theory and practice of 'epic' theatre that is, a theatre that encourages the spectator to view a play not from *within* but from *outside* the dramatised experience; in other words, from a position of critical detachment. Brechtian dramaturgy and theatre, like the numerous non-illusionist forms that it drew upon, delighted in making direct contact with the audience, in frankly acknowledging its presence.

The blatant theatricality of *Waiting for Godot* would suggest a non-illusionist theatre. The author's use of non-illusionist formal devices like the aside, soliloquy and songs, further strengthen this impression. However, this impression is deceptive because, within the strictly self-enclosed structure of the play these asides and soliloquies function not as gestures acknowledging the audience's presence but as attempts at greater inclusiveness–so that the auditorium loses its separate identity and becomes part of the play's fictive world, part of the same terrifying emptiness that surrounds the tramps on all sides and provides no sanctuary to a frightened Estragon. This kind of an inclusive gesture towards the auditorium is more reminiscent of Pirandello than of Brecht.[12]

Besides, despite the aura of spontaneous theatricality that the play possesses, its theatricality remains fully controlled and enclosed *within* the confines of what, for want of a better word, may be called the play's thematic frame of *infinite void*. Indeed, it is an integral element in the feeling of boredom, emptiness and meaninglessness that the play as a whole dramatises. All its histrionics, improvisations, antics and verbal games are merely a series of diversions that the tramps consciously and pathetically contrive to while away the time. As such, they are only improvised fillers for an empty time. They also cleverly fill up an otherwise static and eventless play about waiting. For, as Kenner observes, Beckett has "cunningly doubled his play with the absence of a play" (Kenner 1961, 136). Moreover, in the overall design of the play, the sequences of vigorous theatricality are balanced with those dull and gloomy periods when the tramps return to themselves and to an anguished awareness of their hopeless situation. This contrapuntal arrangement, in which bursts of energy and resourcefulness alternate throughout with moments of complete inertia and despair, has a dual effect. On the one hand, it deepens and intensifies the experience of despair, and, on the other, it allows the tramps' resourcefulness to be perceived as man's pathetic and altogether inconsequential endeavours to divert himself from thinking about his 'real' situation in the cosmos. Thus, theatricality, whose essence is vigour, movement and resourcefulness, becomes in Beckett's hands a device for dramatising a singularly devitalising view of human existence.

Reading Beckett, Historically

It is obvious that Godot defies paraphrasing and discussion in terms of the conventional categories of plot, character, theme, or even 'meaning.' The most fruitful approach to such a play is one which focuses on the totality of its experience and, rather than identifying completely and uncritically with that experience, situates it in history.

As Pascale Casanova has correctly cautioned us, it is futile and misleading to search Beckett's works for "any revelations about 'man', the 'world', 'Being', 'God', or 'existence'. The success of *Waiting for Godot* and its inclusion in the theatre of the absurd, she goes on to remark, "doubtless made a major contribution to such misunderstanding, by giving credence to the idea of a hidden meaning as an ultimate truth" (74). This sense of a "hidden meaning" is encouraged by the strong sense of a certain emptiness at the very centre of Godot. This emptiness is both formal and semantic. It is around this vacuity that the play as a whole is organised. It confronts Gogo and Didi all the time as they desperately try to escape or fill it with their verbal and gestural gimmicks. The same vacuity also confronts the spectator/reader and allows the play to be experienced as a passive contemplation of this emptiness. It is not an ordinary, everyday kind of feeling which one sometimes experiences, for example, in waiting for a letter, a friend, or event. Rather, it is that metaphysical emptiness that confronts one when all meaning, all reason, all hope seem to have been removed from life and existence. What is more, in the socio-historically non-specific and abstract terms of Beckettian dramaturgy–in which 'nowhere-nowhen' becomes synonymous with all places and all times and a pair of 'pseudo-couples' with all mankind–this experience is offered as a universal phenomenon, as the human condition.

Some writers tend to uncritically identify with Beckett's position and would have us see the play as an expression of the general human condition. It is important, however, to ask ourselves whether the experience of Gogo and Didi is a universal phenomenon true for all human beings at all times and in all situations. Or, in Darko Suvin's words: "Has the author, as many apologists claim, in his nightmares and fears just happened to hit upon some archetypal horrors of the self, presumably identical in–and relevant for–a Vietnamese peasant, a Yugoslav worker, a French intellectual, an American businessman...?" (Suvin, 214). We can go on adding to this list from our own specific perspective but the answer will firmly remain 'No." Because the world, and therefore, human experience are characterised by a plurality which are consequent upon the differences in historical and material circumstances of social and individual existence. It is to these differences that all ideas about man, world and reality–no matter how abstract and ahistorical–are ultimately linked in a complex relationship of cause and effect. This being so, all attempts to homogenise human experience into one universal category of the human experience are a negation of history. Furthermore, such a negation of history is usually itself a historical gesture in the sense of being a particular response, at the conscious or unconscious level, to some specific situation or experience; it often signifies the individual's flight, in difficult times, from the seemingly incomprehensible nightmare of history into some realm of pure, metaphysical abstraction.

The next question that arises is: if Godot is not an expression of a universal condition, then precisely whose perception of human condition does it express? Kenneth Tynan provides a clue in this respect. Writing about the plays in the Beckett-Ionesco tradition, he says they are "essentially Western, addressed to and written by members of a sophisticated intelligentsia in countries with a high standard of living. The question they pose could be summarised thus: once a man's physical needs are satisfied, what is the purpose of living?" (Tynan, 186). Tynan here relates correctly the philosophical orientation of this kind of drama to the point of view of a section of a socially smug and spiritually disturbed middle-class intelligentsia in the post-industrial Western societies. However, his remarks are too generalised. They imply a general accusation of complacent philosophising against these writers. He overlooks, for example, the important fact that most of the *avant-garde* writers, Beckett included, are vehemently anti-bourgeois in their conscious moral stance and that the sense of alienation and anguish that underlay their writings are often genuine and deeply felt. The unreality and irrationality in their artistic creation is deliberate and possibly a response to a world which appeared to have lost its reality and rationality.

In one way or another, all significant examples of modern European literature, particularly since the 19th century, respond to a world that seemed to be falling apart and becoming increasingly meaningless in the wake of the brutal advance of capitalism, rampant individualism and the consequent loss of community, large-scale devastations of the world wars, threat of a nuclear holocaust, and the destruction of the liberal traditions of hope and faith in man's innate goodness, rationality and progress. These writings, their individual richness notwithstanding, can be broadly classified in terms of their world views and ideological orientations, into three categories. One, the mythico-religious response (exemplified by writers like W.B. Yeats and T.S. Eliot), which sees hope only in a revival of religious faith and spiritual values, thus implying an escape into some glorified past or transcendental realm from the horrors of the present. Two, the historical, materialist response (best exemplified in Bertolt Brecht but also in, Bernard Shaw, Sean O'Casey, Mayakovsky, John Arden and Dario Fo) which tries to analyse and understand the existing situation historically and, asserting the changeability of the world, stresses the possibility and desirability of turning it into a happier place through collective effort. The third kind of response is what may be described as a subjective and idealist response that contemplates the world in abstract philosophical terms and finds it not only unchanging but also unchangeable. It usually ends up accepting meaninglessness, loneliness and disintegration as the immutable and universal condition of human existence itself.

All these responses were historically available in Beckett's time. It is significant that he chose the subjective-idealist alternative. In this he was influenced not only by his own psychopathological disposition towards morbid solipsism but also, and perhaps mainly, by certain philosophical and literary traditions of his time. The so-called Absurdist (or Existentialist) position, with which his name is often associated, is itself a specifically 20th century European development of what is generally recognised as a pessimistic tradition in Western philosophy, going back from Heidegger to Kierkegaard and Schopenhauer, and characterised by extreme subjectivism and hostility to dialectical thought (of Hegel and Marx), rationalism and history.[13] This tradition became particularly strong in the period between the two world wars and enjoyed wide influence among writers and artists. Its ideological influence is reflected in the feelings of *angst*, boredom, alienation, meaninglessness and fear that pervades a whole tradition of literary writing from Proust, Musil and Kafka to Camus, Sartre and, of course, Beckett.[14]

We have noted how Beckett's writing developed towards an increasingly interiorised and monologised form. This withdrawal into self was itself a response to the external conditions of his time—no doubt the deeply gloomy response of one, who for the most part, refused to be actively involved in any organised attempt to intervene in the situation with a view to altering it. Some of his non-literary writings of the mid-1930s clearly link this understanding of the existing situation to a preference for an irrational and subjectivist kind of art. For example, in a letter to a friend, he 'railed against the mechanistic age in which he found himself living and praised what he called "the deanthropomorphisation of the artist" (Bair, 192–23). He expressed his complete agreement with artists 'who chose to portray human beings as blobs of colour and form because he thought this intensified the dehumanisation of mankind.... People, he thought, were totally alone; there was no community of thought and feeling, only the inner man had any importance. Each was as alien to all others as to a protoplast or God, incapable of loving or hating anyone but himself."

This view of the world and art becomes crystallised, a few years later, into a consciously solipsistic position in an unpublished essay under the title 'Les Deux Besoins' ('The Two Needs'). Developing the idea of a totally subjectivist art, Beckett asserts that 'art results from the artist's quest to rid himself of extraneous knowledge in order to refine his perception into a clear, distilled version on the fundamental inner being: art comes from the abandonment of the macrocosm for the pursuit of the microcosm" (Bair, 294-45). It is this rejection of the macrocosm in favour of an exploration of the macrocosm that characterises the entire body of Beckett's writing. Subjectivism, despair and deliberate distortion or rejection of the external world of objective reality are some of its most persistent emphases. But they are not unique to Beckett and constitute an essential part of the modernist thinking which, as Lukacs points out, implies an image of man, not as a social being (Aristotle's *zoon politikon*), but as "by nature solitary, asocial, unable to enter into relationships with other human beings" (Lukacs, 20). An important and ironical consequence of this position in literature is that it leads not only to an attenuation of the objective reality but also to a fragmentation and eventual dissolution of the inner being (or subjectivity) itself, leaving nothing but a painful sense of emptiness in its wake. In Beckett's specific case, this is precisely what has happened. His subjectivism has led him to a morbid preoccupation with nothingness, to a conviction in his own words, "that there is nothing to express, nothing with which to express, nothing from which to express, no power to express, no desire to express, together with the obligation to express."[15]

It is this mysterious, inner obligation to express nothing, with nothing, and from nothing, that seems to be at work in *Waiting for Godot*.

NOTES

1. An earlier version of this chapter appeared as "Introduction" to the student edition of Samuel Beckett's *Waiting for Godot* published by Oxford University Press (New Delhi) in 1989.
2. Our main source for this part of the chapter are the two biographies of Beckett. Bair's work has the distinction of being the first detailed biography of the author. It was followed in 1996 by Knowlson's which has the status of the first authorised biography because the author was Beckett's chosen biographer.
3. See Kenner 1961, 56.
4. This first play dealt with Dr. Johnson's relationship with Mrs. Thrale. It was never completed and only published years later when Ruby Cohn included the incomplete text as an appendix to her book *Just Play*.
5. Nonetheless, talking about why he joined the Resistance, Beckett once said: 'I was so outraged by the Nazis, particularly by their treatment of the Jews, that I could not remain inactive.' (Bair, 308).
6. All these works were in French. They were translated into English by Beckett himself over the next several years. However, we have here used the English titles for the sake of convenience.
7. Soon after the war, a friend suggested to Beckett that he should write about the heroism of the people fighting against Hitler. Beckett's answer was: 'I'm not interested in stories of success, only failure.'
8. This impression of circularity in Pozzo and Lucky's wanderings is sometimes further strengthened in performance by making them enter from the same side in both Acts.
9. See Eliot's *Murder in the Cathedral*.
10. Earlier writers like Shakespeare had no need to write stage directions because they were connected with practical theatre and had some control over the performance of their plays. Moreover, they wrote directly for performance and not for publication. For a detailed discussion of this topic, see my "Drama and Theatre" elsewhere in this book.

11. It is significant that in the 19th century the word 'theatrical' itself acquired the pejorative sense of false, fake, or spurious.
12. As Duckworth has correctly observed, in Beckett's plays, 'the characters perform the function of each other's audience, and it is only for each other that they go on playing their parts, "since off the stage there is nothing, non-being". This includes the auditorium, and any director who makes the actors play out to the audience has not begun to understand that *we do not exist* to Estragon, or Hamm, or Winnie...' (49–50).
13. These three major European philosophers of the 19th century had one thing in common. All of them were anti-rationalists. Arthur Schopenhauer (1788-1860) opposed Hegel and regarded himself as a true successor to Kant. He propounded a philosophy of pessimism. Denying the possibility of scientific cognition and historical progress, he counterposed metaphysical idealism to the scientific understanding of the world and regarded blind and irrational 'will' as the world's essence. His ideal was the Buddhist 'nirvana', end of the will to live. In art, he opposed realism and valorised desireless and passive contemplation of artistic intuition. Beckett read Schopenhauer during the mid-30s. Almost likewise, Soren Kierkegaard (1813–55) believed that 'Truth is subjectivity' and counterposed his own subjectivist 'existential dialectics' against Hegel's dialectics. A supporter of individualism and moral relativism, he preached despondency, fear and hatred of the masses. Martin Heidegger (1889-1976), a neo-Kantian, was strongly influenced by Kierkegaard and was, centrally concerned with the problem of being which he links to temporality. Heidegger's thought, like that of Kierkegaard and Schopenhauer, is characterised by a profound pessimism and hostility to science and rationalism. Although he himself rejects the label, he is considered a major source of 'existentialist' influence in modern literature. Interestingly, he supported Hitler during the early years of the latter's reign.
14. For a detailed discussion of this modernist tradition in literature, see Lukacs 1963.

15. These famous words were spoken by Beckett in a conversation with Georges Duthuit published in 1949 under the title "Three Dialogues", reproduced in Esslin. (17) In Beckett's novel *Malone Dies*, too, we are told that "nothing is more real than nothing."

WORKS CITED

Bair, Deirdre. 1978. *Samuel Beckett: A Biography*. London: Jonathan Cape.

Casanova, Pascale. 2006 *Samuel Beckett: Anatomy of a Literary Revolution*. London/New York: Verso.

Cohn, Ruby. 1973. *Back to Beckett*. Princeton: Princeton University Press.

____ . 1980. *Just Play: Beckett's Theatre*. Princeton: Princeton Univ. Press.

Duckworth, Colin. 1972. *Angels of Darkness: Dramatic Effects in Samuel Beckett with Special Reference to Eugene Ionesco*. London: George Allen and Unwin.

Esslin, Martin, ed. 1965. *Samuel Beckett: A Collection of Critical Essays*. Englewood Cliff: Prentice Hall.

Fergusson, Francis. 1955. *The Idea of a Theatre*. Garden City, New York: Doubleday.

Kenner, Hugh.1961. *Samuel Beckett: A Critical Study*. London: John Calder.

____ .1973. *A Readers Guide to Samuel Beckett*. London: Thames and Hudson.

Knowlson, James. 1996. *Damned to Fame: The Life of Samuel Beckett*. Simon and Schuster. New York.

Lukacs, Georg. 1963."The Ideology of Modernism" in his *The Meaning of Contemporary Realism*. London: Merlin Press.

Suvin, Darko. 1984. *To Brecht and Beyond: Soundings in Modern Dramaturgy*. Sussex: Harvester Press.

Tynan, Kenneth. 1964. *Tynan on Theatre*. Harmondsworth: Penguin.

5

Drama And/As Theatre: From Written Text to Performance Text[1]

> "Literature creates a virtual past, drama creates a virtual future. The literary mode is the mode of memory; the dramatic mode is the mode of destiny.
>
> Susan Langer

In everyday conversation, we often use "drama" and "theatre" interchangeably. But sometimes we also use these terms to mean two different things. In the latter usage, the term "drama" is reserved for a printed work while "theatre" denotes activity. This distinction is perfectly valid, for drama is read while theatre is watched; drama has readers while theatre has spectators. Drama's mode of existence is literary and it often takes the form of a written script. The theatre's mode of existence, on the other hand, is predominantly visual and auditory. It takes the form of a live public event.

However, our suspicion that drama has something to do with the theatre, a suspicion which lies behind our casual use of the terms interchangeably is not wrong either. For, their distinctive features notwithstanding, there has always existed a close connection between drama and theatre. Drama, written verbal text in dramatic form, is usually a blueprint for the performance. It is an initial step in a process which reaches its fulfilment only in a stage show. At the same time, a theatrical production, too, is often semantically dependent upon the former. Of course, there are plays that are pure literature and nothing else just as there are kinds of theatre which do not need any script or verbal text. But most of the worthwhile and durable plays are written with a view to staging and most stage productions are based on written scripts.

The connection between playwriting and play performing was particularly active and close in the periods before the advent of the printed word. The distinction between the playwright/poet and the stage performers–a distinction that we customarily make today–did not exist then. All great playwrights from the Greek tragedians to Shakespeare and Moliere were writers as well as theatre persons. In fact, they were, above all else, practical men of theatre. They were themselves performers, or wrote for, and in active collaboration with, those who performed their plays. What they wrote did not have an independent public existence as "text." That is why there is an absence of what we today know as "stage directions" in these ancient texts. What the playwright wrote was liable to be constantly modified during rehearsals and even during performance. The verbal text and the performance text were thus neither divorced from each other nor hierarchical in importance. The play (in the sense of a totality of dramatic performance) was, as Hamlet puts it, "the thing."

However, with the arrival of the printed word, it became possible for a playwright to write his plays in seclusion from the practical stage and publish them as books. This had the effect of creating a distance (in terms of space and/or time), or at least weakening the relation, between the two, traditionally interdependent activities: namely, playwriting and performing. Drama, in the sense of verbal or written text, was no longer regarded exclusively as a provisional draft for stage performance but also acquired an independent public existence. Now it could be accessed also as "literature" and even included in literary syllabi.

In due course, this influenced the art and the craft of playwriting as well. Since plays could now be read as well as staged (that is, viewed) and since reading and viewing are two qualitatively different experiences, dramatists began to write for their readers as well as for the possible performers of their works. It was in view of the fact that the plays could now be read or produced without direct involvement of or consultation with the playwright caused a new element, stage directions to be introduced in the play texts for the benefit of the reader as well as that of the future or distant stage performer and director. For example, remarkably extensive stage directions in Bernard Shaw's plays suggest a preoccupation with the reader.

Following this hiatus between the functions of the playwright and the performer, gradually the idea of the primacy, the supremacy, and even the sacredness of the written text arose. The playwright's text came to be seen as the "commanding form" (Langer, 80) of the performance. All the resources of theatre–scenery, costume, properties, music, and, above all, the actor's physical and psychic energies–were made subservient to the written word. A production came to be regarded mainly as a visualisation, at best a re-interpretation, of the playwright's text. Any deviation from this was–and in many orthodox circles still is–frowned upon. In a way, the strong tendencies towards a valorisation of blatant theatricality (or theatricalism, as it is sometimes termed) towards an improvisational, unscripted kind of theatre can be seen as a reaction to this "tyranny" of the written word. As early as in the mid-1940s, Antonin Artaud called for a rejection of the written poetry of the verbal text in favour of what he called the "unwritten poetry of the theatre." The call that he issued in *Theatre in Its Double* was: "Let us do away with the foolish adherence to texts, to written poetry." A major contemporary trend towards more or less unscripted and improvisational performances, a trend which became particularly strong during the 1960s, can also be regarded as an attempt to rid theatre of the dominance of the written text.

However, despite the impact of the publishing industry on the nexus between playwriting and playacting, despite also the angry reactions against the written text, playwrights, at least the significant ones, continued to write with reference to, and in terms of, the practical stage. Some wrote in more or less active association with their directors and their theatres. It is difficult, for example, to think of Chekhov without thinking of Stanislavski too. Similarly, the work of the so-called "angry young" English playwrights was made possible by their association with the recently established English Stage Company and the Royal Court Theatre which encouraged new playwrights. There have also been playwrights who belonged to the old tradition in which the writer was directly associated with the staging of his script. The most influential among these was Bertolt Brecht who, like the classical Greeks, Shakespeare and Moliere, was both a writer and a practical man of theatre. Simultaneously, he was also a theoretician whose theory of drama and theatre profoundly influenced and altered our thinking about theatre and its social function. In more recent times, we have the example of Dario Fo, a performer par excellence who is also the "maker" of the plays he performs. In India too we find similar examples in Utpal Dutt, Habib Tanvir and Badal Sarcar.

Thus, in spite of a relative separation in modern times of playwriting from playacting, a more or less close connection between drama and theatre continues to exist even today. What is more, this connection is also written into the dramatic text and manifests itself in a number of formal and stylistic features which signify the performance possibilities inherent in it. Similarly, the performance text,too, cannot escape carrying traces of its indebtedness to the written text that lies at its basis. These intertextual traces point to the fundamental relatedness of these two otherwise distinct texts.

As a distinct genre, drama has its own specific features. We know that for drama to take place at least two characters are necessary. The development of relationships in a fictive time and space through a process of action and reaction is the essence of the dramatic form. This gives the dramatic text a polyphonic quality. It embodies a multiplicity of voices and diverse experiential and existential perspectives. Each character speaks in her or his own voice and creates his or her own immediate interest and focus. In other words, there is no division of self and the other but, instead, each character is an "I", a subject in his/her own right. This does not leave much scope for a discursive hierarchy and for privileging any particular viewpoint above others. Thus what we have in the democratic artistic economy of a dramatic text is a dialectical pattern of multiple co-emphases.

This also points to the written text's alertness to the needs of a theatrical performance, and links it to what semioticians call the text's "stage potentiality." The stage directions that, as was already mentioned, have only recently been added to the dramatic text also indicate this alertness, for after all they are precisely what they are called, stage directions. Even dialogues and other verbal components, which we often regard as fit subject for literary analysis, are but primarily performable acts. Paola Pugliatti, argues that "units of articulation" in a written dramatic text should not be regarded simply as "units of the linguistic texts [that are] translatable into stage practice." In fact, it is more appropriate to read them as a "units of linguistic transcription of a stage potentiality which is the motive force of the dramatic text" (Elam, 209).

In other words, even as a written or literary text, or a published work with an independent public existence as literature, the dramatic text has stylistic and structural features which not only distinguish it sharply from other literary forms but also point to its performability, to the possibilities of its visualisation on stage. As Keir Ellam has put it, the written text is "determined by its very need for stage contextualisation, and indicates throughout its allegiance to the physical conditions of performance" (209). On its part, a theatrical performance, no matter how radical its departure from, or its reinterpretation of, the original script, cannot entirely free itself from the traces of that written text. It not only gives body and voice to its words but also makes its pauses come alive on stage.

Nonetheless, theatrical performance does offer an experience significantly different from that of reading a play. Above all, the experience is characterised by immediacy and ephemerality and by the theatre's ever present now, by its perpetual present. As Keir Ellam says: "The reader is able to imagine the dramatic context in a leisurely and pseudo narrative fashion while the spectator is bound to process simultaneous and successive acoustic and visual signals within strictly defined time limits" (99). In reading we can always turn back and re-read an earlier dialogue, episode or sequence. In a stage-performance we cannot. If we want to review a play or any part thereof, we have to watch another evening's performance which—since the theatre as an art form antedates by far the age of mechanical (or, for that matter, digital) reproduction—is not exactly the same as the one we had witnessed the previous evening. This points to the theatre's unrepeatability as also to its essentially local and ephemeral quality. The verbal text (as also the cinematic performance) has a permanence, a fixity, which the stage performance lacks. Each performance is a new text because the mental and physical states of the performers, the quality, size and make-up of the audience, as well as the physical and climatic conditions of the performance cannot be exactly reproduced from one evening to the next.

Above all, the theatrical experience distinguishes itself from the experience of reading by the direct and collaborative relationship between two live groups of physically present people: the performers and the spectators. In other words, a performance text can be regarded as a stage-audience dialogue. In fact, of all the elements that constitute the theatrical discourse, the only indispensable ones are the performer and the spectator. For theatre cannot happen, cannot come into being, if either of these two is absent.

In its fully developed form, theatre is a composite (or a synthesis) of different arts—literature, music, painting, architecture and mime. Of all these, the only indispensable art is that of acting. The functions of most of the others can be incorporated into the verbal texts as was often done in Elizabethan drama where the dialogue was used to localise the action. But there can be no theatre without the actor. Gordon Craig dreamt of a theatre without actors but could never achieve it. The actor's physical presence—his body and voice—is the central and essential instrument of theatrical communication. It is also the central focus of the audience's attention. Through voice, gestures, movements, facial expression and physical stances, the actor bodies forth and re-presents the playwright's text.

However, in essaying a given role, the skilful actor does not merely visualise it on stage in terms of physical presence but interprets or reinterprets it, sometimes revealing or producing an entirely new dimension of meaning and thus even significantly altering our experience of the play as a whole.[2] Thus she is simultaneously linked to the written text as well as away from it. For example, the famous speech by Kate in Shakespeare's *The Taming of the Shrew* which includes statements like "Thy husband is thy lord, thy life, thy keeper, thy head, thy sovereign" can be rendered in performance in many different ways: tearfully, (so as to express helplessness, anguish and pain); mockingly (so as to give it an ironical edge and to suggest bitterness and anger); playfully (so as to suggest that she is merely participating in a game and playing a role); or remorsefully (so as to represent a reformed and indeed a tamed Kate). Needless to say, the chosen style will have a significant impact on the meaning of the play as a whole.

If theatre cannot happen without the performer, it equally cannot happen without the spectator. As Elizabeth Burns points out in her seminal book on theatricality, acting requires the presence of others and it is essential that these others should be watching the performance from the outside (26-27). The presence of the spectator is thus an essential prerequisite for any performance to take place. For example, if you are dancing or miming in the privacy and solitude of your own bedroom with no one else present, it will not, strictly speaking, be a performance. However, if there was someone watching you through a chink in the door and you were aware of thus being watched, it will approximate the basic condition of a theatrical performance. For you will then be ostending your performance towards that audience of one. In other words, any kind of conscious role playing becomes a performance. This being so, even in everyday life we are playing roles—because there is always an addressee, actually present or implied. For example, the conventionally valorised role of the good, chaste and dutiful wife has the husband, and the in-laws, and beyond them, the entire conventional, patriarchal society as its implied addressee.

But these are impure examples. Not the performance we are discussing here. Real life performances are not necessarily time-bound. They can span a whole lifetime. Nor is the actual, immediate presence of the addressee or a fully conscious orientation towards it necessary. But a theatrical performance is necessarily limited in terms of its duration. How long a performance will last depends on conventions which are historically and culturally specific. Also, in theatrical performance, the physical presence of the addressee is essential and the performance has to be consciously oriented(in semiotics, ostended) towards that spectator. We have all been told about the religious origins of the dramatic or theatrical form. But religious ritual is not drama or performance, precisely because of the absence of an audience, a group detached from the ritualistic event. Normally, in rituals all are participants/worshippers. It is only when non-worshippers or non-participants assemble to watch the ritual and when the ritual performers are conscious of their presence, that it becomes a theatrical performance.

A performance is thus made possible by a conscious and active dialogic relationship between the performer and the audience. It is a complex relationship which involves both collaboration and detachment. On the one hand, there has to be a clearly defined line (whether imaginary or real) separating the performer from the spectator, or the stage from the auditorium. The spectators are expected to follow an unwritten code of conduct. They should not physically intervene in the play for example. At the same time, theatrical discourse requires an active and collaborative relationship between the performer and the spectator. Theatrical communication, in other words, is a two-way traffic. This is invariably so despite the attempt of the naturalist theatre to reduce it to a virtually unilateral process–from the stage to the auditorium–and to restrict the role of the spectator to that of a passive consumer of the finished, theatrical product. In this two-way communication, the addressor in turn becomes the addressee and the other way around.

Thus, between the performer and the spectator, each is both a sender and receiver of messages. Just as the actor, through her/his body and voice communicates meaningful information to the spectators, the latter too send him auditive signals of their "answering understanding", of approval or disapproval. Although by convention the audience's participation in the performance is non-verbal and non-tactile, its response can be easily gauged by a seasoned actor. Besides loud clapping, or booing, or actual walking out, there are subtler signals like coughing, shuffling, fidgeting, whispering, or heavy breathing. All these are consciously or unconsciously registered by the performer and affect the quality of her/his performance. They are what Umberto Eco has called "phatic or emotive messages of control" which make the actor feel that the contact continues.

In short, theatre, which is simultaneously communication, game, and cognition, is fundamentally dialogic and complex in nature and form. Dialogism in theatre operates on several levels. There is the interaction between different characters. There is the dialogue between the performance and the written text, between the actor and his/her role, and, on a more advanced cognitive level, between the playworld (the fictional world of the play with its imaginary time, space and relationships which is called "counter-factual" or "possible world" in semiotics) and the empirical/historical world of ahe given performance.

To sum up, what I am suggesting here is that drama and theatre represent two distinct but also closely related textual categories. Each has its own distinctive features and modes of existence. Nonetheless, each is also connected with the other through a complex web of intertextual relationships. The dramatic text is "motivated" by performability and carries within it the seeds of all possible performances (although not of any actual performance). Similarly, although "Any given performance is only to a limited degree constrained by the indications of the written text," (Ellam, 209) it does usually originate in the written text and translates the chosen elements thereof into stage vocabulary. Each category calls for a different critical approach and strategy. The dramatic text can be accessed and studied as literature, although given the specificities of the dramatic form the conventional critical tools of literary criticism need to be appropriately modified in order for them to be effective. The performance text, on the other hand, is a highly complex and composite text, made up of a whole range of languages or sign systems. Moreover, it exists as a live, local, transient and unrepeatable public event. As such it defies attempts to document and fix it into a text which could then be taken up for study and analysis. The performance text traverses so many different social, psycho-biological, and geographical areas that, despite attempts by semioticians and others, no truly satisfactory method of notating and documenting it in its entirety and all its complexity has been found so far. In short, the performance text remains largely unavailable for academic study and analysis.

NOTES

1. This paper was originally presented at a national seminar on "Mediations: Literature Across Media", held in New Delhi on March 16-19, 2005, under the auspices of the Department of English, University of Delhi.
2. Some critics view this as a restriction of the rich range of possible alternative readings available to the reader of the written text. For example, Egil Tornqvist writes: "While much is added to the drama text in any performance, the polysemic range of the dramatic dialogue becomes narrower in performance by simply being spoken. As readers, we may think of numerous ways of phrasing a speech. As spectators we partake of one of these ways, chosen by the actor." However, Tornqvist also acknowledges the greater richness of the performance text on another level: "In another sense, however, the performance text has a much wider polysemic range than the dramatic text, by virtue of its constant interaction between verbal and non-verbal elements." (2)

WORKS CITED

Burns, Elizabeth. 1973. *Theatricality: A Study of Convention in the Theatre and in Social Life*. New York: Harper and Row.

Elam, Keir. 1980. *The Semiotics of Theatre and Drama*, London and New York: Methuen.

Langer, Susan. 1967. "The Dramatic Illusion", in Daniel Seltzer ed. *The Modern Theatre, Readings and Documents*. Boston: Little, Brown and Co. 73-90.

Tornqvist, Egil. 1991. *Transposing Drama: Studies in Representation.* London: Methuen.

Index